Heroes of the Reformation

EDITED BY

Samuel Macauley Jackson

PROFESSOR OF CHURCH HISTORY, NEW YORK
UNIVERSITY

Διαιρέσεις χαρισμάτων, το δὲ αὐτὸ πνεῦμα

DIVERSITIES OF GIFTS, BUT THE SAME SPIRIT.

BALTHASAR HÜBMAIER

BALTHASAR HÜBMAIER.

THE ONLY KNOWN PORTRAIT.   FROM AN OLD WOODCUT.

Balthasar Hübmaier

THE LEADER OF THE
ANABAPTISTS

BY

HENRY C. VEDDER

PROFESSOR OF CHURCH HISTORY IN CROZER THEOLOGICAL SEMINARY

" Die göttliche Warheit ist untödlich, und wiewohl sy sich
ettwan lang fahen lasst, geyslen, krönen, creützigen und in das
Grab legen, würdet sy doch am dritten Tag wiederumb sygreich
uferston und im ewigkeit regieren und triumphiren."

HÜBMAIER, *Die ander Erbietung*, Schaffhausen, 1524.

AMS PRESS
NEW YORK

Reprinted from the edition of 1905, New York
First AMS EDITION published 1971
Manufactured in the United States of America

International Standard Book Number: 0-404-06755-7

Library of Congress Number: 79-149670

AMS PRESS INC.
NEW YORK, N.Y. 10003

PREFACE

ONLY two biographies of Hübmaier have hitherto appeared. The earliest of these, by Dr. F. Hoschek, was written in Bohemian and published in Brünn in 1867. It is very valuable for the later years, and contains large extracts from the writings published at Nikolsburg. For the earlier years it is less trustworthy. An English translation of the text, omitting notes and illustrative matter, was made by Rev. W. W. Everts, D.D., and published in the *Texas Baptist Historical Magazine* for 1891 and 1892. The other biography, in German, is by Dr. Johann Loserth, Professor of History in the University of Czernowitz, and was published at Brünn in 1893. It has never been translated.

I have leaned heavily on these authorities, and gladly acknowledge constant and great obligations to them, especially to Loserth, but the great reliance has been upon the writings of Hübmaier himself. The collection of these in the library of the Rochester Theological Seminary is nearly complete, and this collection has been generously put at my disposal by the librarian, Rev. Howard Osgood, D.D., by whom it was first made many years ago. But for his assistance and counsel the study of these writings would never have been undertaken, and could not have been successfully prosecuted. A number of the booklets Dr. Osgood long ago translated, and he has permitted me to use these translations freely in this biography. Other of the works I have myself translated, and the pile of manuscript has grown to such proportions as to arouse the hope that at no distant day a volume of the works of Hübmaier may be published, which, if not absolutely a complete edition, will contain everything of importance that his pen wrote.

During the summer of 1904 was fulfilled a long-cherished purpose of visiting the principal scenes of Hübmaier's labours: Augsburg, Ingolstadt, Regensburg, Waldshut, Nikolsburg. As might be anticipated, few actual memorials now remain of labours so remote, and these few are much altered by decay or "restorations," and yet such a visit is by no means valueless. Most of the illustrations of this work were gathered by this means, and investigation of the scene of long-forgotten events was profitable in supplementing knowledge gained from documentary sources, and correcting errors into which one who had never seen the localities would naturally fall.

Besides the authorities named, the other works that have been found directly helpful are sufficiently mentioned in the foot-notes to the text. The actual composition of the biography has occupied such time as could be spared from other engagements for about a year, but it has in reality been twenty years in the making. Let us hope that readers will not find it heavy in proportion!

Crozer Theological Seminary,
May, 1905.

CONTENTS

CHAPTER I

CHAPTER II

THE YEARS OF PREPARATION
1481–1520

CHAPTER III

HÜBMAIER AN EVANGELICAL REFORMER
1524

CHAPTER IV

HÜBMAIER BECOMES AN ANABAPTIST
1524–1526

Contents

CHAPTER VIII

THE SUPPRESSION OF THE MORAVIAN ANABAPTISTS

ILLUSTRATIONS

Illustrations

BIBLIOGRAPHY

HÜBMAIER'S CHIEF WRITINGS

Explanation of signs. The first letter appended to a title indicates the place where the original may be found. B = collection of Dr. Beck, now in Vienna. MA = Moravian Archives. V = Vienna, Hofbibliothek. R = copy in the library of the Rochester Theological Seminary. The letters H, L, S, appended in addition, signify that the document is reprinted by one of Hübmaier's biographers, Hoschek, Loserth, or Schreiber. For convenience these writings are frequently cited in the following pages by their numbers, as *Op. 1*, *Op. 22*, etc.

1. *Achtzehn Schlussrede*, so betreffende eyn gantz Christlich Leben, woran es gelegen ist. Disputiert zu Waldshut, von Doctor Balthassar Fridberger. 1524. B. H. L.

2. *Eine ernstliche Christliche erbietung* an einen ersamen Rath zu Schaffhusen, durch doctor Baldazar Hubmör von Fridberg Pfarren ze Walshut beschehen. 1524.

Original in Schaffhausen Archives. L., *Beilage*, No. 2.

3. *Uon ketzern vnd iren verbrennern* vergleichung der Gschrifften, zusammengezogen durch doctor Balthazer Fridbergern pfarren zu Waldsshut. 1524. B. R.

Reprinted in this volume.

4. *Schlussreden* die Baldazar Fridberger Pfarrer zu Waltzhut ein Bruder Huldrychs Zwinglis dem Joanni Eckio zu Ingoldstatt die meysterlich zu examinieren furbotten hat. Zürich, 1524.

Library of University of Basel. H. L. S.

5. *Von dem Christlichen Touff der Gläubigen* durch Balthasarn Hüebmör von Friedberg, yetz zu Waldshut ausgangen. 1525. B. R.

6. *Ain Sum ains ganzen christlichen Lebens*, durch Baldasaren Frydberger, Predicant, yetz zu Waldshut, etc. 1525. B. R.

7. *Ettlich beschlussreden* von Doctor Paltus Fridberger zu Walzhut, allen Christen, von Undericht der Mess. Zurich. 1525. L. S.

8. *Balthazars Friedbergers zu Waldshut offentliche erbietung* an alle christgläubige menschen, an andern tag des Hornungs beschehen. 1525.
Original in the Archives of St. Gall. S.

9. *Ein wahrhartig Entschuldigung und Klag* gemeiner Stadt Waldshut von Schultheiss und Rath allda an alle christgläubigen Menschen, ausgegangen anno 1525.
Original in the Archives of Basel. Reprinted by Strickler, *Actensammlung*, i., No. 932.

10. *Ein Gesprech* Balthasar Hubemörs von Fridberg auff Mayster Ulrichs Zwinglens zu Zürich Tauffbüechlen von dem Khindertauff. Nicolspurg. 1526. V. R.

11. *Ein Christennliche Leertafel* die ein eydlicher mensch ee und er im Wasser getaufft wird vor wissen solle. D. Balthasar Huebmör vonn Fridberg. Nicolspurg. 1526. V. R. H.

12. *Der Uralten und gar neuen Leeren Urtail* das men die iungen khindlen nit tauffen solle bisz sy im glauben unnderricht sind. Nicolsperg. 1526. V. R.

13. *Ein kurze entschuldigung* D. Balthasar Huebmörs von Fridberg an alle Christglaubige menschen das sy sich an den erdichtenn unnwahrhayten so im sein miszgöner zu legen nit ergern. Nicolspurg. 1526. V. R.

14. *Ein kurzes vater unser*. D. Balthasar Hubmör von Fridberg. Nicolspurg, 1526. V. R.

15. *Ein einfeltiger unnderricht* auff die wort. Das ist der leib mein in dem Nachtmal Christi D. Balthasar Huebmörs von Fridberg. Nicolspurg. 1526. V. R. H.

16. *Grund und Ursach*. Das ein eydlicher mensch der gleich in seiner khindheit getaufft ist. schuldig sey, sich recht nach der Ordnung Christi ze tauffen lassen. ob er schon hundert jar allt were. D. Balthazar Hubmör von Fridberg. Nicolspurg. 1527. V. R.

17. *Von dem Khindertauff.* Ekolampadius, Thomas Augustinianer Leesmaister M. Jacob Immelen M. Vuolfg. Weissenburger Balthasar Hubmör von Fridberg. Nicolspurg. 1527. V. R. H.

18. *Die zwelf Artikel christenlichs glaubens* ze Zürch im Wassertthurn. in Bett weis gestellt. D. Balthasar Huebmör. Nicolsburg. 1527. V. R.

19. *Ein Form ze Tauffen* im wasser die unnderrichten im glauben. D. Balthasar Hübmör von Fridberg. Nicolspurg. 1527. V. R. H.

20. *Ein Form des Nachtmals Christi.* D. Balthasar Hübmör von Fridberg. 1527. V. R. H.

Reprinted in Calvary's *Mittheilungen.*

21. *Von der Briederlichen straff.* Wo die nit ist, da ist gewiszlich auch khain Kirch ob schon der Wassertauff und das Nachtmal Christi daselbs gehalten werdent. D. Balthasar Höebmöer von Fridberg. Nicolsburg. 1527. MA. H.

22. *Von dem Christlichen Bann.* Wo derselb nit auffgericht und gebraucht wirdt nach dem ordenlichen und ernstlichen bevelh Christi, daselbs regirt nichts, denn sünd, schand und laster. D. Balthasar Huebmör von Fridberg. Nicolspurg. 1527. MA. R.

23. *Von der Freyhait des Willens.* Die Gott nach sein gesendet wort anbeut allen menschen und ihnen darin gewalt gibt seine khinder ze werden auch die waal natur seind ze bleiben lassen. G. Balthasar Huebmör von Fridberg. Nicolspurg. 1527. MA. R. H.

24. *Das ander Biechlein von der Freiwilligkeit des menschens.* In welchem Schrifft bezeugt wirdt, das Gott durch sein gesenndt wort allen menschen gwalt geve seine Kinder zu werden, und die wal guttes zu wollen und ze thon frey haym setze. Auch darbey die gegenschrifften des Widertayls auffgelöset. Balthasar Hübmör von Fridberg. Nicolspurg. 1527. MA. R. H.

25. *Von dem Schwert.* Ein Christennliche erklerung der Schrifften, so wider die Oberkeit (das ist, das die Christen nit sollent im Gwalt sitzen, noch das schwert siern) von etlichen Brüedern gar ennstlich angezogen werdent. D. Balthasar Hüebmör von Fridberg. 1527. MA. R. H.

26. *Rechenschaft seines Glaubens* an den König, in 27 Artikeln.
Original in the Archives, Vienna ; reprinted by L., somewhat abridged.

OTHER SOURCES

BECK, *Geschichts-Bücher der Wiedertäufer* in Oesterreich-Ungarn, Vienna, 1883.

This volume of invaluable extracts from the scattered Anabaptist chronicles, and other original sources, is duly appreciated in the Preface. Dr. Beck's collection is in the possession of his family (he died in 1890), but it has been put at the disposal of Dr. Loserth and other investigators. It is the richest collection of Anabaptist literature in existence, and contains copies of a large number of scarce or unique writings.

EGLI, *Actensammlung zur Geschichte der Zürcher Reformation* in den Jahren 1519–1533. Zürich, 1879.

Contains several valuable documents concerning the process against Hübmaier at Zurich.

FABRI, *Vrsach warumb der Widertauffer Patron uund erster Anfenger Doctor Balthasar Huebmayr zu Wien auff den zehnten Martii Anno 1528 verbrennt sey.* Vienna, 1528.

Unique and invaluable account of the Vienna process, sentence, and execution of Hübmaier. Reprinted by Loserth, as *Beilage* No. 10.

FABRI, *Adversus Balthasarum Pacimontanum, Anabaptistorum nostri sæculi primum authorem, orthodoxæ fidei catholicæ, defensio.* Leipzig, 1528.

A small tractate of only 22 leaves. The tone is polemic, and but few facts are added to our knowledge by it.

FÜSSLIN, *Beiträge zur Erläuterung der Kirchen-Reformations-geschichte des Schweizerbundes.* 5 vols. Zürich, 1741.

A storehouse of documents of the highest value, well known to every student of the period.

Bibliography xix

GEMEINER, *Chronik von Regensburg.* Regensburg, 1800–1803.
Reprinted in vol. xiii. of *Chroniken der deutschen Städte* vom 14 bis ins 16 Jahrhundert. Leipzig, 1824. All important facts are given by Loserth.

GEMEINER, *Geschichte der Kirchenreformations in Regensburg.* Regensburg, 1792.

KESSLER, *Sabbata.* Chronik der Jahre 1523–1539. St. Gall, 1870.
The diary of the Zwinglian pastor at St. Gall ; abounds in valuable matter, some of it to be received with caution.

Mittheilungen aus dem Antiquariate von S. Calvary & Co., Berlin. Berlin, 1870.
This, the first volume of a projected series that was unfortunately not continued, contains a nearly complete list of Hübmaier's writings and a reprint of his tract, *Ein form des Nachtmals Christi.*

OSTROFRANCUS, *de Ratisbona, metropoli Bojoariæ et subita ibidem Judæorum proscriptione.* Augsburg, 1519.
A valuable account, by a monk of the cloister of St. Emmerau, contemporary and eye-witness, of the agitation against the Jews.

SCHELHORN, *Beiträge* zur Erläuterung der Geschichte besonders der schwäbischen Kirchen und Gelehrten. 4 Parts. Memmingen, 1772–1775.
Part iv. contains material of use for the biographer of Hübmaier.

Schultheiss und Rath der Stadt Waldshut an die Statthalter, Regenten, und Räthe im Oberelsass. Bericht über die Thätigkeit Imers und Ulrichs von Habsperg der Auslieferung des Doctors Balthasar Hubmaier. Waldshut, 1523.
Reprinted in *Archiv für österreichischer Geschichte*, vol. lxxxvii., 95–99. Very valuable.

STRICKLER, *Actensammlung zur Schweizerischen Reformationsgeschichte* in den Jahren 1521–1532. 5 vols. Zürich, 1878–1884.
This collection does for all Switzerland what Egli so well does for Zürich only. Contains some documents omitted by Egli.

WIDMANN, *Chronik von Regensburg.* In vol. xv. of *Chronik der deutschen Städte.* Leipzig, 1878.

With the chronicle of Gemeiner, this constitutes our chief source of information regarding Hübmaier's work in Regensburg.

ZWINGLI, *Werke, erste vollständige Ausgabe* durch Melchior Schuler und Joh. Schulthess. 8 vols. Zürich, 1828-1861.

ON HÜBMAIER'S BIOGRAPHY

HOSCHEK, *Balthasar Hubmaier* a počátové novokřestěnstva na Moravě. Brünn, 1867.

A wonderfully sympathetic study, seeing that the author is a Roman Catholic, but not always to be relied on in matters of fact, and still more frequently astray in its interpretations.

LOSERTH, *Doctor Balthasar Hubmaier* und die Anfänge der Wiedertäufer in Mähren. Brünn, 1893.

Though a Protestant, the author is less sympathetic than Hoschek, but more accurate. His study of the sources and literature has been exhaustive, and but for the help derived from his book this volume could never have been written.

SCHREIBER, *Hubmaier, der Stifter der Wiedertäufer* auf dem Schwartzwalde, in his *Taschenbuch für Geschichte und Alterthum in Süd-Deutschland.* 1839, pp. 1-130; 1840, pp. 153-234.

This, the first serious attempt to write a biography of Hübmaier, still has value. It is an incomplete sketch, a promised third part, to tell the story of the work in Moravia, never having been published.

Besides these formal biographies, there are a number of excellent biographical sketches in various works of reference: Cunitz, in Herzog-Plitt, *Real Encyclopädie*, vi., 344 sq. Hegler, in Herzog-Hauck, *Real Encyclopädie*, vii., 418 *sq.* Stern in *Allgemeine deutsche Biographie;* Veesenmeyer in Staudlin and Vater's *Kirchenhist. Archiv*, 1826.

SOME INDISPENSABLE BOOKS

ARNOLD, *Unparteyische Kirchen- und Ketzer-historie.* 3 vols. Schaffhausen, 1740–1742.

An old and deservedly esteemed work, not yet entirely superseded.

BAX, *Rise and Fall of the Anabaptists.* London, 1903.

The author writes from the socialistic point of view, and is too anxious to show that the Anabaptists were the forerunners of modern socialism. All of his facts are selected, and some are distorted, to prove this thesis. Had the author been able to resist this advocacy of a theory, he would have produced a very valuable book. As it is, his book cannot be neglected by any student of the Anabaptists.

BULLINGER, *Der Widertouffen* ursprung, fürgang, Secten, wasen, furnemen, und gemeine jrer leer Artikel. Zurich, 1561.

BULLINGER, *Reformationsgeschichte.* 3 vols. Frauenfeld, 1840.

The first-named of these two works is much the more important for our purpose. It is exceedingly valuable, when due allowance for the personal equation is made. Bullinger was strongly prejudiced against the Anabaptists, and his testimony demands critical examination and frequent correction.

BURRAGE, *History of the Anabaptists in Switzerland.* Philadelphia, 1882.

Still the best monograph on the subject, in any language.

CORNELIUS, *Geschichte des Münsterischen Aufruhrs.* Leipzig, 1855, 1860.

The work of a Roman Catholic (in his later years an Old Catholic), remarkable for learning and candour, but unfortunately never completed. It contains valuable documents in the Appendix to either Part.

EGLI, *Die Züricher Wiedertäufer.* Zürich, 1878.

A book whose value is in inverse ratio to its size. (It is a booklet of 104 pages.)

FÜSSLIN, *Kirchen- und Ketzer-geschichte der mittelalterischen Zeit.* 3 vols. Erlangen, 1772–1774.

This supplements the author's *Sabbata,* and contains much documentary and other information, both interesting and valuable.

HAGENBACH, *J. Oekolampads Leben* und ausgewählte Schriften. Elberfeld, 1859.

An interesting biography of one who was an early friend of Hübmaier, and never became his enemy.

HEATH, *Anabaptism,* from its rise at Zwickau to its Fall at Münster, 1521–1536. London, 1895.

A book to which may be applied all that is said of the work of Bax above.

JACKSON, *Huldreich Zwingli,* the Reformer of German Switzerland. New York, 1903.

The best biography in English. Chap. xii. contains a clear and candid account of Anabaptism at Zürich and Hübmaier's treatment there.

JACKSON, *Selected Works of Huldreich Zwingli.* Philadelphia, 1901.

KAUTSKY, *Geschichte des Socialismus,* von Plato bis zu den Wiedertäufern. Stuttgart, 1895.

The author gives a valuable appreciation of the Anabaptists, but exaggerates the importance of the socialistic group among them.

LOSERTH, *Die Stadt Waldshut* und die vorderösterreichische Regierung in der Jahren 1523–1526, in the *Archiv für Oesterreichischer Geschichte,* lxxxvii., 1 *sq.*

LOSERTH, *Zur Geschichte der Wiedertäufer in Mähren,* in the *Zeitschrift für allgemeine Geschichte,* 1884, Heft 6.

LOSERTH, *Der Communismus des Mährischen Wiedertäufer* im 16 und 17 Jahrhundert. Vienna, 1894.

These three are all valuable, the last invaluable. The first is practically reprinted in the biography of Hübmaier.

NEWMAN, *History of Anti-Pedobaptism,* from the Rise of Pedobaptism to A.D. 1609. Philadelphia, 1897.

This gives the best account in English of the rise and general history of Anabaptism. Chaps. vii., viii., x., and xiv. include a brief, accurate, and appreciative account of Hübmaier's career.

OTT, *Annales Anabaptistici.* Basel, 1672.

Like Catrou's *Histoire des Anabaptistes* (Paris, 1615) this is now superseded, and valuable chiefly for the documents it contains, some of which are important and not easily found elsewhere.

SCHREIBER, *Der deutsche Bauernkrieg.* 3 vols. Freiburg, 1863–1866.

A rich and instructive collection of documents rather than a history.

SEIDEMANN, *Thomas Müntzer.* Dresden, 1842.

While still the best single book on the famous agitator, it demands considerable correction in the light of later investigations.

STÄHELIN, *Huldreich Zwingli : sein Leben und Wirken.* Basel, vol. i., 1895 ; vol. ii., 1897.

The standard biography in German.

STERN, *Ueber die Zwölf Artikel der Bauern.* Leipzig, 1868.

A monograph of considerable value, but the author's hypothesis that Hübmaier composed the Articles, though widely adopted as if a proved fact by writers hostile to Hübmaier and the Anabaptists, has been fully disproved by later investigation.

STROBEL, *Leben, Schriften und Lehren Thomä Müntzers* des Urhebers des Bauernaufruhrs in Thüringen. Nürnberg, 1795.

This small and now very scarce book is an unskilful piece of biography, but the collection of documents is of the greatest value. They include reprints of Münzer's most important writings.

USTERI, *Darstellung der Tauflehre Zwinglis,* in *Studien und Kritiken* for 1882, p. 205 *sq.*

WIEDEMANN, *Dr. Johann Eck.* Regensburg, 1865.

An excellent biography of Hübmaier's teacher, that contains original documentary matter illustrating the relations of master and pupil to about 1520.

WOLNY, *Die Wiedertäufer in Mähren* in *Archiv für Kunde österreichischer Geschichts-Quellen.* 1850.

BALTHASAR HÜBMAIER

BALTHASAR HÜBMAIER

CHAPTER I

THE ANABAPTISTS AND THE REFORMATION

FEW people have fared so hard at the hands of historians as the Anabaptists. Until a generation ago, writers of every school did little more than repeat the rash and unjust and often slanderous statements of the contemporaries of this sect. For these sixteenth-century denunciations there are some obvious excuses to be made. The Anabaptists were the most universally troublesome of all the anti-Catholic parties. They were most vexatious to the Romanists, because they were the most logical, consistent, thorough-going, and determined opponents of the Papacy and all its works. They were equally vexatious to those who conducted the reformations in the various states, because these

were all more or less illogical, lukewarm, and inclined to compromise with the old order, for the
sake of obtaining the support of princes and governments, without which support reform was believed
to be, and perhaps would have been, impracticable.
It was natural that such a party, a veritable Ishmael
among the reformers, should come to be disliked,
distrusted, feared by all, and that it should be denounced with commensurate warmth and energy.

Then, too, certain groups of this party, falling
under the spell of preachers whose learning and
sense were no match for their eloquence, and misled
by a certain specious but false exegesis of Scripture,
were betrayed into a fanatical expectation of the
immediate Parousia and the founding of Christ's
millennial kingdom.   Under the stress of this fanaticism these Anabaptists fell into disorders and excesses, the stigma of which would in any case have
fallen upon the rest, even had not their opponents
eagerly seized upon this pretext to involve the
whole party in a condemnation as fierce and bitter
as it was undiscriminating and often unjust.

Certain groups among the Anabaptists, led astray
by a too literal interpretation of Christ's words and

of apostolic precedent, professed principles of non-resistance, avoidance of oaths, non-payment of taxes, community of goods,—doctrines that might easily be supposed, even by the sincere among their contemporaries, in their application to involve the entire subversion of the existing civil and social and religious order. That men should shrink from a revolutionary programme so comprehensive and radical need surprise nobody. The surprising thing would be if these Anabaptist vagaries had found any favour in the sixteenth century. They barely find tolerance now, to say nothing of favour.

But, worse than all, the Reformation coincided with a time of great social changes and deep social unrest. Many things had helped to bring about the decay of feudalism and the decline of the knights and lesser nobles, but the invention of gunpowder had dealt the final blow. In the last analysis, social and political supremacy, in the case of any order, rests on force. So long as the mailed knight on his mailed horse was the invincible force, to him fell honours and wealth, lands and power. But the arquebus and cannon changed all this. Knighthood had to give place to manhood. The meanest peasant with a gun in his hand became more than the military equal of the knight, whose armour was no protection against bullet or ball, and whose lance, sword, and mace lost all their terrors for the man in leather jerkin. Infantry, not cavalry, became the strength of armies. With this decline of the military power of the knights began also the decay of their social and political importance. They fought against their fate desperately, but they might as well have set themselves against the tides.

The first result of this social change was a marked increase in the power of kings and ruling princes. Feudalism made for decentralisation: it was anti-national, the apotheosis of individualism. That is to say, feudalism was this in practice. The great feudatories were always turbulent, always rebellious against the authority of their nominal suzerain, the king, so that the royal authority was a mere shadow. But in the sixteenth century this was rapidly changing: the power of the nobles was declining, while the royal authority was becoming a thing to be reckoned with and feared.

Parallel with this decline of the nobility, and contributing much to hasten the process, was another great social change, the accumulation of large fortunes by the more enterprising among the burgher class. The multi-millionaires of our day have their counterpart, on a smaller scale, among the merchants, manufacturers, and printers of the free cities of the sixteenth century. Many of these so prospered that they were able to live in a splendour that vied with that of kings and far outshone the state of ordinary nobles. While the castles of the knights still lacked what we should now reckon the ordinary necessaries and decencies of life, the town house of the wealthy merchant or tradesman was the abode not only of comfort but of luxury. The attempts of the nobles to equal this splendour of apparel, this sumptuousness of living—attempts all the more determined because the high-born noble despised his burgher rival—only resulted in their more rapid impoverishment and more speedy extinction.

As the drowning man clutches at the proverbial straw, the knights in their distress tried to wring more money out of the class dependent upon them, the peasants. For a time, therefore, the lot of these long-suffering people, whose emancipation was in the end to come out of this very turmoil, grew

worse rather than better.   They had been scourged
with whips before, now they were scourged with
scorpions.   The result was that the peasantry were
seething with dissatisfaction, ready for any de-
sperate revolt at the first promise of betterment of
their fortunes, only too willing to lend eager ears
to any who would prophesy that the good time
coming was almost here.   And with this state of
things the first throes of the Reformation and the
circulation of Luther's brave early demands for
freedom exactly coincided.   It is no marvel that
the peasants expected more than was then possible,
that they were misguided by fanatics into a prema-
ture uprising.   Nor is it any wonder that some of
the Anabaptists were drawn into this movement.
Many of them were from this peasant class, knew
fully their wrongs, sympathised with their hopes and
aspirations, and, it must be added, became par-
takers of their errors and excesses.

A scapegoat for these errors must be found.
The Roman Catholic writers of the period were inclined to lay all the blame on Luther and his writings.   This was unfair, but Luther and his followers
became greatly alarmed lest the princes of Germany

should adopt this view of the case and decline to support his reformation.   They therefore fixed upon the Anabaptists as the party that should be made to bear all the reproach of the social disorders of the time.   The rest was easy.   It was only necessary to make the name Anabaptist a general term of opprobrium, like "scoundrel," "villain," "heretic," and apply it recklessly to any party or to any man disapproved by the speaker or writer, to all who had published unorthodox opinions or been guilty of unworthy deeds.   This was done for generations by writers who repeated these whole-sale slanders without taking the least trouble to discover the facts.   What wonder that the name Anabaptist still reeks with foul suggestions, after standing through more than three centuries for the sum of all wickedness, the synonym of all that is falsest in doctrine and vilest in practice?

One of the earliest notes of dissent from this un-sparing condemnation, if not the first of all, was sounded by a Roman Catholic writer, Dr. Cornelius, of Bonn.[1]   He first spoke an effective word in

---

[1] A captious critic might object that Dr. Cornelius should not be described thus, since he belonged for the last thirty years of his life

mitigation of judgment upon the Anabaptists, and declared that their real history had yet to be written. His contributions to our knowledge of the Münster affair are not only of great value in themselves, but his labours encouraged other scholars to delve among the records for the facts regarding a much-misunderstood and greatly abused people. The next great service was rendered by Dr. Josef Beck, Counsellor of the Austrian Supreme Court of Judicature, whose *Geschichts-Bücher der Wiedertäufer* (Historical Writings of the Anabaptists)[1] marks an epoch in the study of these people. With great industry he gathered from archives and libraries a vast mass of original Anabaptist literature, to which he added a rich collection of his own; and from these sources he collated, condensed, and edited a volume that for the first time gave the world an inside view of Anabaptist teaching and history.

It is not practicable, nor is it necessary, to speak

to the Old Catholics. But at the time he wrote this book he was in full communion with the Roman Church, had shown no symptom of separation from it, and was, so far as anything appeared, in full sympathy with all its doctrines. What else but a Roman Catholic should one call him in 1855 ?

[1] This was published in 1883, as vol. xliii. in the *Fontes Rerum Austriacarum*, Second Series, and also reprinted separately.

of all who have since laboured in this field with diligence and success. One writer should be noted, however, as easily surpassing all others during the past two decades in the extent and value of his work,—Dr. Ludwig Keller, State Archivist at Münster. Dr. Keller's special contribution has been to show the genetic relation of the Anabaptists of the Reformation period to the older reform-parties. And if at times his conclusions have outrun his facts, and depended for their soundness rather on his historical insight than on any definite proofs he has been able to bring forward, this cannot be said to vitiate the greater part of his work.

Whether documentary proofs will ever be forthcoming to establish a clear historical connection between the Anabaptists and the older evangelical sects who taught similar doctrines and practices, is a question that for the present had better be relegated for discussion to such as are confident that they possess the gift of prophecy. That there is a genetic connection we are fairly entitled to assume, by the practice of all historical investigators, not as a thing completely proved, but as a convenient and safe working hypothesis. Take a parallel case. It cannot be said to be established, by satisfactory historical proof, that there is a genetic connection between the heretical groups or parties known as Paulicians, Bogomils, and Albigenses. They are widely separated in time and space, and visible links to connect them there are none. Yet the Manichæan element common to their theology and organisation is so distinct as to make it certain that a genetic connection subsists between them, whether it can be traced or not. Documentary proof is only one method, after all, of convincing the human reason as to historical fact: there are other methods that are both effective and valid. Historical investigation, though it is quite right to rely mainly on documents, cannot altogether ignore other methods of reaching truth.

The characteristic feature of all these older reform-parties is that, beginning in each instance as a revolt from a corrupt and impure Church, and attempting to return to the Scriptural ideals of faith and practice, these parties reach at length an identical conclusion: that a pure church cannot exist except on the basis of believers' baptism, and that the baptism of infants is totally unwarranted by the

Scriptures. In many other details these parties differ; in this they are a unit. This was the conclusion of the earliest of these parties, the Petrobrusians; as to that, the testimony of their great Roman Catholic opponent, Peter the Venerable, leaves no possibility of doubt. The same conclusions were reached by the followers of Peter Waldo—by those, at least, on the French side of the Alps, if we may accept the unanimous testimony of their contemporary Roman critics and persecutors. Neither of these bodies is called Anabaptist by their contemporary and hostile chroniclers. This may be because they did not commonly rebaptise adults who had (in their view) received a null-and-void so-called baptism in their infancy.[1] They may never have seen that logical consistency required this of them—we know that for a time such was the case with the Swiss Anabaptists—and they may have contented themselves with making their

---

[1] That some of the Petrobrusians, at any rate, rebaptised is proved by the fact that Peter puts these words into their mouths: " We wait for the proper time, after a man is prepared to know his God and believe in him; we do not (as you accuse us) rebaptise him, but we baptise him who can be said never to have been baptised."—*Contra Petrobrusianos Hæreticos*, Migne's *Latin Patrology*, clxxxix., 729. These words might be taken from a treatise of Hübmaier, so well do they express his ideas.

protest against the baptism of infants. Or, it may
be that they rebaptised, but the Roman writers
were ignorant of the practice, or did not think it
worthy of mention. Neither of the last two suggestions seems very probable.

These earlier evangelical parties, though severely
persecuted,—perhaps in consequence of such persecution,— had spread themselves widely abroad.
Originating in Southern France, they had not only
made their way across the Alpine passes into
Northern Italy, but had sent their missionaries
throughout Switzerland and Germany. Roman
Catholic literature testifies unmistakably both to
the extent and to the success of this evangelisation.
Communities of Waldenses were gathered everywhere, and the severest persecution did not succeed
in utterly eradicating these heretics from the regions
in which they once obtained a foothold. That a
secret existence of the sect was maintained in many
quarters is proved by the fact that the authorities
occasionally lighted upon such a case. The possibility, the credibility even, of many such survivals
down to the Reformation era, is sufficiently established by the history of the Unitas Fratrum, which

was preserved in secret, even the due succession
of its bishops being maintained, for more than a
century. The close correspondence in doctrine and
practice between Petrobrusians and Waldenses, between Waldenses and Anabaptists, even in the absence of definite documentary proofs, warrants the
conclusion that in these successive sects we really
study the history of a single evangelical movement,
which, in various regions and under different names,
has persisted without a break from the twelfth century (and perhaps earlier still) to the present day.

If such is the case, the Anabaptists of the sixteenth century are not so related to the Reformation as has generally been supposed. They are not,
that is to say, an offshoot of the Reformation,
though they might, indeed, be called its root, since
they are both older and more primitive in practice.
Among the "Reformers before the Reformation "
whose labours deserve to be better recognised are
those evangelical preachers who for centuries had
been gradually leavening Central Europe with the
truths of the gospel, and preparing the way for the
great spiritual revolution to come. A history of
their labours cannot indeed be written; material

may never be discovered for such a history, though doubtless large additions will yet be made to our present knowledge by scholarly diligence. The broad outlines even are vague and conjectural. We can only infer from a few known facts, and from certain observed phenomena in connection with the Reformation, that the influence of this evangel upon the people has been too lightly estimated by many who have passed for critical historians.

However scholars may finally agree upon the question of the origin of the Anabaptists, certain things concerning them are now comparatively plain. The great majority of them were peaceable folk, law-abiding people, asking nothing but that they might be permitted to worship and serve God in their own way, and wishing no harm to those who held to different ways. There was a mystical element in their doctrines, the foundation stone of which was the conviction that to be a Christian is to be united by faith to the Son of God, so as to be a partaker of his nature. This cannot be, save by a complete change of nature, character, life. One cannot be a Christian, therefore, by inheritance, by education, by sacraments; repentance, faith, regeneration, are necessary to produce this intimate personal relation with Christ.   Flesh and blood cannot inherit the kingdom: to enter it one must be born again.

This notion of the essential nature of Christianity led them to their idea concerning the Church.   This outward embodiment of the kingdom should be, so far as is humanly possible, composed of those only who have been regenerated by the Spirit, who have become vitally one with Christ by faith, and are continuing in such union with him, as is shown by their bringing forth the fruits of the Spirit.   Such a Church could not possibly exist if it were ruled by princes and town councils; hence the Anabaptists insisted on the sharp separation between the secular and the spiritual—as we should say, between Church and State.   The civil magistrate, in their view, had nothing to do with matters of religion.   He had discharged his full duty when he had protected the innocent and peaceable, and punished the evil-doer. For this he bore the sword and was a minister of God; anything more was a usurpation.   And it equally followed that entrance into such a Church as they contemplated must be made by the voluntary act of the individual concerned, and could not possibly be accomplished for him by another. Infant baptism was therefore objectionable to them, not only because they found it to be neither taught by precept nor warranted by example in the Scriptures, but because it was essentially an impertinence, the anticipatory doing by others of that which it was alike the privilege and the duty of every believer to do for himself. As an act performed without faith, it was to them null and void. Hence they always resented the name Anabaptist (*re*-baptisers), and protested that it was a complete misnomer, since they administered the first and only real baptism—the baptism of a believer—and that the so-called baptism of an unbeliever is no baptism at all, but an empty and meaningless form. As Hübmaier pithily put it for all of them, "Water is not baptism, else the whole Danube were baptism, and the fishermen and boatmen would be daily baptised."

There was but one other principle on which all Anabaptists were agreed: the supremacy of the Scriptures as a rule of faith and practice. They rather assumed than asserted a doctrine of inspira-

tion, and confined themselves generally to an assertion of the authority of the Bible without defining
the grounds on which such authority rested.   They
made no such distinction as is attributed to certain
heretical sects between the Old Testament and the
New.   They received the whole Bible as equally
authoritative, but not equally authoritative for all
purposes.   Here they made a distinction, namely,
that the New Testament is our sole source of knowledge of all that pertains to the Christian Church,
and they would not admit the validity of arguments drawn from Jewish institutions to prove
what should exist under the gospel.

The mystical element in Anabaptist teaching is
apparent in what some of them say about the interpretation of Scripture.   A special illumination is
not only promised to every believer, but is indis-
pensable for the understanding of the word of God,
since the natural man cannot comprehend the things
of the Spirit, but spiritual things must be spiritually
discerned.   Though we may trace some likeness
here between their teaching and the doctrines of the
earlier Montanists and the later Friends, we miss
altogether that exaggerated notion of an inner light

of the Spirit which is superior in authority to the external word. This inner light, according to the Anabaptist, is bestowed not to supersede the written word, but to make it possible for the humblest believer to understand and follow that word. With the Friend, the seat of authority is and must be within himself; he must listen to the voice of the Spirit speaking to his own soul, though it supplement, even if it contradict, the written word. With the Anabaptist, the seat of authority is the declared will of God in the Scriptures, and the light of the Spirit is given to make these plain to him; and he is always to test the supposed voice of the Spirit to his soul by comparing these utterances carefully with the written word.

And yet, in spite of this admirably sane theory of the Scriptures and of the office of the Spirit, groups among the Anabaptists fell into grievous errors, which were most unfortunate in their results. For one thing, they greatly weakened the party by the divisions and the controversies that naturally ensued; and then the follies and excesses into which some fell, in consequence of error in interpreting Scripture, covered the whole party with opprobrium and gave a decent pretext for persecuting all with unrelenting fury, as has already been pointed out. Even from their persecutors, however, we may frequently discover that there was no real ground for so severe treatment—or, rather, that the real ground of these persecutions differed from the grounds alleged. The real offence of the Anabaptists was not that they were seditious, turbulent, fomenters of social revolution, and therefore dangerous subjects, potential rebels even when not in actual rebellion. That was true of a few among them, but nobody ever seriously believed this of the majority. The real offence of the Anabaptists was that they were Anabaptists—that they held and taught just such things as are above set forth. Their doctrines were too Scriptural, too spiritual, too incompatible with those that in many places were being forced on unwilling people, in the name of reform, by irreligious rulers obviously actuated by ambition and greed. Their doctrines were too often eagerly received by the common people, who lacked the learning requisite for the perversion of the plain sense of Scripture, and found their Bibles and the Anabaptist teachings to agree wonderfully. There was, in fact, no reconciling these teachings with those of state churches, set up, as they often were, by unworthy princes and ungodly town councils— churches in which little or no attempt was made to discriminate between regenerate and unregenerate. These were reasons enough—these were the real reasons — why governments everywhere tried to harry the Anabaptists out of their lands.

Time, which works so many changes, is bringing about the vindication of these greatly wronged people. It is now known, and every year sees the fact more generally acknowledged, that they were treated with a cruelty as unjust, unnecessary, and unwise as it was brutal. The brutality may be excused in part as the universal sin of the age. The folly and injustice are not so easily forgiven, since many of those in places of influence and power sinned against light. The Anabaptists experienced the fate that usually befalls any man who has the misfortune to be out of joint with his times. Not all their teachings, it is true, have won their way to general acceptance—some of them may never gain such a victory—but many of their fundamental contentions are commonplaces of Christian thought

to-day, and their ideal of the total separation between the spiritual and the temporal is inwrought
into the texture of American institutions. The
time is rapidly approaching when the Anabaptists
will be as abundantly honoured as, in the past four
centuries, they have been unjustly contemned.

If this is true of the Anabaptists as a whole,
what shall be said of their leaders? These have not
escaped the general fate of the party. They were
burned, they were drowned, they were beheaded,
they were tortured, they were beaten with rods;
while they lived they wandered as outcasts from
city to city, or dwelt in caves of the earth; and
after they had sealed their testimony to the truth
with their blood, men whom the world calls great
in piety and good works often conspired to cover
their names with undeserved infamy.[1] Not a few
of these leaders were men of the highest culture,
the broadest learning of their times—scholars not

---

[1] A case in point is that of Ludwig Hätzer, beheaded at Constance
in 1529. The Anabaptist chroniclers are unanimous in saying that
he "was condemned for the gospel, and witnessed in knightly
fashion for the truth with his blood." Nevertheless, the Archives
of Constance say that he was condemned for bigamy, which he had
confessed. Everything in his life and writings gives the lie to this
record, which is open to suspicion from the fact that Anabaptism

unworthy of a place beside Erasmus and Melanchthon, preachers whose eloquence was not inferior
to that of Luther or Zwingli. It was their misfortune to be on the losing side of a great controversy,
and they were obliged to pay for their allegiance to
truth and righteousness not only life and fame, but
honour. Their very names are known only to a
few curious scholars, and their writings — if any
have escaped the zeal of rival persecutors, Catholic
and Protestant—are to be found in dusty archives
or the dark corners of libraries and museums.

It is with the hope of doing something to rescue
from his undeserved oblivion one of the greatest
Anabaptist leaders that this biography has been
undertaken. The rage of persecution did not succeed, in his case, in destroying what his busy pen
sent forth, and we have fairly adequate materials
for a biography. Not quite every line, but nearly

---

was not then a capital offence in Constance, and some other pretext
must be found to put him to death. In later years Hätzer was accused of advocating polygamy, and of having as many as twenty-four
wives ! We find no contemporary attestation to these slanders
where we should most expect it if there were any truth in them.
For example, Capito's letters to Zwingli (Zwingli, *Op.*, vii., 420,
422, 455, 456, etc.), though they accuse Hätzer of many things, do
not mention immorality. Füsslin rejects the charge altogether.
Neue und unpartheyische Kirchen und Ketzerhistorie, iii., 269.

DR. JOHN ECK.

TRADITIONAL PORTRAIT.

so, of his printed writings has survived, and the chief events in his career are otherwise well attested. Of no other leader of the Anabaptists can so much be said; biographies of the greater part of them must for ever go unwritten, because materials no longer exist for more than the meagrest of sketches. There has been no attempt in these pages at idealising Hübmaier. What he was and what he did will be found plainly set forth, and as far as possible in his own words, with no concealment of his errors, no apology for his faults. His life and teachings, his character and fate, will speak for themselves, and the biographer need add nothing further.

CHAPTER II

THE YEARS OF PREPARATION

1481–1523

GREAT obscurity envelops the early life of Hübmaier. Certain record remains of but one fact relating to his origin: he was born in Friedburg, an ancient town on the Ach, some five miles east of the city of Augsburg. He sometimes called himself, and was called by others, an Augsburger. More frequently he was known in his earlier years as Friedburger or Pacimontanus; later he is usually called by his surname of Hübmaier. The year of his birth can only be conjectured; it was probably 1480 or 1481.

Of his family we know absolutely nothing. It was evidently of peasant origin, as is witnessed by its meaning, "the farmer on the hill." [1] From the

---

[1] Hübmaier = Hübel (provincial for Hügel) meier.

circumstance that his parents lived in the town of Friedburg and were able to give their son more than the ordinary education of his day, it might be plausibly conjectured that they had risen to the artisan or small-merchant class. Yet, as there are not a few instances in the sixteenth century of sons of poor peasants obtaining a university education, little confidence can be placed in any such inference. That the family was of no importance may be more certainly inferred from the fact that no record of it remains, and that no trace of it is to be found to-day. It may perhaps be still further inferred that, as Hübmaier never visited his parents after he came of age, and never refers to them in his writings, they had died during the years of his education. In his case, however, silence means nothing, for he says singularly little about himself, only in two or three instances, hereafter to be cited, referring to anything in his past life, and then for apologetic reasons.

Everything in the character and life of Hübmaier goes to show that he received a careful religious training in his tender years. From the first he seems to have been inclined to piety and the service

of God, and we shall not go astray if we attribute
this inclination of heart to the influence of a Christian mother.   As to his education, it was no doubt
begun, according to the customs of the time, in
some local school, but at an early age the lad was
sent to the Latin school of Augsburg, then a famous
institution for the training of boys.   Of the Augsburg of Hübmaier's days there remain few traces
except the cathedral, parts of which are of the
tenth century.   The most diligent search has failed
to discover even a tradition as to the location of the
school that he attended.   That he made unusual
progress in his studies and was already singled out
as a boy of exceptional promise, is all that we now
know of this part of his career.

It is clear, however, either that he began his
studies in preparation for the university somewhat
later than was customary, or that they were frequently interrupted by poverty or illness.   The
former is the more probable, for there was little
difficulty of a financial sort in the way of a bright
boy's education in those days.   Now there are
scholarships and funds of various kinds to smooth
the way of such; then, the Church was ever on the

THE UNIVERSITY OF INGOLSTADT, AS IT IS TO-DAY.

lookout for promising youths to enter the ranks of the priesthood or one of the celebrated orders. But Hübmaier was past twenty years of age before he was ready to enter the university, and past thirty before he took his baccalaureate degree, as we should say. Luther and Eck, some years his juniors, had already been lecturing for several years in their respective universities, while Hübmaier was still an undergraduate.

The first written record that we have of Hübmaier is his matriculation at the University of Freiburg, under date of May 1, 1503. In the matriculation book he is described as "Baldesar Hiebmayr de Augusta" *i. e.*, from Augsburg. This university, established in 1456, was but little older and hardly more famous than the much nearer University of Ingolstadt, and why the more distant institution should have been sought is not easily conjectured. Here the usual studies of the period were pursued with ardour and success, until the taking of his Master's degree, probably in 1511. On the occasion of his taking a later degree an oration was delivered, according to the academic custom of those days, by his master, Dr. Eck, which gives us practically all that is known concerning this part of his life:

" Well grounded in the rudiments of grammar and the easier subjects taught, he came to the Freiburg high school and became a student there. It is wonderful to say with what circumspection and eagerness he acquired the doctrines of philosophy, how he hung upon the lips of his teacher and zealously wrote down the lectures—a diligent reader, an unwearied hearer and an industrious repetitor [1] of other hearers. So he obtained the Master's degree with the greatest honour. Many had advised him to pursue the study of medicine; to whom he answered: he would rather seek theology as the holiest mistress, and say with the prophet, I have long since chosen her, and will prepare her a dwelling in the sanctuary of my mind. [2] And although the narrow means of his father's house [3] was so embarrassing to him that he had to leave

---

[1] It was the custom in Hübmaier's day for bright students to give private lectures to their fellows, repeating the substance of what the professor had taught. Such a course was called a *Repetorium*, and the lecturer was a *Repetitor*. The custom has its analogue in the " quiz " classes in the medical schools of the present day. At the present time a *Repetitor* in a German university corresponds pretty nearly to a tutor in an American college.

[2] Hoschek gives (p. 120) a somewhat different version of Hübmaier's praise of theology : " Her alone have I chosen, her before all others have I selected, and for her will I prepare a cell in my heart." But for the original see Wiedemann, *Dr. Johann Eck*, Regensburg, 1865, p. 451.

[3] This reference to his father's poverty might be taken in itself to negative the above-mentioned conjecture regarding Hübmaier's family, but some sudden reverse might have overtaken a man hitherto prosperous.

A LECTURE-ROOM (POSSIBLY HUBMAIER'S) IN THE OLD UNIVERSITY OF INGOLSTADT.

the high school for a long time, and, to protect himself
from want, became a school-teacher in Schaffhausen, yet
he returned at the first favourable opportunity to his accustomed studies and under my guidance. What progress he then made, his learned lectures, his sermons
before the people, and his scholastic exercises give a
sufficient testimony.''

This eulogy was returned with interest three
years later, when Eck published the text of a disputation held by him at Bologna, for which occasion
Hübmaier, like Silas Wegg, "dropped into poetry":

" O felix nimium felix Germania, quæ nunc
    Doctiloquos gignis multisciosque viros.
Cleopatream priscus satis extulit umbram
    Objicient doctum sæcula nostra virum.
Eckius is meus est Germano sydere natus
    Illo nimirum Theutona terra nitet.
Theologus rarus, juris Sophiæque peritus
    Sæpius in populum semina sacra serit.
Nodosam Logicen (si mavis) Rhetoris arma
    Quæque mathematicus, Astronomusque docent
Quicquid habet Rhetor, Historia, culta poesis
    Dispeream si non singula solus habet.[1]

These verses, if they contain words that would
have made Quintilian stare and gasp, have at least

---

[1] Wiedemann, *Dr. Johann Eck*, pp. 462, 463. The lines may be
rather freely englished thus: " O happy, too happy Germany, that
now producest men of so great eloquence and learning ! Antiquity
brought forth beauty as her choicest product, our age presents the

the merit of brevity, and are not much worse than
the specimens that Eck's biographer gives us from
the most famous scholars of that age.

From another source we learn more about the
Schaffhausen episode of which Eck speaks: the
official records of the city inform us that Baltisar
Hubmer of Augsburg was a temporary resident of
the town in 1507, and had taken the prescribed
oath of obedience to the laws.[1] Beyond this, little
or nothing can be added to the words of Eck. Of
Hübmaier's university career only one other detail
can be supplied, and that is told us by himself, in
one of his rare autobiographic passages. In his last
known writing, he says that twenty years before,
he held a disputation at Freiburg on the question
whether it is allowable to increase the number of
feast days, himself taking the negative. His enemies accused him in Zürich, in 1526, of stealing
gowns while he was at Freiburg; it is possible there

---

scholar. My Eck, sprung from the stars, is surely the bright orna-
ment of this German land. A rare theologian, skilled in law and
wisdom, he often sows the good seed among the people. A knotty
logician, a master of sentences, whatever mathematician or astrono-
mer teaches, all that orator, historian, or poet knows—I 'll be hanged
if this single man does not know it all!"

[1] Loserth, p. 15, note 4.

CHURCH OF THE VIRGIN, INGOLSTADT.

Liebfrauenkirche

was some escapade on which such a construction could be placed by an enemy, for students then were full of their pranks as now, but the high repute that he always maintained makes it certain that there could have been nothing more than this in the charge.

The most important fact regarding his course at Freiburg is that it brought Hübmaier under the influence of John Mayer, better known as Eck, a surname assumed because he was born in the Swabian town of that name. Though five or six years the junior of his pupil, Eck was farther advanced, having already gained fame for his scholastic and patristic learning, and still more for his readiness and skill in dialectics. He was, in addition, the more strenuous and masterful spirit; and had the two men remained in close connection we might have seen on the Catholic side during the Reformation struggle a pair closely approximating the characteristics and influence of Luther and Melanchthon on the Protestant side. Eck was at this time principal of Peacock Hall,[1] one of the students' societies or

---

[1] Hoschek says (i., 120) that, by the influence of Eck, Hübmaier himself was elected superintendent of Peacock Hall, but this appears to be an error. *Cf.* Loserth, p. 16.

Bursen, and it is morally certain that Hübmaier was a member of this body. It was the general custom of the universities of that day to give much attention to disputation, as a means of fixing acquirements in memory and making one's entire mental resources instantly responsive to any demand. So great a master of dialectics, so eager a disputant as Eck proved himself to be during his whole life, would certainly magnify this part of his work as a teacher. From many sources we learn that his students were constantly exercised in debating disputed questions in theology, and such exercises were more than grateful to Hübmaier. Here he imbibed that ardent love of religious controversy which all his life was quite as characteristic of him as love of the truth. All his writings show that he revelled in discussion for its own sake, though also without doubt as a means of eliciting truth.

It was in 1511, apparently, that Hübmaier received the master's degree, of which Eck makes mention in the words already quoted. According to the customs of the time, this degree in itself gave him the right to teach, but he seems in addition to have received a formal recognition as a member of the Freiburg faculty. Here he might have remained but for a quarrel that broke out between the university and Eck concerning the latter's salary. The pupil espoused his teacher's quarrel with more zeal than discretion, and the result was that both soon left the university. Eck received an appointment in the University of Ingolstadt, and his influence was sufficient to secure a position also for his devoted pupil and friend.

The University of Ingolstadt had been established in 1472 by Duke Lewis the Rich, and was already a famous institution. It became still more celebrated through Eck's connection with it, and by the end of the sixteenth century is said to have had four thousand students. The town is a small one, and though now one of the great fortresses of the southern frontier of the German Empire, is a place of slight commercial importance, and its population of about twenty thousand is little if any in excess of its mediæval size. Being thus outstripped in growth by other towns, it became less desirable as an educational centre, and since 1826 the university has been merged in that of Munich.

The original university building, however, is still

3

standing, and the exterior has evidently suffered little alteration. It is in a quiet part of the town, a few squares distant from the chief market-place, where the old-fashioned horse-car deposits the visitor whom it has brought from the railway station, two miles away. The interior of the building is more modern than the outside, but the arrangement of the rooms is unchanged, and one easily believes the assurance that it has undergone only such refitting as was necessary to adapt it for its present purpose, a gymnasium or high school for boys. The Aula, where disputations were once held and degrees conferred, is now a museum and library ; and in rooms where once echoed lectures and discussions on theology are now chemical and physical laboratories. The name of Eck is still remembered and honoured by the teachers, but that of Hübmaier is forgotten, and the mention of it is greeted with a stare.

On his first coming to Ingolstadt, Hübmaier was entitled, by virtue of his master's degree, to lecture only on philosophy, but he was speedily made a Doctor in Theology. On September 29, 1512, the degree was conferred, Dr. Eck presiding and delivering an oration *De Sacerrima Theologia* (Concerning

MEMORIAL TABLET TO DR. JOHN ECK, IN THE CHURCH OF THE VIRGIN, INGOLSTADT.

Most Holy Theology) which contains the already cited passage on the candidate's scholastic life. At about this time Hübmaier was also made university preacher and chaplain of the Church of the Virgin. This, the most interesting of the churches now found in Ingolstadt, had but recently been completed in his day. It is a fine old Gothic edifice, with two tall square towers; and the interior, apart from its interest as the place where Hübmaier preached, attracts those who wish to see the last resting-place of Eck. He died in Ingolstadt in 1543, and his body lies beneath a huge slab in a little chapel of the north aisle, above it a bronze tablet bearing his portrait and a suitable Latin inscription. The Church of the Virgin was the university church in the sixteenth century. The receiving of this important appointment warrants at least two inferences: that Hübmaier had been ordained to the priesthood some time before, and that he had already won some reputation as a preacher. The making of the appointment would otherwise be incomprehensible. Not even the influence of Eck would have induced the authorities to bestow a post so important upon a wholly untried man.

Hübmaier's various talents enabled him speedily to take a leading position at Ingolstadt, and he approved himself on trial as not only an eloquent lecturer and preacher, but a good man of affairs. At Easter, 1515, he was made vice-rector of the university. The rector at that time was the Margrave Friedrich von Brandenburg, but the rectorship of a nobleman must have been merely nominal and ornamental, and the real manager of the affairs of the university was Hübmaier. We have only one recorded incident of his administration of this office: an annalist of the city narrates that on one occasion he was fined ten ducats and confined to his house three days for releasing a student who had been imprisoned for assaulting a woman.

The growing fame of Hübmaier as a pulpit orator secured for him a call to Regensburg as chief preacher in the cathedral. The Danube with its tributaries was the great commercial highway of Southern Germany before railways were known; and Regensburg, or Ratisbon, situated at the confluence of the Danube and Regen, was then as now a much more important town than Ingolstadt. The cathedral, which was then nearing completion, is

surpassed in spaciousness and beauty only by that
of Strassburg among the cities of that region. We
have no information as to the motives that induced
Hübmaier to accept this call; he was doubtless ambitious, and the new position seemed to him one of
greater influence, and a quicker road to promotion,
than a chair of theology. Possibly he had become
conscious that his vocation was that of preacher and
agitator rather than teacher. The decision to leave
Ingolstadt was, at any rate, the turning-point in his
life. Hitherto he had been under the influence,
not to say control, of a stronger nature than his
own; henceforth he becomes independent, free to
develop according to the laws of his own nature.
One other thing is also clear: Ingolstadt parted
with him unwillingly. In later years, when he had
to defend himself against many aspersions, the university and town council gave him written testi-
monial of his innocence. During his residence
there he had made many warm friends, some influential,—among them the Count Palatine John.
He left Ingolstadt January 25, 1516, after labouring
there three years and five months.

On his arrival at Regensburg he found an anti-

Jewish movement in progress among the citizens, and he threw himself into the contest with ardour. In fact, he soon became the leader, and advocated his cause in the pulpit, in the street, in the market-place, before the magistrates. There had been a strong anti-Jewish feeling in Regensburg for more than a generation, due in large part to the peculiar position occupied by the Jews in the city. They lived in one of the oldest parts of the town, surrounded by a wall, and enjoyed many special privileges. They were lodged in what we should now call tenement-houses,—high, narrow buildings,—beneath which were cellars and secret passages where they could hide from the officers of civil and religious courts. At times, when the persecution was severe, they dared not go outside their own region, and then opened only a little gate through which could be passed the necessaries of life and the pledges of Christians who wished loans. Sometimes at Easter even this loophole was closed for a week or more.

The Jewish quarter of Regensburg disappeared long ago so completely that no trace of it is now to be found; but the city of Augsburg contains a

THE CATHEDRAL, REGENSBURG
HERE HÜBMAIER WAS CHIEF PREACHER, 1516–1520

quarter that helps the modern traveller comprehend what it must have been. In Augsburg one of the most interesting sights is the "Fuggerei," a section of the town endowed in 1519 by John Jacob Fugger, the Rothschild of the sixteenth century, to furnish free homes for the poor. The Fuggerei is a little walled city within the city, the gates of which are shut at night; and in this quarter are fifty-three houses, of two and three stories each, still tenanted at a merely nominal rent by poor Roman Catholic citizens of Augsburg—for the Fuggers were good Catholics, and the trust has been faithfully administered, as the founder intended it should be. But the Fuggerei is a model city quarter—clean, quiet, and orderly, while the Jewish quarter of Regensburg, by all accounts, was dirty, noisy, and unsanitary.

Although the Regensburg Jews were hard pressed by taxes and exactions of every sort, by the Emperor, the Duke of Bavaria, the bishop of the diocese, the city,—and the city tax was higher for the Jews than for the burghers, — nevertheless, through their enterprise and system they had managed to get into their hands the principal part of the

city's business, and the whole town and even the
region about was in their debt. They had mort-
gages on many of the surrounding estates in their
coffers. It was charged, probably with truth, that
they were receivers of stolen goods, and the plate on
their boards was often made of vessels taken from
the altars of Christian churches. But their chief
crime, no doubt, was that they were too rich. The
people saw only too clearly that, while their affairs
went from worse to worst, while the public finances
became more and more embarrassed, while the trade
and manufactures of the city more and more declined, the Jews continued to prosper. What was
more natural than that they should lay the blame
for all this on the Jews? The priests, therefore,
found willing ears to listen to their denunciation of
the usury of this people, and the citizens flocked to
hear such sermons.

The Regensburg Jews were under the special protection of the House of Austria, and at the meeting
of the Reichstag at Cologne in 1512 they appealed
for protection against the constantly increasing persecutions. It was the Imperial policy to hold this
movement in check, and accordingly the fanaticism

that Hübmaier and others had aroused could not
fail in time to bring the city into sharp collision
with the Imperial Government.   This actually happened in 1517.   The first appeal of the Jews to the
law was unavailing.   Palgrave John, the administrator of the bishopric, threatened with excommunication any who should compel a Christian to pay
usurious interest to a Jew.   Papal confirmation of
this decision was obtained, and Hübmaier preached
from the pulpit: "We have brought a bull from
Rome, the effect of which is to put under the bann
every one who helps a Jew to his usurious interest."
The Jews on their part obtained an Imperial mandate commanding the people of Regensburg to
molest these people no further, and the next year,
when the Reichstag met at Augsburg, the Jewish
question was thoroughly discussed in a secret
session.

Hübmaier was sent to Augsburg to defend the
clergy, and the city also had its representative there.
The presence of this hated preacher against their
race roused the Jews to special efforts, and they did
everything in their power to secure his expulsion.
So well did they use their influence and money that

an Imperial messenger was sent to Regensburg, demanding Hübmaier's recall. The messenger moreover bore a mandate that the administrator should
not summon Jews before his court again; that the
priests should cease preaching against them; and
declared the papal bull, having been issued without the Emperor's consent, to be null and void.
The council attempted to temporise, saying that
Hübmaier was not at Augsburg as a representative
of the city, but as a cleric, and therefore not under
their jurisdiction. The Imperial messenger refused
to accept this disclaimer; he replied that the council
had the keys of the city, and if Hübmaier persisted
in remaining at Augsburg, against their command,
they could lock the gates against him. Reluctantly,
we may presume, the city did as required.

The decision of the Reichstag was in favour of
the Jews; a special court and judge were appointed
to try their cases. Hübmaier in the meantime appears to have contumaciously remained at Augsburg, and he had some difficulty in obtaining
permission to return. Only the intercession of
powerful friends, and a pledge on his part that he
would henceforth show greater moderation, made

INTERIOR OF THE REGENSBURG CATHEDRAL.

THE TOMB IN THE NAVE IS IN MEMORY OF BISHOP PHILIP WILLIAM, DUKE OF BAVARIA, AND
WAS ERECTED IN 1598.

his peace with the Emperor and enabled him to return. It throws some light on his character at this time that he promised the city council on his arrival that he would do just the contrary, that he would not slacken his efforts against the Jews; while, as for his pledge to the Emperor, he said, the Church would hold him guiltless, and would defend him! It is true that this was the common morality of ecclesiastics in his day, though a less frank avowal of perfidy was usual.

It is difficult, from the facts we have at hand, to infer the motives that led Hübmaier to take so active and so discreditable a part in this agitation. It is extremely probable that he honestly shared the prejudices of his time against the Jews, and even believed that persecution of them was a mark of a good Christian. Even after he had become more enlightened as to the true spirit of the gospel, he expressed no regret for his course, but rather gives it tacit approval, though he by no means tells the whole story of his misdeeds. In 1526 he makes this allusion to the matter: "When I was preacher in Regensburg, I saw the great oppression that the population suffered from the Jews; I saw that ecclesiastical and secular statutes gave law and sentence against this. Then I said to the people from the pulpit, that they ought not to suffer in this wise for the future. But nobody repented, and all remained as before." [1]

The agitation against the Jews in Regensburg dragged until after the death of Emperor Maximilian. In the spring of 1519 they were driven out, and their synagogue was turned into a Christian chapel, dedicated "to the beauteous Mary" (*zur Schönen Maria*). Shortly after, miracles were said to be wrought at this shrine, great excitement arose, people began to make pilgrimages to this altar, and gifts poured in. It was decided to build a church, and the corner-stone was laid September 9th. On this, besides the name of the administrator and suffragan-bishop, appeared the name of Hübmaier, the first chaplain of the "beauteous Mary." On September 16th he gave to the council a list of fifty-four testimonies to the miracles wrought at this shrine. The fame of these rapidly extended through all the neighbouring district, and even

---

[1] From his examination while in prison at Zürich, Egli, *Actensammlung zur Geschichte der Zürcher Reformation*, S. 432.

farther, throughout Austria, Bohemia, and Moravia, and from everywhere came the throngs of pilgrims. Grave mischiefs and abuses accompanied these pilgrimages; all the population seemed to be affected. When they went through a town by night women crowded to see them, often in their nightclothes; by day men left their business and followed as if they, too, would go on pilgrimage, some with a hayfork in their hands, others with a scythe. The more sensible thought the people had all gone crazy. Impostors appeared, and at length the Regensburg council found itself compelled to adopt some measures of repression, or at least of control.

These pilgrimages aroused much attention and discussion in the whole Empire. As to Hübmaier's exact part in them there is almost nothing to warrant an inference. One of his biographers[1] has accused him of fomenting the fanaticism, and says that good Catholics blamed him for his excessive zeal. Another[2] says that he preached against the fanaticism and did what he could to moderate it. Neither seems to have any grounds for so positive assertion; all that is certain is that Hübmaier's

---

[1] Loserth, p. 25.   [2] Hoschek, i., 123.

attitude, so far as known, was favourable to the pilgrimages, since he professed a complete faith in the miracles, and has left no record of his disapproval.

In the year 1542, when the Reformation had extended to Bavaria, the chapel of the "beauteous Mary" became a Lutheran church. The statues, pictures, and relics that had been accumulated were removed and for the most part destroyed. The chapel was enlarged, and the new edifice became known as the *Neupfarrkirche*, which name it still bears.[1] A few of the relics and pictures have been preserved, and among these the curious visitor may still see an old and much-dimmed oil painting, that shows the original chapel, with its altar and relics, and a crowd of adoring pilgrims kneeling before it.

The authorities of the city were not the only ones aroused to action by these pilgrimages. Regens-

---

[1] The photograph from which the illustration of the *Neupfarrkirche* is made shows from the east side the church as it now exists. This end of the church, with its apse, is comparatively new ; the original chapel is the western part, from the line of the two towers, which are little altered. A transverse aisle separates the new portion of the interior from the old, and a gallery has been built in recent times within the latter. It would hardly be possible for any building to undergo a greater transformation than this chapel of the "beauteous Mary" shows—only the western walls and towers remain in substantially the former condition.

THE MODERN NEUPFARRKIRCHE, REGENSBURG.

THE FARTHER PART, WITH THE TOWERS, IS PART OF HÜBMAIER'S CHAPEL ZUR SCHÖNEN MARIA.

burg was the home of one of the largest, richest, and most famous Dominican monasteries in Europe. It had been made famous by the lectures of Albertus Magnus, next to Thomas Aquinas the greatest of the mediæval scholastics. Though not formally a university, this had always been a celebrated school, and was still an important seat of learning. There were also two Benedictine abbeys: one originally founded by followers of Columban, and hence still known as the *Schottenkirche;* the other, St. Emmeram, founded in the seventh century, was also one of the oldest monastic establishments in Germany. These orders had for three centuries been the dominant religious force in Regensburg, and had for a still longer period been accustomed to absorb all the surplus wealth of the faithful. It was not to be reckoned that they would submit without a struggle to this sudden and startlingly successful rivalry of a new shrine and an upstart preacher belonging to none of the orders.

The great income of the chapel through the gifts of the pilgrims quickly roused the jealousy of the orders, especially of the Dominicans, and they began to attack the whole affair in their sermons.

From the same cause, there began a strife in 1520 between the chapter of the cathedral and the city council over the patronage, which the city claimed, and its claim was confirmed by the court attorney of Nürnberg.   Hübmaier undertook to play the part of mediator, and set forth in behalf of the chapter that before there was any thought of building the great church, offering-boxes had been placed under the pulpit in the cathedral and in the country churches, and liberal gifts for the building had been thus collected.   It was evident therefore, that the new chapel had been erected not from the resources of the city, but from alms, and, this being the case, the council had no legal title to the patronage.   In spite of the general esteem in which he was held among the citizens, this attempt at mediation was a failure.   In consequence, the numerous grudges that were entertained against him among the clergy began to manifest themselves.   He and his chapel were the object of their jealousy, and they preached against both with renewed vigour.

It may have been these troubles that decided the question of Hübmaier's longer stay in Regensburg. There is no ground whatever for the assertion of his biographer, Hoschek,[1] that he had already become infected with heresy, and left in order that he might find a field where the Reformation was more likely to succeed than in Regensburg. So many circumstances conspire to negative this hypothesis, that it may be confidently pronounced unworthy of serious consideration. We know, both from his own testimony and from other sources, that he left Regensburg with the esteem of its citizens and the powerful friends that he had made. In 1526, replying to the charge of his enemies that he secretly ran away from the city, he said:

"How I departed from Ingolstadt and Regensburg know his serene highness, prince and lord John, Count Palatine and administrator at Regensburg, my especially gracious lord; also the most noble, honourable and wise captain, city treasurer and council of that city; also the university and the honourable council at Ingolstadt, all of whom gave me letters testifying my innocence of such invented and base untruths. Also William Wyeland, burgher and councilman at Regensburg, took me and my furniture on his iron-boat, and at midday starting from Regensburg brought me to Ulm. I was also exempted from all customs and tolls by reason of the letters of assistance which my gracious lord at Regensburg gave me."[2]

[1] Hoschek, i., 122.
[2] Hübmaier, *Ein kurze Entschuldigung*, Nikolsburg, 1526. *Op.* 13.
4

He might have added that the city gave him, in grateful recognition of his distinguished services, a parting gift of forty gulden. This of itself is sufficient proof that he departed with no odour of heresy or misdeed clinging to his garments. He left behind him the repute of being an unusually faithful and zealous son of the Church. It is indeed surprising that neither at this time, nor for some time later, does Hübmaier show any sympathy with the Reformation; not even do his words or acts betray the consciousness that any such movement was in progress. The final persecution of the Jews in Regensburg was coincident with the posting of Luther's theses, and the miracles and pilgrimages happened in the year of the Leipzig disputation. The old friendship between Eck and Hübmaier showed as yet no signs of fracture, and one would have thought this would have been sufficient to attract the latter's attention to a controversy in which his former master was taking so prominent a part. Perhaps his attention was attracted, perhaps he read what was printed on both sides of the controversy, but if so his own personal concerns so far absorbed his attention that no immediate result

DOMINICAN MONASTERY, REGENSBURG.

was produced, whatever effect might have followed later.

From Regensburg Hübmaier went to Waldshut, a little town in the Breisgau, on the Rhine, beautiful for situation but of no commercial significance. Its military importance was considerable, and might be again in certain contingencies, as it completely commands the Rhine, and could be held by a relatively small force. This living was part of the patronage of the convent of Königsfeld, in the canton of Aargau, and how the choice fell upon Hübmaier is not known.[1] Nor is it easy to see how he came to choose such a field of labour in preference to Regensburg. The walls of Waldshut have been long since removed, and the town has spread somewhat beyond its ancient limits, but even now it must have a population considerably below four thousand, and a walk of ten minutes will take one from one end to the other of the "city." There

---

[1] Loserth (p. 25) conjectures that he secured the place through the favour of the Count Palatine ; Hoschek (i., 123) is sure that the intercession of the Swiss reformers obtained it for him. Against the latter supposition the known facts are decisive : it was certainly not until after his settlement at Waldshut that the acquaintance between Hübmaier and the Swiss leaders began, as we shall presently see.

seems to be but one church—the same that stood in Hübmaier's day and in which he preached—and it is apparently quite ample for the needs of the town.

Possibly the character of the people, rather than the size of the town, constituted the attraction for Hübmaier. They were thoroughly German in blood and speech, and had the characteristics of that people; but, in addition, their proximity to Switzerland and their dwelling among the mountains had given to them a passionate love of liberty. They were a strong, resolute, simple people, loyal to the House of Hapsburg and the religion of their fathers. They had no intention of being disloyal to prince or religion, as they had inherited the authority of both, and they had every intention of maintaining stoutly what they regarded as their own privileges and rights.

In such a town and among such a people Hübmaier began his work in the spring of 1521, and soon found himself quite at home among them. For two years he remained a zealous Catholic, continuing the observance of all the ancient practices, and even introducing new ceremonies. In great thunder-storms he stationed himself at the church

door with the Host and blessed the clouds; at
Easter and on other occasions, as when the Host
was carried to the sick, he saw to it that everything
was done with much pomp and state; he was particular that two communicants from the council
should be present at the sacrament; to Mary and
all the saints he paid great veneration.

But during these same two years a great change in
his religious convictions was beginning, and perhaps
these outward marks of zeal were only attempts on
his part to confirm himself in a faith that was
wavering. He was giving his leisure hours to the
study of the Scriptures, in which, so far as we
know, he was now beginning for the first time to
take a real interest. How much he became absorbed in this study his letters prove. He devoted
especial attention to the Pauline epistles, first reading the letter to the Romans, and then the letters
to the Corinthians. There could be but one result
of such study, and though we have no definite
record of Hübmaier's conversion, his life from this
time indicates that at about the end of the year
1522 he had come to see that the Catholic Church
had departed, in doctrine and practice, from the

teachings of the apostles; and he had also, in consequence of his study of the New Testament, come to a clear understanding of the gospel, and sought his personal salvation from Christ himself, and not from the Church and its sacraments.

A visit to Switzerland, in June, 1522, was an important factor in producing this change. He first journeyed to Basel, where he made the acquaintance of Busch, Glareanus, and Erasmus. He conferred with the latter on the doctrine of purgatory, and some dark places in the Gospel of John, but received little aid. He was not at all pleased with Erasmus, in fact, and said of him afterwards, "Erasmus speaks freely but writes cautiously." From Basel he went to (the Swiss) Freiburg. "I have found this quite other than its name implies," he writes; "it is not free but imprisoned, and rent with faction and narrowness." In Basel he noted that the cloisters were becoming more empty from day to day, and that the nuns were marrying. Switzerland was seething with disaffection to the old faith, and on the eve of a religious revolution. Hübmaier returned to Waldshut and plunged anew into the study of the Pauline epistles. At about this time

WALDSHUT AND THE RHINE.

also we find that he is reading some of the tracts of Luther that had been so widely scattered among the German people.

At this juncture of affairs, his friends at Regensburg recalled him to be preacher at the chapel of the "beauteous Mary." The old dispute between the chapter and the council had been compromised, through the intervention of the Duke of Bavaria. The bishop was to have spiritual jurisdiction over the church, and the right of confirmation and investiture of all foundations, besides an indemnity in ready money; on the other hand, the council had the patronage of the chapel and the management of its income. Hübmaier began his work there on Advent Sunday, 1522,[1] and found the chapel well filled with both clergy and laity, especially the council, to his great pleasure. His salary was fixed at fifty gulden, besides thirty kreutzer for the week-day services. In return he was to sing or have sung three masses a week, preach as often as the provost required, have processions, and contribute of his means to the aid of pilgrims.

He began preaching from the Gospel of Luke

---

[1] Egli, *Actensammlung*, No. 911.

and promised a course of sermons from that book.
There is no doubt that he was now strongly inclin-
ing to the new doctrine and that his preaching was
of the evangelical type, though he practised the
rites of the Church.   In a letter written at this time
to a friend in Ulm, he says that Christ is preached
in unadulterated fashion in Nürnberg, in spite of
the opposition of Frederick of Austria and other
princes, and adds: "Also among us in Bavaria is
the gospel preached."   But with him this return to
Regensburg was an experiment, as is shown by the
fact that he had taken care not to resign his pastor-
ate at Waldshut, and had so provided himself a way
of retreat.   Inclined as he now was to the reformed
doctrine, he could see little prospect of its progress
in Bavaria; Waldshut offered a more hopeful field.
Accordingly, before the close of his trial year,
March 1, 1523, he gave up his position at Regensburg and returned to Waldshut.   That he was still
held in high esteem by the Regensburgers is shown
by the fact that they presented him at his departure
with fifteen gulden.[1]

---

[1] A special resolution of the council makes mention of this pledge
of their friendship. *Cf.* Loserth, p. 21.

On taking up his work anew at Waldshut, Hübmaier almost from the first gave decisive proofs of
his change of religious convictions. In a month
after his return we find him in active communication
with the Swiss reformers. He visited Zürich and
conferred with Zwingli on various subjects, especially on the baptism of infants, of which he had
been able to find no trace in the New Testament.
From Zürich he went to St. Gall, and made the
acquaintance of Joachim Watt, known as Vadianus.
He had established for himself the reputation of an
evangelical preacher, and was asked to preach.
This he did several times, to the great pleasure and
edification of the people. It was on his return to
Waldshut that he seems to have made known his
change of views and begun to introduce innovations.

It first becomes clear, however, that he has broken
forever with the old faith from the part that he
took in the second religious disputation at Zürich,
held by order of the Government in the council
hall, October 26–28, 1523. This discussion had
been forced on Zwingli and the council by the more
radical members of the reforming party at Zürich,
who wished for an immediate and thorough-going

reformation of religion, on the basis of the Holy Scriptures. Zwingli was till then in sympathy with the aims of this radical element, so far as they had been formulated and were understood by him, but it was his opinion that they were too precipitate in action and were inclined to press the work of reformation too rapidly. So far, however, the difference was concerning methods rather than principles, nor did the discussion develop a more serious difference than this.

The questions discussed at this gathering were the use of images and the celebration of the mass, two of the three days being given chiefly to the first subject. On the first day, after Zwingli, Leo, and others had quite fully discussed the matter,—all being agreed in principle that images are contrary to the gospel order, but Zwingli counselling moderation in action,—Hübmaier spoke as follows:

" He who is the omnipotent and eternal God has commanded us, through his servant Moses, thus: ' If thou meet thine enemy's ox or ass going astray, thou shalt surely bring it back to him again. If thou see the ass of him that hateth thee lying under his burden, thou shalt forbear to leave him, thou shalt surely release it with him ' [Ex. xxiii., 4, 5.]. And Christ admonishes us to the same effect: 'Which of you shall have an ass or an ox fallen into a well, and will not straightway draw him up on a Sabbath day?' [Luke xiv., 5].   And much more we ought to pity that man who has gone astray in those things that pertain to his salvation, or who has fallen into some deep ditch of error, so that our labours may release him and bring him back.   And it is as clear as day that for ages infinite errors and abuses have been brought into the Christian Church by Satan, who never rests; for he is certainly concerned with the business of images and the mass.   I can only praise, therefore, the most reverend council of this ancient town, which ordered that this friendly gathering should be held to discuss these matters, so that the sharp differences of many concerning religion might be adjusted in a friendly way and without any disturbance.   That surely cannot be done in a more fitting way, than by hearing passages from both Testaments produced in the midst of us.   For in all disputes concerning faith and religion, the Scripture alone, proceeding from the mouth of God, ought to be our level and rule.   For the Lord Himself has put that judge on the throne: 'And in a controversy they shall stand to judge: according to my judgments shall they judge it' (Ezek. xliv., 24).   Wherefore the Lord has ordered that the Scriptures shall be searched, and commanded that we hear Moses and the prophets; for he will not receive the testimony of man.   Christ has said the same, likewise Paul and all the apostles.   For, however often they had to contend against Satan or men evidently wicked, they pressed upon such the Scriptures, as the most fitting judge of every controversy, and by means of these alone they won the victory.   For the Scripture is the sole light and is a true lantern, by whose light all the fictions of

the human mind may be discovered and all darkness be
dispelled. The prophet David testifies to this in the saying, 'Thy word is a lamp to my feet' [Ps. cxix., 105].
And Christ Jesus warns us that we should take the lamp
of that saving word in our hands, that, when the bridegroom comes, we may enter with him to the eternal
marriage feast. Wherefore also, those errors that have
sprung up concerning images and the mass should be examined and corrected by the sole rule of the word of God.
Moreover, whatever shall be founded on this will endure
forever; for the word of God is eternal and immortal.''

On the second day he spoke somewhat more at
length and in less general terms against images:

" That images ought never to be made or retained was
sufficiently proved yesterday from the holy Testaments.
And for my part, I wish none had ever been brought
into a church of Christians. For what Ex. xx., 4, says,
is as clear and plain as it is valid and incontrovertible.
For by two eloquent laws it is forbidden not merely to
worship images, but even to make them. What is written in Deut. v., 6 *sq.* is even plainer, for there in three
commands God removes and overthrows everything of
the kind: 'I am the Lord thy God, who brought thee
out of the land of Egypt, out of the house of bondage.'
Secondly, 'Thou shalt not make unto thee a graven
image, the likeness of any form that is in the heaven
above, or that is in the earth beneath, or that is in the
water under the earth.' Thirdly, 'Thou shalt not bow
down thyself unto them nor serve them; for I, the Lord
thy God, am a jealous God, etc.' Whence he orders
them to burn with fire and curse him who makes such

things.   And all the people shall answer and say Amen
(Deut. xxvii., 15).[1]   I will add another two-horned argument that will easily overturn images.   To have images
is either commanded or it is not commanded.   If it is
commanded, let the Scriptures be produced and at once
all strife will be ended.   But if it was never commanded
that we have them, they are certainly of no use.   For
whatever God does not teach, either by his word or his
works, is altogether vain and useless.   For as God alone
is good so it follows that what is good comes from God
alone.   He that has said other than this charges false-
hood against God the Father, Christ the Son, and the
holy Paul.   God the Father: ' What thing soever I command you, that shall ye observe to do: thou shalt not
add thereto, nor diminish from it ' [Deut. xii., 32].
Christ the Son: ' Every plant which my heavenly Father
planted not shall be rooted up ' [Matt. xv., 13].   Paul:
' Whatsoever is not of faith is sin ' [Rom. xiv., 23].
Another thing also follows these.   One thing or the
other must be granted: images are either useful or useless to the Church.   But if they are of no use, what are
they for, I pray?   But if they are of some profit, shall we
say that God has proclaimed less than the truth when he
teaches in Is. xliv., 9, that they are profitable for nothing?   In view of these things, it is blasphemy if we
teach that images call, move, and draw our souls to piety.
For it is Christ who calls the sinner, who moves him to
what is good, invites him to the heavenly marriage feast;
God the Father draws those who come to Christ.   Since
then images, O woe! have at some time been brought
into the Church, there is need of great care and prudent

---

[1] Hübmaier, or his reporter, has combined Deut. vii., 5, with the
passage cited by him.

consideration lest any one be made to stumble and the general peace of believers be disturbed. For up to the present there are many who hold firmly to images. It is fitting, therefore, to quote diligently to such the word of God from both Testaments, and to place it before people's eyes. For so it will exert its own force and potency, so that all images will soon fall down. For it is impossible that, if the word of God be preached, it should not bring forth fruit in the place where God has sent it (Is. lv., 10, 11). Paul said this at Athens and many other places, as the Acts bear witness. Therefore, if this be done, individual believers will learn that images are of no value, and so it will come to pass that by common consent of the whole Church, without any trouble, it will be ordered that images be removed. And then it will be said that the word of God has accomplished the very thing for which it was sent."

The discussion of the third day related exclusively to the mass—a subject also discussed somewhat on the afternoon of the second day. This came home to all the participants and aroused great interest, as was manifest in the exceptionally lively debate. Zwingli was cautious in his statements, for while he repudiated the idea of actual sacrifice in connection with the mass, he seemed to admit that the euchar-ist might be a representation of Christ's sacrifice, though not a repetition. Hübmaier spoke again, making this contribution to the discussion:

"Although there are still several abuses left in the mass (which I prefer to call Christ's Testament, or the memorial of his death) this will certainly be seen to be the chief cause of all these: that we celebrate mass as a sacrifice. But, to mention that about which my mind is employed (though I am always ready to be taught better), I cannot announce it in any other way than Zwingli and Leo have done—by saying that the mass is no sacrifice, but rather a publishing of Christ's Testament, in which is celebrated the memorial of his death, through which he no doubt offered himself once for all on the altar of the cross and cannot be offered again. And whoever celebrates mass otherwise, undertakes to seal a document not yet written. The reason that moves me to say this is found in Matt. xxvi., Luke xxii., Mark xiv., 1 Cor. xi., Hebrews vii. and ix. Christ says, 'This do,' but not 'This offer.' Whence it follows, first, that the mass, if it is held to be a sacrifice, profits neither living nor dead. For as I cannot believe for another, so it is not permitted me to celebrate mass for another; since truly this was instituted by Christ as a sign, in which the faith of believers is confirmed.

"Secondly, since the body and blood of Christ are seals and tokens of Christ's words that it is customary to recite in the mass, priests ought to use and proclaim nothing but the pure and clear word of God, of which these are signs. Whoever celebrates the mass otherwise errs from the truth.

"Thirdly, he who does not proclaim the word of God does not celebrate the mass. Christ acknowledges the same, and Paul, his disciple: 'This do in remembrance of me.' 'As often as ye do this, ye do show forth the Lord's death.' Therefore it is necessary either that Christ yield his declaration, or our conclusion is true.

" Fourthly, the mass should be read in Latin to the Latins, in French to the French, and in German to the Germans. For there can be no doubt but that Christ used a language at the supper with his disciples that could be understood by all of them. And likewise when the mass is celebrated, it is ridiculous to recite Latin words to a German who knows nothing of the Latin language. What else is this than to hide the Lord whom we ought to proclaim ? Paul wishes so to speak in the Church as to be understood by all, and he would rather speak five words with the understanding than thousands in an unknown tongue (1 Cor. xiv., 19).

" Fifthly, he who undertakes to celebrate mass truly ought to feed not only himself, but also others hungering and thirsting in spirit, and that under both kinds. Christ taught this by both word and deed (Matt. xxvi., 27). Whoever therefore shall teach otherwise and administer otherwise, insolently violates Christ's Testament. This even an angel from heaven has no right to do, still less a man (Gal. i., 8).

" These, brethren, are my opinions concerning images and the mass, which I have learned from the Holy Scriptures. But if there is any error in them, I pray and beseech you, by Jesus Christ our only Saviour, and the day of his last judgment, to condescend to set me right through the Holy Scriptures in a fraternal and Christian manner. I can err, for I am a man, but I cannot be a heretic, for I am willing to be taught better by anybody. And if any one will teach me better, I acknowledge that I shall owe him great thanks; I will confess the error, and in accordance with the decision of the divine word I will

gladly and willingly, with greatest obedience, submit myself to you and follow you most carefully, as followers of
Christ. I have spoken. It is yours to judge me and set
me right. I will pray Christ to give you his grace for
this purpose.''

The decision of the Zürich council [1] was studiously
moderate—far too moderate to satisfy the radical
reformers, who now began to distrust Zwingli and
to draw away from him. The removal of the images
was not ordered, and as for the mass, each priest
was left to do as he liked, celebrate it or not, according to his own conscience and understanding of
the word of God—in short, the council wished to let
matters drift a while longer before taking vigorous
action.

On the whole, in these addresses Hübmaier shows
himself to be in agreement with the radical party
that was now fast developing in Zürich. His views
are more like those of Conrad Grebel, the spokes-
man of this party, than Zwingli's; yet his attitude
is not one of antagonism to the Zürich leader. But
it is evident that his views have undergone a great

---

[1] For the text of the decree, which was dated November 17th, see
Egli, *Actensammlung*, p. 173, No. 436; *cf.* Füsslin, *Beyträge*, ii.,
43–46.

5

transformation since his coming to Waldshut—he is now an evangelical, in the fullest significance of the term. Once for all he has taken his stand on the principle that for him the voice of Scripture is the only voice of authority, and consequently the only voice that he will obey.

A careful reading of the account of the disputation [1] confirms the idea that Zwingli did not at any time differ so much in doctrine from Grebel and Hübmaier, as in policy. He was in favour of proceeding slowly with the reform in Zürich, for many reasons. He had no objection to the radical programme as an ultimate goal,—he only objected to the attempt to realise it at once. He was probably calculating carefully just how fast the council could be persuaded to go, and just what changes the Zürich people would approve. The difference between them lay in the sphere of politics rather than in the domain of theology, but this the radicals could not see.

Excursus on the Spelling of Hübmaier's Name

It is no easy matter to decide how the name of the subject of this biography should be spelled. He lived

---

[1] The full account of this second disputation may be found in Zwingli's *Op.* i., 481 *sq.*

in an age when men had only vague ideas of orthography, especially in the matter of proper names. The oldest known form of the name is in the matriculation book of the University of Freiburg, where it is entered under date of May 1, 1503, as Baldesar Hiebmayr. The Christian name is spelled by contemporaries Balthazar Baldazar, Baldasar, Baltassar, and even Walthausar, while of the surname one finds not fewer than twenty spellings, namely, Hubmär, Huebmär, Huebmaier, Huebmer, Hubmejer, Hubemör, Hubmör, Huebmör, Hubmaier, Höebmöer, Hüebmör, Hüebmär, Hübmör, Hubmeyer, Hubmoyer, Huebmayr, Hiebmaier, Hubmer, Hübmer, Hubmair—to say nothing of such forms as Hilcmerus, Isubmarus, etc.

This ought not to surprise us, since it is well-known that there are more than threescore ways of spelling the name Shakespeare. Generally speaking, the principle should no doubt be recognised that a man knows best how to spell and pronounce his own name. But what are we to do if he knows how to spell it in several ways? Such is the case with the man with whom we have to do. In the only existing autograph (so far as known), which is preserved in the archives at Schaffhausen, and bears date of 1524, his signature is Baldasar Hüebmör. In his printed works he later adopted for the first name the spelling Balthasar, and as to that all are now practically agreed. During the last two years of his life he published seventeen tracts that are now in existence, and on the pages of thirteen of these he prints his name Huebmör, or Hübmör, essentially the same spelling.

Examination of the variant spellings shows that they are all attempts, more or less careful, to represent the same sounds. There is no real question as to how the name sounded in the ears of contemporaries. The first syllable is so frequently spelled Hieb, Hüb, or Hueb, as to leave no doubt that the vowel sound was that of *ü*, and the cases of variation are easily explicable on the theory that the umlaut was often carelessly dropped. The first syllable cannot possibly have sounded as Hoob. The vowel sound in the second syllable was obscure, and as it fell upon different ears might be represented almost equally well by mayr, meyer, maier, mör, or mär.

On the whole, therefore, the spelling Hübmaier seems to come nearest to reproducing the true sounds in accordance with modern usage.

CHAPTER III

1524

RETURNING from the disputation at Zürich committed to the work of reform, and full of the proverbial zeal of the new convert, Hübmaier set to work with energy to teach his townspeople the pure gospel. It was natural that he should attempt to apply the method that had been successful in Zürich, and accordingly one of his first steps was to invite all the clergy of the district to a disputation. As a preliminary, he drew up a series of theses, which appeared in print the following June, in this form:

" 1. Faith alone makes us just before God.
" 2. This faith is the knowledge of the mercy of God, which he manifested to us through the giving of his only begotten Son. Thereby are overthrown all sham Christians, who have only 'a historical faith' in God.

" 3. This faith cannot remain dead, but must manifest itself toward God in thanksgiving, toward our fellow-men in works of brotherly love. Thereby are all ceremonies destroyed, tapers, psalms, holy-water.

" 4. Only those works are good that God has commanded, and only those are evil that he has forbidden. Thereby fall fish, flesh, cowls, plates.

" 5. The mass is no sacrifice, but a memorial of the death of Christ. Hence it may be offered as a sacrifice neither for the dead nor for the living. Thereby fall masses for souls and the like.

" 6. When this memorial is celebrated, the death of our Lord should be preached in their mother tongue to believers. Thereby fall private masses.

" 7. Images are good for nothing; wherefore such expense should be no longer wasted on images of wood and stone, but bestowed upon the living, needy images of God.

" 8. Just as every Christian should believe and be baptised for himself, so it is his privilege to judge from the holy Scriptures if the bread and wine are rightly given him by his pastor.

" 9. As Christ alone died for our sins and we are baptised in his name alone, so should we call upon him only as our mediator and intercessor. Thereby fall all pilgrimages.

"10. It is better to explain a single verse of a psalm in the vernacular of the people, than to sing five whole psalms in a foreign language not understood by the people. Thereby vanish matins, prime, tierce, nones, vespers, compline, and vigils.

" 11. All doctrines not planted by God himself are profitless, condemned, and must be rooted up. Here fall to the ground Aristotle, the Scholastics, as Thomas, Scotus, Bonaventura and Occam, and all teachers who in their origin are not from God.

"12. The hour is coming and is already here, in which no one will be considered a priest but he who preaches the word of God. Thereby fall the sayers of early mass, suffragists, requiemists, sayers of intercessory masses.

"13. It is the duty of church-members, to whom the pure word of God is clearly preached, to provide food and clothing for the ministers. Thereby go to the ground the courtiers, pensioners, incorporators, absentees, liars and dream-babblers.

"14. Whoso seeks purgatory, the trust of those whose god is the belly, seeks the grave of Moses—it will never be found.

"15. To forbid priests to marry and wink at their carnal lewdness is to release Barabbas and put Christ to death.

"16. To promise chastity in the strength of man is nothing else than to fly over the sea without wings.

"17. Whoso for worldly advantage denies or remains silent concerning the word of God, sells the blessing of God, as Esau sold his birthright, and will also be denied by Christ.

"18. Whoso does not earn his bread by the sweat of his brow is in condemnation, [and] is not worthy of the food that he eats. Herewith are all idlers condemned, whoever they may be."

Although the title-page of the four-page pamphlet in which these theses appeared informs us that they were "disputed at Waldshut by Dr. Balthassar Fridberger in 1524," there is reason to doubt whether such a disputation actually occurred, though doubtless the author expected a discussion when he sent the writing to press. There is no reason to doubt, however, that he proceeded to reduce the doctrine of the theses immediately to practice, with the consent of the people of Waldshut. One exception should be made to this statement, and it is an important one: the eighth thesis clearly implies the doctrine and practice with which the name of Hübmaier afterwards became inseparably associated, but this was clear neither to him nor to others at this time.

From various sources, mostly hostile, but in this case seemingly well informed, we learn that the actual religious reforms made in Waldshut during the early months of the year 1524 were about as follows: the services of the church were held in German, especially the sacrament of the Eucharist, which was administered in both kinds, the people being taught that they received only bread and wine as a memorial of Christ's death. Pictures and images were banished from the church, and in

some cases at least burnt.[1] Tapers were banished
from the altar, and the costly vestments, chalices,
and jewelled ornaments were sold. The people
were allowed to eat meat on Fridays, the observance of holy days was greatly abbreviated, and the
rule of celibacy for the clergy was abrogated. In
pursuance of this last reform, Hübmaier anticipated the acts of Luther and Zwingli by marrying
the daughter of a burgher named Elizabeth Hüg-
line, who with rare fidelity and bravery shared his
later fortunes. The wedding was celebrated with
a great feast, given by their townsmen in their
honour.

In this work at Waldshut he ranged himself by
the side of the other evangelical reformers. By all
the writers of the day, friendly or hostile, he is now
classed with Luther and Zwingli. In his general
ideal of practical reform, as well as in the doctrines
that he preached, he was in substantial agreement
at this period with his fellow-workers. Owing
doubtless to his closer proximity to Zwingli, he

---

[1] That Hübmaier was no fanatical iconoclast we know from Faber,
who informs us that after the catastrophe at Waldshut there were
found a costly and beautiful Joachim, besides a vesper picture and
a Sebastian. Quoted by Loserth, p. 44.

was more influenced by the Swiss reformer than by
the German; and perhaps they had more in common in their method of interpreting the Scriptures.
It required another year to make the differences
that were from the first potential show themselves
clearly in thought and action.

In the meantime, Hübmaier was to learn that the
path of the reformer is by no means strewn with
roses. His visit to Zürich had attracted the attention of the Austrian authorities, and his conduct
after his return was closely scrutinised. Moreover,
though he carried the people of Waldshut with him
in his reforms, and to the last had their complete
confidence and warm affection, he was not without
opposition from the clergy. He would have easily
surmounted this difficulty, however, had there been
no interference from without. Interference there
was, beginning early, increasing in vehemence, and
at length bringing disaster upon him and his work.

Not long after his return from Zürich commissioners from Prince Ferdinand came to Waldshut,
and summoned the mayor and council of the town
to a meeting. Three charges were presented
against them: (1) The city was disobedient to the

Imperial and episcopal commands, in that they tolerated a Doctor who preached things opposed to the Emperor and bishop. This Doctor the Emperor would no longer suffer to remain in Waldshut. (2) The Doctor preached the gospel to his believers according to his own notions, and gave great scandal to the people and neighbourhood. (3) At the debate in Zürich, he gave himself out as a representative of the four cities and the Black Forest, a thing most distasteful to Emperor and princes, and injurious to the cities and Black Forest. Especially he had called himself "of Waldshut," which he had no right to do.

The mayor and council replied in substance: All the Imperial and episcopal mandates had been duly published; they were not aware that Hübmaier preached anything contrary to them—that was only a groundless report of his enemies. That he misinterpreted the gospel they did not know; they knew his intention to be to preach nothing but the unadulterated gospel. That he had preached this and nothing else, the dean and all the clergy of Waldshut would testify. That he had represented himself as a delegate of the four cities at Zürich there was no proof; they believed he had not done it, since he had conducted himself always so truly and honourably at Waldshut that they could believe no such thing of him. They added that it would be hard on Hübmaier to send him to Constance to the bishop. It would be better, they suggested, for the commissioners to hear the Doctor, then they could give a veracious report of all these things.

The commissioners were surprised and enraged at this firm answer. They replied that they had no authority to make such an inquiry, and demanded anew the immediate expulsion of the offending Doctor. To this the authorities would not consent, and with warnings of what might happen for such contumacy the commissioners went to make report to their master. From that time Ferdinand was the implacable enemy of Hübmaier, and sought his life; he was also determined to reduce Waldshut to obedience. Whatever the preacher said or did was made the subject of accusation by his enemies, of whom he had some in the town and many outside of it, both to the prince and to the bishop. It must be admitted that these accusations were not wholly malicious; Hübmaier was openly attempting

WALDSHUT.

SHOWING OLD TOWER AND HÜBMAIER'S CHURCH.

to subvert the Catholic doctrines and practice,[1] and
it is no wonder if those who still believed in the
Catholic doctrine and practice should look upon his
course with grief and even determine to stop him if
they could.

There was an apparent respite from these troubles
offered him by a new invitation from his old flock
at Regensburg to visit them again. To their letter
he returned the following response:

" I am quite conscious that I should have put myself
again at the disposal of your wisdom, yet for my own
safety it cannot be exactly on the Sunday after Easter
[the time they had specified]. In the meantime so great
plague and pursuit has befallen those who preach the
divine, true and pure word, that I have not dared to
venture. Further, I hear with great sadness how in
your city of Regensburg more men preach vanity than
the pure word of God. That makes my heart ache; for
what does not flow forth from the living word is dead
before God. Therefore says Christ, Search the Scriptures. He does not say, Follow the old customs —
though I did nothing else when I was the first time
with you. However, I did it ignorantly. Like others,
I was blinded and possessed by the doctrine of men.

---

[1] For example, his sermon on April 10th, in which he said, on the
text " I am the good shepherd ": " Those who do not enter in by
the door and are thieves and robbers are those pastors who preach
the legends, untruths, and dreams of the monks, [and] withhold the
gospel from the people, which is the true soul-murder."

Therefore I openly confess before God and all men,
that I then became a Doctor and preached some years
among you and elsewhere, and yet had not known the way
unto eternal life. Within two years has Christ for the
first time come into my heart to thrive. I have never
dared to preach him so boldly as now, by the grace of
God. I lament before God that I so long lay ill of this
sickness. I pray him truly for pardon; I did this un-
wittingly, wherefore I write this. I wonder if your
preachers now will say, I am now of another disposition
than formerly, that I confess and condemn all doctrine
and preaching, such as were mine among you and elsewhere, that is not grounded in the divine word. And if
they cast at you the holy councils, believe it not; men
will deceive you, as they have taunted us a year and a
day, by promising to hold a council, but it does not
appear. They know well that a single woman—such as
the pious Christian woman, Argula von Stauff [1]—knows
more of the divine word than such red-capped ones will
ever see and lay hold of. Yield yourselves to God, trust
him, build on his word, and he will not forsake you.
Whether he gives a short life or a long, you will have
eternal life yonder. And should men call you heretics,
be joyful, for your reward will be great in heaven. The
sophist-heads at once called us heretics, but since they
make us heretics in their writings, they let the stone lie

---

[1] Of Argula von Grumbach, born Freiin (baroness) von Stauff,
little is known save what may be gathered from several references
to her in Hübmaier's writings, and a single entry in the Chronicles
of Regensburg. She was evidently a pious woman of high rank,
well read in the Scriptures, and an ardent promoter of the new
evangelical doctrine. She rebuked the Regensburg council for their
lukewarmness in the work of reformation, though Cardinal Cam-
peggio praised them highly for their course.

there. Fools along with us it appears are Nürnberg, Nördling, Augsburg, Ulm, Reutling, Konstanz, St. Gall, Appenzell, Zürich, Schaffhausen, Basel, Strassburg, Worms, Speier, Maintz, and almost the whole of the land of Saxony."[1]

For what reason Hübmaier declined the invitation from Regensburg we can only conjecture. He probably was unwilling to leave the work at Waldshut in this crisis, and if he sought merely his own personal safety and comfort, there is nothing to show that he would have been more secure in preaching evangelical doctrine at Regensburg than at Waldshut. The former motive seems, from all the evidence we have, to have been controlling. The people of his town, the flock for whom he had come to have a strong affection, were loyal to him under circumstances of great trial; it was not for him to desert them.

The effort to dislodge him from the city increased in strength and persistence. On April 13th the Austrian Government addressed a letter to the council of Waldshut, in which it was said: "It is understood that your Doctor and preacher in all his sermons holds forth the Lutheran doctrines, praises

[1] Written April 4th. Quoted by Loserth, p. 41.

and defends them, buys Lutheran books and tracts, and brings them home among his people. Hence we would advise, with all earnestness, that within a month's time you expel the said Doctor and preacher from the city, and choose in his place another suitable and pious preacher, who does not hold Luther's condemned doctrines."[1] Not content with using the secular power against him, the enemies of Hübmaier also invoked the authority of his ecclesiastical superiors. He was accused to the Bishop of Constance, who had jurisdiction over the city of Waldshut, and this prelate wrote letters of remonstrance to the town authorities, rebuking them for tolerating the preaching of a Lutheran heretic, instead of hearing only one who would preach the "holy gospel." These having no effect, he summoned the offending preacher to Constance. This summons Hübmaier refused to obey, saying, as it is reported, "It was none of his duty to appear before that hypocrite."

As time passed, however, not only was there no relenting in the attitude of his opponents, but the pressure on Waldshut to abandon him to his fate

---

[1] Loserth, p. 42.

became increasingly great, and it was at length evident that if the town persisted in upholding him the Austrian Government would resort to force to maintain its authority. As the one contention of that Government up to this time had been that the city should dismiss their heretical preacher, Hübmaier was brought to face the question whether he should not sacrifice himself for the sake of giving peace to the city. His townspeople would defend him to the last extremity, that was evident; but ought he to bring the horrors of war against Waldshut, when his withdrawal would remove the cause of controversy with Austria? We cannot wonder that he decided that it would be best for him to leave the city, at least for a time, and he evidently won the consent of his more influential friends to this course. On the 1st of September, 1524,[1] he left the town, three armed knights escorting him to the frontier, where some knights from Schaffhausen met him and conducted him to their city. These precautions not only indicate that the withdrawal was carefully planned, but that his friends

---

[1] Hoschek says August 16th, but this is an error of computation, as Loserth shows, p. 48.

6

considered Hübmaier to be in serious danger of capture *en route*.

If he thought to secure his own safety by thus retreating to Schaffhausen, he was still ignorant of the intensity of Austria's hatred. His choice of Schaffhausen as a refuge was plainly enough dictated by the fact that he had been domiciled there before, and had friends in the city. He probably counted on them to ensure him protection, and not without reason. For though the Austrian Government pursued him even here, and made repeated and almost threatening demands for his surrender, the council of Schaffhausen firmly refused to give him up. While the matter was still pending, Hübmaier addressed three letters to the council, in which he besought them to permit him to abide peaceably in their town. In the third and most elaborate of these letters, after setting forth at length reasons why his petition should be heard, he goes on:

"Why have I made so long a preface? Because I am called a disturber of the people, a stirrer-up of strife, a Lutheran, a heretic, and so forth, and the pious, honourable city of Waldshut because of my teaching is slandered high and low, which truly pains my heart. No

VIEW OF SCHAFFHAUSEN.

one could ever be more ready and willing than I am to give all men an account of my doctrine, as I have preached it these two years past. If I have taught only truth, why abuse me? If error, any man may set me in the right way with the spiritual word. As man I may very well err, but will be no heretic. I am conscious that in the whole two years past I have not preached a single letter that is not grounded in God's word. I herewith further pledge myself, where the necessity of this my defence presses me, here at Schaffhausen, I will before the court give and receive justice. Only one should not offer violence, either to me or to the pious city of Waldshut. Moreover, I beg you to permit neither me nor other Christian teachers to be urged and compelled, but hear me in the face of my opponents, who accuse me so shamefully. But should this prayer of mine find no hearing, which once I would not have expected of Turks, and I should be tortured by prison, rack, sword, fire, or water, or God otherwise withdraw from me his grace, so that I speak otherwise than now, then do I herewith protest and testify that I will suffer and die as a Christian." [1]

The plea found favour with the council, which returned but one answer to the numerous demands made for the surrender of this now notorious heretic. Nevertheless, it was a position of much uncertainty regarding the future in which Hüb-maier found himself. Schaffhausen's attitude in this matter, though doubtless approved in secret by

[1] Dated September 9th. and quoted by Loserth, p. 51.

Zürich and Basel, and possibly one or two other cantons, aroused much indignation among the majority of the Swiss cantons, which were still Roman Catholic. It was an open question whether Schaffhausen would not be compelled to yield in the end, however unwillingly. In the meantime, Hübmaier could not be in the least in doubt as to his fate should the council finally decide to surrender him to his foes. It was while in this condition of peril and doubt that he composed one of his most characteristic tracts, "Concerning Heretics and Those who Burn Them." It is the earliest plea that has come down to us for complete toleration; and for this reason, as well as for its biographical value, it is herewith given in full:

"1. Heretics are those who wickedly oppose the Holy Scriptures, the first of whom was the devil, when he said to Eve, 'Ye shall not surely die' (Gen. iii., 4), together with his followers. 2. Those also are heretics who cast a veil over the Scriptures and interpret them otherwise than the Holy Spirit demands; as those who everywhere proclaim a concubine as a benefice, pasturing and ruling the church at Rome, and compelling us to believe this talk. 3. Those who are such one should overcome with holy knowledge, not angrily but softly, although the Holy Scriptures contain wrath. 4. But this wrath of the Scriptures is truly a spiritual fire and

zeal of love, not burning without the word of God.
5. If they will not be taught by strong proofs or evan-
gelic reasons, then let them be, and leave them to rage
and be mad (Tit. iii., 2, 3), that those who are filthy
may become more filthy still (Rev. xxii., 11). 6. The
law that condemns heretics to the fire builds up both
Zion in blood and Jerusalem in wickedness. 7. Therefore will they be taken away in sighs, for the judgments
of God (whose right it is to judge) either convert or
harden them, that the blind lead the blind and both the
seduced and the seducer go from bad to worse. 8. This
is the will of Christ who said, 'Let both grow together
till the harvest, lest while ye gather up the tares ye root
up also the wheat with them' (Matt. xiii., 29). 'For
there must be also heresies among you, that they that
are approved may be made manifest among you' (1
Cor. xi., 19). 9. Though they indeed experience this,
yet they are not put away until Christ shall say to the
reapers, 'Gather first the tares and bind them in
bundles to burn them' (Matt. xiii., 30). 10. This
word does not teach us idleness but a strife; for we
should unceasingly contend, not with men but with
their godless doctrine. 11. The unwatchful bishops
are the cause of the heresies. 'When men slept, the
enemy came' (Matt. xiii., 25). 12. Again, 'Blessed
is the man who is a watcher at the door of the bridegroom's chamber' (Prov. viii.),[1] and neither sleeps nor

---

[1] Hübmaier's quotations of Scripture are usually very accurate,
and his references can almost always be easily identified, though, as
the verse divisions had not then been made, he refers only to chapters. But there is nothing in Prov. viii. in the least corresponding to
the above words. Had they not been given as a verbatim quotation,
they might have been received as an allusion to some text like Matt.

'sits in the seat of the scornful' (Ps. i., 1). 13. Hence
it follows that the inquisitors are the greatest heretics of
all, since, against the doctrine and example of Christ,
they condemn heretics to fire, and before the time of
harvest root up the wheat with the tares. 14. For
Christ did not come to butcher, destroy and burn, but
that those that live might live more abundantly
(John x., 10). 15. We should pray and hope for repentance, as long as man lives in this misery. 16. A
Turk or a heretic is not convinced by our act, either
with the sword or with fire, but only with patience and
prayer; and so we should await with patience the judgment of God. 17. If we do otherwise, God will treat
our sword as stubble, and burning fire as mockery
(Job. xli.). 18. So unholy and far off from evangelical
doctrine is the whole order of preaching friars (of
which variegated birds our Antony is one), that hitherto
out of them alone the inquisitors have come. 19. If
these only knew of what spirit they ought to be, they
would not so shamelessly pervert God's word, nor so
often cry, 'To the fire, to the fire!' (Luke ix., 54–
56). 20. It is no excuse (as they chatter) that they give
over the wicked to the secular power, for he who thus
gives over sins more deeply (John xix., 11). 21. For
each Christian has a sword against the wicked, which is
the word of God (Eph. vi., 17), but not a sword against
the malignant. 22. The secular power rightly and
properly puts to death the criminals who injure the
bodies of the defenceless (Rom. xiii., 3, 4). But he
who is God's cannot injure any one, unless he first
deserts the gospel. 23. Christ has shown us this clearly,

---

ix., 15, or John iii., 29. As it is, they are an insoluble puzzle.
The reference to Job, under Article 34, is also puzzling.

saying, 'Fear not them that kill the body' (Matt. x.,
28).   24. The [secular] power judges criminals, but not
the godless who cannot injure either body or soul, but
rather are a benefit; therefore God can in wisdom draw
good from evil.   25. Faith which flows from the gospel
fountain, lives only in contests, and the rougher they
become, so much the greater becomes faith.   26. That
every one has not been taught the gospel truth, is due
to the bishops no less than to the common people—these
that they have not cared for a better shepherd, the
former that they have not performed their office properly.   27. If the blind lead the blind, according to the
just judgment of God, they both fall together into the
ditch (Matt. xv., 14).   28. Hence to burn heretics is in
appearance to profess Christ (Tit. i., 10, 11), but in
reality to deny him, and to be more monstrous than
Jehoiakim, the king of Judah (Jer. xxxvi., 23).   29. If
it is blasphemy to destroy a heretic, how much more is
it to burn to ashes a faithful herald of the word of God,
unconvicted, not arraigned by the truth.   30. The
greatest deception of the people is a zeal for God that
is unscripturally expended, the salvation of the soul,
honour of the church, love of truth, good intention, use
or custom, episcopal decrees, and the teaching of the
reason that come by the natural light.   For they are
deadly arrows where they are not led and directed by
the Scriptures.   31. We should not presume, led away
by the deception of our own purpose, to do better or
more securely than God has spoken by his own mouth.
32. Those who rely on their good intention and think
to do better, are like Uzziah and Peter.   The latter
was called Satan by Christ (Matt. xvi., 23), but the
former came to a wretched end (1 Chron. xiii., 10).

33. Elnathan, Delaiah and Gemariah acted wisely in withstanding Jehoiakim, the king of Judah, when he cast the book of Jehovah into the fire (Jer., xxxvi., 25). 34. But in that, after one book was burnt, Baruch by the express direction of Jeremiah, wrote another much better (Jer. xxxvi., 27-32), we see the just punishment of God on the unrighteous burning. For so it shall be that on those who fear the frost, a cold snow falls (Job. vi., 16?). 35. But we do not hold that it was unchristian to burn their numerous books of incantations, as the fact in the Acts of the Apostles shows (Acts xix., 19). It is a small thing to burn innocent paper, but to point out an error and to disprove it by Scripture, that is art. 36. Now it is clear to every one, even the blind, that a law to burn heretics is an invention of the devil. 'Truth is immortal.' "

The world was not ready for this doctrine in the year of our Lord 1524; indeed, now that a large part of the world has come to profess this same faith, those who really believe it are a lamentably small remnant. The old zeal for persecuting still survives, and often breaks out in utterly unconscious manifestations in the midst of every religious body. We do not really believe that the ark of God is safe unless our hand occasionally steadies it. We have no real confidence at bottom in the ability of the truth to conquer error in a fair field, and are impelled from time to time to lend our invaluable aid—always, of course, on the side of right and truth and justice.

Another fruit of the stay at Schaffhausen was due to a controversy that had broken out between his old teacher and friend, John Eck, and his new friends, the Swiss reformers, especially Zwingli. Thirsting for the fray, Hübmaier prepared a series of theses which were printed in Zürich the following November, in both German and Latin, the latter edition having the title: "Fundamental articles, which Baldazar, the fly of Fridberg, brother in Christ of Huldrych Zwingli, has proposed to John Eck, the elephant of Ingolstadt, for masterly examination." These articles are of special interest, as showing the relations that obtained at this time between the author and the Zürich leader:

"1. Every Christian must give to him who demands it an account of his hope and also of his faith.

" 2. For only him who fearlessly confesses Christ before men will he also confess before his Father.

" 3. With the heart one believes unto righteousness, but with the mouth he makes confession unto salvation.

" 4. When you have not faith, how can you understand this: ' I have believed, therefore have I spoken'? How will you believe him whom you have not heard ?

" 5. The decision, which of two holds the right

opinion, belongs to the church, which is conceived in the word of God and born in faith.

" 6. For the sake of order and to avert strife, three or four men may be chosen by the church, as once Peter and Paul, Barnabas and James.

" 7. The apostles of Christ held councils, not to settle the doctrine of faith, but to maintain unity among the brethren.

" 8. Their decision appears according to the 'level' of the Scripture.

" 9. It searches, therefore, the divine Scripture, not papal dogmas nor councils, nor Fathers, nor schools, for the word of Christ will judge all things.

" 10. Those only should be judges who are taught and inspired by God.

" 11. They are such when they put away worldly passion and search the Bible.

" 12. That is, they are not to contend with unspiritual verbosity, even to hoarseness, but to explain the dark places of the Scripture by the clear.

" 13. Those who do that are blessed.

" 14. And to them one should hearken.

" 15. Their judgment will be sanctioned by the silence of the multitude.

" 16. The church should be heard in things relating to strife and brotherly love; but in disagreement regarding the faith the Scripture is the only standard.

" 17. It may well be that all men should especially teach, so that every one may learn and all receive comfort.

" 18. Therefore has God given to the prophet the spirit of truth-speaking, and he is a teacher not of strife but of peace.

" 19. He guards them also against false prophets; they mislead with flattering words the hearts of the innocent, after they receive from the Pope twelve times a hundred ducats.

" 20. Beware of them, they are sons of hell.

" 21. In this conflict, every one must teach equipped with the armour of the Holy Spirit.

" 22. And the women must be silent and learn at home of their husbands.

" 23. But if the men through fear have turned to women, then must these do men's deeds, like Deborah, and Argula of our own time.

" 24. The judges should therefore be true theologians, not ' invested and provided with cowls,' but such as wear, according to the divine injunction, the ' breastplate ' of Aaron.

" 25. The learned therefore are to hear; the learned are they who daily read the book of the law, and have Moses and the prophets.

" 26. They who do not read this book ought not to be judges.

" Where now is this wise man, this Biblical scholar? Where is the disputer of this world? Is it Eck? Let him come to us, that renowned Hercules, from Ingolstadt. If I do not deceive myself, he will be taken with a 'herculean' sickness, he will suffer danger in the 'fray of the faith.' If he comes, we will praise him."

To this challenge, of course, Eck paid not the slightest attention — indeed, there is nothing to show that he ever saw it. The value of the document consists solely in the light that it throws on

Hübmaier's opinions and connections. It has not always been correctly interpreted; it is reading the author's subsequent history into the articles to see in them doctrine "entirely in the direction of the Anabaptists." [1] The principle that the Scripture is to be the arbiter of all questions, the sole rule of faith and practice, did, indeed, become later the fundamental contention of the Anabaptist party; but it was at this time also the fundamental avowal of the Swiss reformers, and had been such from the first. It was upon this basis that the first Zürich disputation was conducted, and in all their writings Zwingli and Œcolampadius had been setting it forth as the corner-stone of their reformation. Luther, too, up to this time had been advocating the same principle with all the vigour of his voice and pen. It had not yet been shown that the reformers would be unwilling to follow this principle to all lengths. It was their ultimate refusal to do this, their partial surrender again to the tradition they had so vigorously repudiated, that led to the division of the reforming party and developed the minority radical group, to whom the name "Anabaptist" was gener-

---

[1] Hoschek, i., 146.

THE MÜNSTER, OR CHIEF CHURCH OF SCHAFFHAUSEN.

ally given.   There is nothing in the above theses, fairly interpreted in the light of contemporary events, that foreshadows any serious difference of opinion between Hübmaier and Zwingli.

The next that we learn of Hübmaier is his sudden return to Waldshut on the 29th of October.[1]   He had probably become more than ever doubtful of his continuance in safety at Schaffhausen, but it had also become perfectly evident that his leaving Waldshut had accomplished nothing.   So far from bringing peace to the city, his going away had apparently increased its trouble with the Austrian Government.   At first the demand had been only that the heretic preacher should be expelled, but, after he had voluntarily withdrawn, other concessions were demanded.   The negotiations were long

---

[1] A contemporary chronicle quoted by Loserth (p. 70) says that he was received with extravagant manifestations of joy, being greeted with drums, pipes, and horns, "just as if he were an Emperor." The council, according to Faber, looked with little sympathy on this demonstration, but the people welcomed him.   The reception ended with a feast in the market-house, in which the Swiss contingent participated.   Further alterations in public worship were now made. Hübmaier himself reassumed his office of chief pastor and preacher, and his salary was fixed at two hundred gulden (Egli, *Actensammlung*, No. 911).   He did not hesitate, also, to take his part, like any other citizen, in the defence of the town, and bespoke armour, an arquebus, and a broadsword, that he might keep his watch at the gate.

and tiresome, and it would be profitless for our purposes to go into their details. It is enough to say that the people of Waldshut speedily learned from Austria that before they would be left in peace they must return fully to the Catholic religion and submit to whatever other exactions that Government chose to impose. The truth is, that the city was in a condition of political as well as religious unrest and revolt; of this Austria was fully conscious, and was determined to reduce the town to submission. On the other hand, the citizens desired such liberties and immunities as the neighbouring Swiss towns possessed, such as were enjoyed by the free cities of the Empire, and they would be satisfied with nothing less. But as Austria was determined to grant nothing of the kind, it is evident that here were all the conditions of an irrepressible conflict, the issue of which could only be decided finally by the sword.

The strife seemed an unequal one—on the one side all the power of Austria, on the other, this small town. But Waldshut knew that she did not stand alone. The fact that she had entered on a reformation similar in spirit and method to that of

Zürich gained for her the warm sympathy of that
town, as well as of several other Swiss cities.   For
prudential reasons, this sympathy might not take
the form of openly aiding ·a rebellion against Austria, but secret aid was doubtless promised and was
certainly given.   On several occasions when Austria
menaced Waldshut with an armed force, men from
Zürich came to her aid and caused the invaders to
retire.

But there was a special reason just now for Austrian forbearance towards Waldshut, and for the
triumphant return of the favourite preacher thither.
Hans Muller and his band of insurgent peasants
were in the immediate vicinity of the town, and had
more or less fraternised with the citizens, and the
Austrian Government was trembling at the possible
consequence of this uprising.   Archduke Ferdinand, with his usual treachery, was instructing his
officers and governors to temporise with the peasants until he could collect a sufficient military force
to crush them; in the meantime, it was evident
that he could do nothing against Waldshut.

It is not easy to determine exactly what were the
relations between Hübmaier and this movement.

His enemies busied themselves afterwards in making
all sorts of charges against him, some of which are
contrary to documentary evidence and others absurd in themselves. He confessed under torture at
Vienna in 1528 that he had revised and commented
on the peasants' articles, which were sent him from
the camp for the purpose. The statement would
imply a certain amount of sympathy with the general purposes of the uprising, and would at the same
time restrict his actual connection with it to very
narrow limits. It is now tolerably certain that
those who credited him with the original composition of the articles were astray.[1]   All that we know
of Hübmaier's life, and the general tenor of his
writings, alike point to the conclusion that he was,
first of all, a preacher of the gospel, and that his
interest in political and social reforms was slight in
comparison with his zeal to teach men the true religion of Christ, as he understood it. To him the
gospel was the one remedy for all the ills of man.
It would not only save men from God's wrath and
condemnation, but save them from sin. It would

---

[1] See Bax, *The Peasants' War in Germany*, p. 75 *sq.*, London,
1889. For the opposite view, Stern, *Ueber die zwölf Artikel der
Bauern*, esp. p. 89 *sq.*

not merely fit men for heaven, but for their life upon earth. Consequently, while he no doubt believed the cause of the peasants to be just, and wished them well, and even gave them his more or less open approval, he was not the man to become their leader, like Münzer, to whom the gospel came to mean social reform far more than individual regeneration.

How does this attitude of Waldshut and of Hübmaier agree with his later assertions that the only grievance of Austria against the town and him was on account of the gospel?

" With us neither tax nor tithes has ever been spoken against with the least word, but it has been sought to force us from the word of God by violence and against all right. That has been our only complaint. Here I defy all men on earth and all devils in hell, that there was no other occasion against Waldshut but alone, alone, alone the word of God. God grant that they may acknowledge it, and illumine those who denied us before the prince [Ferdinand]. As I now speak I could prove to the prince when he was at Breisach in Breisgau. Those in Waldshut proffered this orally and in writing to the prince. Also to other princes and lords who were there personally, and especially to the Christian town of Constance, in which the last diet was held, those from Waldshut publicly promised that they would to the prince and all others do all things as they were

7

done before, as their forefathers have done; and much more, they offered to pour out their body, life, honour, goods, and blood for the sake of the honourable house of Austria; and if there were a stone at Waldshut ten fathoms deep under the earth which was not good Austrian, they would scratch it out with their nails and cast it into the Rhine. They have always been the first to pay to the prince their obedience and tribute, but have ever asked with weeping eyes for God's sake that they be allowed the simple, pure, clean word of God.

" The councillors of the prince gave this answer at Constance: 'It shall not be done at all. If that were allowed them, it would be the same as if one fire were put out and others lighted. Other cities afterwards would desire the same.' I know all those who gave this answer, but I will not now indicate them. The messengers of the cities of Zürich, Basel, and Schaffhausen were present at this answer." [1]

This was, no doubt, the manner in which the question always presented itself to the mind of Hübmaier; to him the great question, the sole question, was the preaching of a pure gospel. But there is considerable evidence at hand, which need not be given here in detail, to show that this was not the matter uppermost in the minds of Waldshut citizens generally, nor does this statement of the matter agree with the idea that the Austrian Govern-

---

[1] *A Short Apology of Dr. Balthasar Huebmor of Fridberg, Op.* 13.

PORTRAIT OF ŒCOLAMPADIUS.
FROM AN OLD WOODCUT.

ment had of the things at issue. Religious reform was, indeed, one thing that Austria understood to be demanded by Waldshut, and which she was resolute in refusing to concede; but she had other grievances against the city, that might be summed up in the one word, "contumacy."

Thus affairs remained for months with little change: Austria threatening and occasionally making demonstrations of attack; Waldshut stubbornly resisting, and relying not in vain on her secret allies for continuous moral support and occasional active though unofficial assistance. The relations between Hübmaier and the Swiss reformers during this period were close and warm. He was known not to believe in the Scripturalness of infant baptism, but the reformers themselves were at this time by no means strenuous in maintaining this point, and such difference of opinion as there might have been did not interrupt their friendly intercourse. In one of his pamphlets, as we have seen, Hübmaier describes himself as "brother of Huldrych Zwingli," and Zwingli, Œcolampadius and the other Swiss leaders had only words of sympathy and praise for him. But all this was speedily to change.

CHAPTER IV

HÜBMAIER BECOMES AN ANABAPTIST

1524–1526

THE closing weeks of 1524 saw Zwingli in great perplexity, and the people of Zürich divided in sentiment. The reformation in that city was begun by the systematic exposition of the Scriptures, and from the first the principle was avowed that nothing was to be preached or practised which was not clearly taught in the word of God. It was inevitable that differences of judgment should arise over the practical application of this principle to the work of actual reform; and even when there was virtual agreement as to what should be done, there would still be room for disagreement as to the time and method of doing it. Every man is by temperament and training a radical or a conservative, and a party on the whole agreed in policy has always its Left and its Right wing. Zwingli had the experience common to all leaders: whatever he did or left undone, some were certain to accuse him of going too fast, while others would assert that he was going far too slow; to one he would seem to be destroying the very foundations of the faith, while another would complain of him as only a half-hearted reformer after all.

A radical wing or group gradually developed in the party of reform, and by the beginning of the year 1525 they were demanding with much insistence that Zwingli should adhere with more consistency to his avowed principle of conformity to the Scriptures, and should move more quickly in the direction of a complete reform of the Church. They demanded that he should "separate himself from the godless, and gather a pure church, a congregation of the church of God." [1] The only church of which they could find mention in the New Testament was a congregation of true believers in Christ, and it seemed plain to them that conformity to the Scriptures required that the church of Zürich should be reorganised on that basis. They had also discovered not only that the

---

[1] Bullinger, *Reformationsgeschichte*, i., 224. *Cf.* Zwingli, *Op.*, II., i., 372 ; Egli, *Wiedertäufer*, p. 10 *sq.*

baptism of infants is nowhere commanded in the New Testament, but that there is no clear case recorded there of the baptism of any but a believer on his personal profession of faith. The intimate connection of these things, and the bearings of them on their own conduct had not yet been apprehended by this radical group, but they were already quite clear as to what the Scriptures did and did not teach.

There was thus raised the weightiest question that arose for solution during the entire Reformation period—a question that goes deeper than any other, and has more momentous consequences than any other, according as one answer or the contrary is given. It was this question that became fundamental with this party, and held that position throughout the history of the Anabaptists.[1] Anabaptism was but a necessary corollary from the answer given to the question, What, according to the Scriptures, is a church of Christ, and of whom should it be composed? The radicals could find

[1] The name "Anabaptist" is not applied to the radical party here or elsewhere before they actually adopted the practice of rebaptism. It is believed that considerable confusion is avoided by maintaining carefully this distinction.

but one answer: A church of Christ is a congregation of true believers, giving token that they have been born again of the Spirit of God by living in accordance with the precepts of their Lord. A church composed of the regenerate only was the ideal of this party, and they pressed upon Zwingli the adoption of this as his programme.

To Zwingli this seemed an impracticable ideal. His was an eminently practical mind, and he saw clearly what was likely to be successful and what would almost certainly fail. He had begun his work with the approval and support of the town council of Zürich; he reckoned the continuance of support by the council to be an absolute necessity to him, if he was to succeed; and he was certain that he could not carry the council with him in any such programme as that urged by the radicals. It is not necessary for any who, on the whole, agree with the radicals that to be right is even more important than to succeed, to question the sincerity of Zwingli in the course that he took. Though a zealous reformer and an ardent patriot,— or perhaps one should rather say, because he was both these,—he was not a radical; no policy of

"Thorough" could under any circumstances have had his entire approval.   And he was able to argue from the Scriptures against the radical position with an exegesis that was ingenious if not correct. He insisted that the tares should be allowed to grow together with the wheat, that the strong ought to bear the infirmities of the weak, and the like.

The question of infant baptism seemed to Zwingli at first open to doubt.   He avows that for a time his mind was not at rest on this question,[1] and the like was true of his friend Œcolampadius.   But when they saw later the practical bearings of the

[1] " For the error also misled me for several years, so that I thought it would be much better to baptise children first when they had come to a good age."   *Vom Touff, vom Widertouff, und vom Kindertouff*, Zwingli, *Op.* II., i., 245.   " Although I know, as the Fathers show, that infants have been baptised occasionally from the earliest times, still it was not so universal a custom as it is now, but the common practice was, as soon as they arrived at the age of reason, to form them into classes for instruction in the word of salvation (hence they were called catechumens, *i. e.*, persons under instruction).   And after a firm faith had been implanted in their hearts and they had confessed the same with their mouth, then they were baptised.   I could wish that this custom of giving instruction were revived to-day, viz., since the children are baptised so young, their religious instruction might begin as soon as they come to sufficient understanding. Otherwise they suffer a great and ruinous disadvantage, if they are not as well religiously instructed after baptism as the children of the ancients were before baptism, as sermons to them still preserved show."—Quoted by Jackson, *Huldreich Zwingli*, p. 243.

question, they convinced themselves without much trouble of the Scripturalness of the practice, and thereafter remained its firm advocates. This accounts for their friendly attitude towards Hübmaier and others when this question first began to be disputed, and it also accounts for other things to be related soon. It is absurd to attribute the rise of this question in Zürich to the agency of Thomas Münzer. Those who have conjectured, on the weak authority of Bullinger,[1] that he instructed Grebel and others in this matter, would hardly be prepared to admit that Münzer inspired the doubts which at the same time disturbed Zwingli and Œcolampadius. It is not necessary to have recourse to any outside agency to explain this very simple matter. The Zürich people were studying the Scriptures attentively to learn what they

---

[1] Weak because of Bullinger's strong prejudice against Anabaptists and his readiness to record anything to their discredit. *Reformationsgeschichte*, i., 224, 237 ; followed by Egli, *Widertäufer*, p. 19 ; Loserth, *Hübmaier*, p. 73, and others. On the other hand, the circumstantial narrative of Kessler is quite inconsistent with this theory. *Sabbata*, i., 265 *sq.* Hübmaier opposed the baptism of infants as early as May, 1523, and the earliest time that can with probability be assigned for his meeting with Münzer is after September, 1524, as we know from a letter of Münzer's to Œcolampadius.—Siedemann, *Thomas Münzer*, p. 136 *sq.* ; *cf.* Jackson, *Huldreich Zwingli*, p. 243, n.

taught, and no long study is needed to disclose the fact that infant baptism certainly does not lie on the surface of the New Testament writings.

Those who hold that the Swiss Anabaptists had derived their views from Münzer cannot have read attentively the letter written by Grebel, Mantz, and others, September 5, 1524, in which they request from him a statement of his ideas regarding baptism; and, after expounding their own doctrine at some length, go on to say:

"We believe . . . that all children, who have not yet come to know the difference between good and evil . . . are saved by the sufferings of Christ, the new Adam. . . . Also that infant baptism is a silly, blasphemous outrage, contrary to all Scripture. . . . Since . . . you have published your protestations against infant baptism,[1] we hope you do not act against the eternal word, wisdom, and command of God, according to which only believers should be baptised, and that you baptise no children."[2]

This is hardly the language of disciples to a master, and the whole letter is similar in tone. In a word,

[1] On the practice of Münzer regarding the baptism of infants, see his statement to Œcolampadius in Herzog's biography, i., 302. It did not differ much from that of Hübmaier before Röublin's visit and the definite adoption of Anabaptism—a point to which Münzer never came.

[2] Cornelius, *Gesch. des Münsterischen Aufruhrs*, ii., 240 *sq.*

the writers roundly rebuke Münzer for his errors, especially singling out his teaching about the sword for reprobation. Grebel and the others had evidently learned that the teaching and practice of Münzer did not in all respects agree, and so far from looking up to him as one from whom they had learned something valuable, they take him to task as an erring brother.

This theory would probably never have been broached but for the fact that the name of Thomas Münzer was loaded with obloquy, on account of his doings in Mühlhausen during the rebellion of the peasants, and therefore to establish any sort of connection between him and the Anabaptists is to discredit the latter—which is a thing that many writers, from Bullinger to our own day, have busily attempted to do. It should also be borne in mind that Münzer was not himself an Anabaptist, though often incorrectly called by that name. Though he asserts in one of his tracts that infant baptism cannot be proved from Scripture, he never abandoned the practice, and his teaching on this subject was purely academic, and filled no large place in his horizon.

By this time Hübmaier had become thoroughly convinced, not only that the baptism of infants is contrary to Scripture, but that he ought to combat the practice. This we learn from a letter that he wrote to Œcolampadius, under date of January 16, 1525:

" For we have publicly taught that children should not be baptised. Why do we baptise children? Baptism, say they [Zwingli and Leo], is a mere sign. Why do we strive so much over a sign? The meaning of this sign and symbol, the pledge of faith until death, in hope of the resurrection to the life to come, is to be considered more than a sign. This meaning has nothing to do with babes, therefore infant baptism is without reality. In baptism one pledges himself to God, in the Supper to his neighbour, to offer body and blood in his stead, as Christ for us. I believe, yea, I know, that it will not go well with Christendom until Baptism and the Supper are brought back to their own original purity. Here, brother, you have my opinion; if I err, call me back. For I wish nothing so much that I will not revoke it, yea, cut it off, when I am taught better from the word of God by you and yours. Otherwise I abide by my opinion, for to that I am constrained by the command of Christ, the word, faith, truth, judgment, conscience. Testify to the truth, you can in no way offend me. I am a man and can fall, since that is human, but from my heart I desire to rise again. Write we whether the promise in Matt. xix., 14, 'Let the little children come to me,' etc., especially belongs to infants. What prompts me to that is the word of Christ, 'for of such is the kingdom of heaven,' not 'of them.' I have sent letters to Zwingli by the captain of our volunteers. Instead of baptism, I have the church come together, bring the infant in, explain in German the gospel, 'They brought little children'; then a name is given him, the whole church prays for the child with bended knees, and commends him to Christ, that He will be gracious and intercede for him. . But if the parents are still weak, and positively wish that the child be baptised, then I baptise it; and I am weak with the weak for the time being until they can be better instructed. As to the word, however, I do not yield to them in the least point. I have written twenty-two theses with sixty-four remarks, which you will soon see."[1]

The last sentence seems to imply a purpose of publication, but, so far as is known, it was not fulfilled. On February 2nd, however, he did issue a leaflet entitled *The Open Appeal of Balthazar of Friedberg to All Christian Believers*, which shows the increasing firmness of his tone regarding the baptism of infants:

"Whosoever wills, let him show that one ought to baptise young children, and let him do this in German, with plain, clear, simple Scriptures, relating to baptism, without addition.

"Balthazar of Friedberg pledges himself, on the other hand, to prove that the baptism of infants is a work without any ground in the divine word, and that he will

---

[1] Zwingli, *Op.* II., i., 338.

do this in German with plain, clear, simple Scriptures relating to baptism, without any addition.

"Now let a Bible fifty or a hundred years old be opened, as the right, orderly, and truthful judge between these two propositions; let it be read with prayerful, humble spirit, and then this disagreement will be decided according to the word of God, and finally settled. Then shall I be well content, for I shall always give God the glory, and permit his word to be the sole arbiter—to him will I surrender, to him have I devoted myself and my teaching. The truth is immortal."[1]

From this time Hübmaier becomes the champion of the radicals, and it is this championship that brings him into speedy conflict with the Swiss reformers. They could have forgiven him his opinions regarding infant baptism, especially as he did not for a time insist on making his practice perfectly correspond with his theory. What they could not so easily forgive was the aid and comfort that he continually gave to their most troublesome opponents. Zwingli felt that his position was hard enough in Zürich without the interference of such men as the Waldshut preacher to encourage his opponents and make his task still harder. He would have been a remarkable man if he could have retained a friendly feeling for one who was

---

[1] Loserth, p. 76.

thus giving him a great deal of trouble. Hübmaier did not intervene in person for a time, but through the press he made himself felt continually. Many of the Zürich radicals were men of learning and ability; some of them were possibly the superiors of Hübmaier in scholarship; but he had pre-eminently the gift of expression. We owe to his writings the better part of our knowledge concerning the teachings and motives of these men who for a few years played so active a part in the Reformation, and then succumbed to the relentless measures of persecution, only to be misunderstood and vilified for generations afterward.

It was through William Röublin, of Wytiken, that Hübmaier's practice was at length brought into harmony with his theory.[1] Driven out of Zürich, Röublin made his way early in April, 1525, to Waldshut, where he was kindly received. He at once proceeded to expound the principles and practice of Anabaptism to Hübmaier, and found in him a ready hearer and a speedy convert. Of the principles the Waldshut pastor was already

---

[1] This we know from Hübmaier himself. Egli, *Actensammlung*, p. 431.

convinced; the practice seemed to him both logical and Scriptural. Such was his hold upon the people of Waldshut that a large part of them were at once ready to follow him. Röublin baptised Hübmaier and about sixty others, and on Easter day Hübmaier baptised over three hundred men out of a milk-pail filled with water from the well, brought into the church and placed on the font, which soon after was thrown into the Rhine as a papal relic. On Easter Monday the Lord's Supper was celebrated.

The movement towards Anabaptism did not stop with this extraordinary beginning, but went on with little-diminished rapidity. On Monday and Tuesday after Easter Hübmaier baptised from seventy to eighty others, and, on Tuesday, "gave them the bread of heaven and washed their feet." From this and certain other like references in contemporary chronicles, it should seem that the practice of feet-washing in connection with the Supper had been previously introduced at Waldshut, and was still retained. In the attempt to reproduce the exact order of the New Testament churches, there were certain to be some extravagances, resulting from a hasty and unwise literalism.

At about this time Conrad Grebel, one of the chief men of the Anabaptist movement in Switzerland, paid a brief visit to Waldshut, but it does not appear that there was any marked result. The visit is of significance mainly as showing that Hübmaier was now recognised as one of the Anabaptist leaders. Not only did he receive this recognition within the body, but from outside this was henceforth the place of honour or dishonour awarded him. On May 28th appeared Zwingli's tract *On Baptism, Anabaptism, and Infant Baptism*,[1] and though Hübmaier is not definitely named in it as the adversary against whom it is chiefly aimed, it is plainly his position and his arguments that the Swiss reformer has in mind throughout.

The contents of this tract are summarised by Zwingli himself in three theses: (1) No element or outward thing in this world can cleanse the soul; the cleansing of the soul pertains only to the grace of God. Thence it follows that baptism can remit no sins. Since it cannot do this, and nevertheless has been appointed by God, it must be a sign of allegiance of God's people and nothing else. (2) Christian children are not less God's children than their parents, just as in the

---

[1] Zwingli, *Op.* II., i., 230–303.   No translation of this work into English has yet been published.

Old Testament. But if they are God's children, who shall forbid their baptism? Circumcision in the old covenant was the sign that baptism is to us. As that was given to children, so should baptism also be given to children. (3) Anabaptism has neither teaching, example, nor witness from God's word. They who rebaptise crucify Christ afresh, either from selfishness or seeking after novelty.

Hübmaier was not the man to let such an opportunity for debate pass unimproved, and he accordingly prepared an answer under the title of *The Christian Baptism of Believers*, which he seems to have finished July 11th.[1]

This work consists of an introduction and seven chapters. In the introduction the author sets forth his purpose to defend himself and his followers from the imputation that they are schismatics and subverters of government. He is not an Anabaptist, because he was never before baptised—infant baptism is no baptism at all. As to government, he believes that it should bear the sword, and he will obey it in all that is not against God.

In the first chapter he treats of many kinds of bap-

---

[1] Hoschek is clearly wrong in making June 6th the date of publication for this book, for Hübmaier himself announces its coming appearance in a letter to the Zürich council, dated June 10th, in which he begs that Zwingli will consent to debate the question with him. "If I err," he says, "I will gladly retract. If master Ulrich errs, he should not be ashamed to forsake his error, for the truth will ultimately conquer him."

tism, and concludes that Christian baptism, in the name
of Father, Son, and Holy Spirit, is an open confession
and testimony of inward faith and obedience, in which
a man testifies that he is a sinful man and believes that
Christ through his death has removed his sins. The
next two chapters discuss the baptism of John, and contend against Zwingli's idea that it is the same as Christian baptism. If this were so, Hübmaier argues, infant
baptism would be excluded, for all accounts agree that
the order of John was: hearing of the word, repentance
or conviction of sin, baptism, works. John baptised
only those to whom he had first preached, who had
therefore believed, confessed their sins, and promised
amendment of life. Those who received the baptism of
John were rebaptised by the apostle, and that is the true
Anabaptism. Infant baptism, hitherto reckoned the true
baptism, is no baptism, and it is a groundless complaint
against us that we practice rebaptism. Baptism as
practiced by the apostles was the remission of sins.
Those who think children should be baptised as future
believers make a mock of Christ's command, to teach
all peoples and to baptise them then, not before. No
one can tell what a child's will may be later; to baptise
a child as a future believer is like hanging out a hoop as
a sign of future wine. But now, says Hübmaier, they
take a fresh hold and call infant baptism "a sign of
beginning." Beginning of what? Of faith? that cannot be, for they have not heard the word, from which
alone faith comes. Of a new life? That cannot well
be, for the child knows not right from wrong. Let us
say, then, it is a ceremony, as if the child had been
received into an order. But as the monk's gown alone
does not make the monk, so infant baptism makes

nobody a Christian. If they say children are baptised on
the faith of their parents or godfathers, no such baptism
is found in the Bible. Christ says, he who himself believes and is baptised.

The fifth chapter treats of the baptism of Christ. In
his teachings the true order is found to be: the word,
hearing, faith, baptism, works. His command is, "Go,
teach all peoples, and baptise them, etc." There is only
this water-baptism, no other, in the Scripture. Since
infants cannot be taught, they should not be baptised.
Baptism alone does not wash away sins, but only the
answer of a good conscience. In chapter six, the question is raised whether the baptism of infants is forbidden
in the Bible. Yes, says Hübmaier, for it is commanded
to baptise only believers. If the plea is valid that infant
baptism is not forbidden, one might baptise his dog or
ass, circumcise girls, bring young children to the Supper, and the like. If you say to baptise an ass is forbidden, because one may baptise only men, then baptise
Jews and Turks; or if you say, one may baptise only
believers, then why do you baptise children? A second
question raised is, whether (as Zwingli had asserted)
infants had been baptised ever since the days of the
apostles. The first reply is, that even if this were true
infant baptism would not be right. But Hübmaier finds
evidence in papal documents that a thousand years
earlier baptism was administered only twice a year, and
then only to such as could repeat the Creed. Popes and
councils, he contends, have corrupted the faith and
practice of the Church. A third question is also discussed, are unbaptised children damned or saved? To
this the reply is given, that God may through his grace
save young children, because they do not know good

from evil. But the author confesses that he is not ashamed to be ignorant of what God has not revealed.

Chapter seven gives advice as to how a Christian should regulate his life. It is the sum of a Christian life, says the author, that a man should alter and amend his living—hear the command of God, forsake his sins, live according to the rule of Christ, permit the working of God's Spirit in him and be thankful to God for his grace. Christ established a memorial of his death in his last Supper, so that we might not forget him. The bread is nothing else than bread, and the wine is as any other wine; yet is the bread the body of Christ, but only as a symbol, while the wine is the blood of Christ, but only as a memorial. As often as ye eat this bread (mark, he calls it bread, and it is bread), and drink this cup, that is wine (mark, it is wine that we drink), ye show forth the Lord's death till he come.

Though Zwingli was not named in this tractate, yet his teachings were so clearly singled out for criticism and refutation that there was no doubt in his mind, or in that of intelligent readers, as to the aim and purpose of the writing. The clear exposition of Scripture, the moderate tone, the skilful and racy way of putting things, convinced many readers that the teachings thus set forth were Scriptural and true. The best proof of the circulation and effect of the tract is the angry tone that now begins to creep into the private letters of the Swiss reformers when they have occasion to mention Hübmaier, and if a further proof were needed, the tartness of Zwingli's reply furnishes it. His tract was entitled *A True, Thorough Reply to Dr. Balthasar's Little Book on Baptism*, and the preface is dated November 5th.[1] It contains little that is new, reiterating the arguments of his former treatise, with occasional attempts to meet the objections of his adversary. The tone is one of irritation, and though he writes "dear Balthasar" frequently, there is occasionally a betrayal of the fact that their friendly relations had been much strained. He especially complains that Hübmaier writes against him, without mentioning him by name, and says that this is wicked (*böse*); he would much rather have an opponent come out boldly and declare himself such. He presses again the objection that the Anabaptists are schismatics, and that their course will result in the division of the Church and the destruction of the standing order.

This was evidently the main reason for the determined opposition that Zwingli offered to the Anabaptists and their teachings. No doubt he was

---

[1] Zwingli, *Op.*, II., i., 343-369.

correct; and that such consequences impended was reason enough to his mind why the Anabaptists should be resisted, condemned, and punished. To many of the present day the same logic will be convincing; but there are many now, as there were then a few, who will insist on answering: Granted that you state the danger accurately, the question still remains, Ought not this to be risked? Should we not obey the Scriptures, no matter what the consequences promise to be?

The answer of Hübmaier, which concluded this controversy, though prepared at once, was not printed until the following year. It was entitled *A Dialogue between Balthasar Hubmör of Friedberg and Master Ulrich Zwingli, of Zurich, on Infant Baptism.*[1] The Dialogue is a controversial device that has been much employed, but, one suspects, to very little purpose. It is a dangerously simple

[1] *Op.* 10. This Dialogue gives internal evidence of having been rewritten after the author's actual dispute with Zwingli (see p. 126). An extensive extract from it is given in Burrage's *Anabaptists in Switzerland*, pp. 148–152. Hübmaier claims that the words of Zwingli are taken from his published writings. Occasionally the attack is pretty severe, as in this case: "You said in opposition to Faber that all truth is clearly revealed in the word of God. If, now, infant baptism is a truth, show us the Scripture in which it is found. If you do not, the vicar will complain that you have used against him a sword that you now lay aside."

affair; the writer can conduct both sides of the controversy, make the arguments of his imaginary disputant as ridiculous and inconclusive as he pleases, and his own quite overwhelming. But the apparent victory thus gained is the most delusive of all dialectical triumphs, for it is open to his adversary to retort in the same way, and to win victories equally bloodless and equally indecisive. A mere tyro in rhetoric, theology, and all else can easily beat one who is not there to speak for himself. Hübmaier was rather fond of this form of controversial writing, however, which must be admitted to have the merit of interest for the reader, if it is skilfully done; and he had shortly before tried it in a dialogue on the same subject between himself and several adversaries at once, of whom the chief was Œcolampadius.[1] As to literary form, this latter dialogue is the best of his work, and an extract will give a better impression regarding it than pages of description:

" ŒCOLAMPADIUS. Parents will see with pleasure their children put to death in the name of Christ.

---

[1] The disputants were supposed to be, besides Hübmaier and Œcolampadius, Thomas, an Augustinian reader, Jacob Immelen, and Wolfgang Weissenburger.

PORTRAIT STATUE OF ŒCOLAMPADIUS.

CLOISTER WALL OF THE CATHEDRAL, BASEL.

" BALTHASAR. My Œcolampadius, how are children killed in water-baptism ? Bodily ? Then they must be drowned. Do you say spiritually, a killing of the old Adam ? Then I hear indeed that cradle-infants can sin and resist sin, against the clear word of God. (Deut. i. [39].) Ah, God, whither will the truth drive you!

" ŒC. What need is there of division for the sake of the water ?

" BAL. It is not for the sake of the water, but for the high command, the baptism of Christ. Water is not baptism, as the making of idols is not mere stone and wood, but idolatry which by that is practised against the earnest command of God. (Ex. xx. [4], Deut. v. [8].)

" WOLFGANG. Well, in baptism it is not your father's faith that is applied, but that of the Christian assembly.

" BAL. Some of you tell me of the faith of another, of father and mother, some of the faith of godfathers, some of the faith of the Church, and all of this is spoken without foundation in the Scriptures. For if infants are baptised on the faith of their father and mother, why is it forbidden to the father and mother to present their children for baptism ? If it is in the faith of godfathers or of the Church, men may be saved by another's faith. All of which is contrary to the Scriptures, for, the just will live by his own faith. (Hab. ii. [4], Rom. i. [17].) He who himself believes and is baptised shall be saved, not he for whom one believes. (Mark xvi. [16].) Philip demanded the chamberlain's own faith. (Acts viii. [37].) [1] The Christian Church is built on the confession of one's own faith. (Matt. xvi. [16].)

---

[1] Hübmaier could not be expected to foresee that modern textual criticism would cut the ground from under this argument by pronouncing this verse an interpolation.

.   .   .   .

" Œc. I will show you a place in Tertullian, that baptism is not a bond.

" Bal. You tell me much of Tertullian, Origen, Cyprian, Augustine, councils, histories, and old customs. I am compelled to think you are in want of Scriptures. They will not come out of the quiver. Dear Œcolampadius, put together your Scriptures concerning infant baptism, as I have done with the Scriptures concerning the baptism of believers in my little book on baptism printed at Strassburg, and we will together weigh them and soon we will be at one. Do it. Don't forget it."

The time was approaching when Hübmaier was to experience the results of this breach with the Swiss reformers. The long controversy between Waldshut and the Austrian Government reached its crisis in the late autumn of 1525. The complete defeat of the insurgent peasants, and the settlement of some other internal troubles, left the Government free to turn its sole attention for a time to Waldshut, and it was evident that without external help the city could not stand out. But from the one available source of aid, the Swiss cities, Waldshut had cut itself off by its adherence to its favourite preacher. The only terms of peace offered by the Government of Ferdinand were that the city should return to the old faith, and surrender their pastor and eight of the leading citizens to the tender mercies of Austria. These terms were of course refused, and there was nothing left but an appeal to force. There had all along been a Catholic minority in the town, to whom the reforms introduced had been most obnoxious, and now they were emboldened to declare that they meant to surrender the city to the Austrians. Hübmaier felt that all was lost, and, with some of the more timid or more deeply compromised citizens, fled. The Austrian forces occupied the city December 5th, and on the 17th the Vicar-General of the Bishop of Constance, John Faber, entered the city and celebrated the mass. After an interregnum of two years or more, Waldshut was thus forcibly restored to the Catholic faith, and we hear no more of reformation there.[1]

Hübmaier had been ill during these last trying weeks,—so ill that he described himself as sick unto death (*ein todtkranker Mann*),— and his departure was made in the utmost haste. As we know from a letter of Zwingli's, his wife accompanied him, and if we may accept another statement from the

---

[1] Kessler, *Sabbata*, i., 350; Egli, *Actensammlung*, No. 911.

same source they were not ill provided with money.[1]
Why he should have chosen Zürich as a place of
refuge it is not easy for us to guess, since in our
ignorance of the motives that influenced him it
seems now that this was the very last place that he
would or should have chosen. Possibly he still
relied on his former friendly relations with Zwingli,
and did not yet comprehend how complete was the
breach between them, nor know how deep was the
resentment of the Swiss reformer. He must have
known, or at any rate he very soon became aware,
that the Zürich council had now adopted very severe
measures against all Anabaptists, and especially
those foreign to the canton, for every precaution of
secrecy was taken by him and his friends.

About the middle of December he reached the
city, and was given harbourage (contrary to law) by
Henry Aberli, an Anabaptist preacher, and was by
him taken to an inn called the Green Shield, kept

---

[1] "When he went away [from Zürich] he so worked on these good
men's feelings that they gave him ten gold pieces. And yet either
he or his wife had more gold than they had silver. . . . I see
in him (I trust I am mistaken) nothing more than an immoderate
thirst for money and notoriety." Jackson, *Huldreich Zwingli*, p. 256.
With this compare the statement of Hübmaier himself in his recantation, p. 138 *sq.* In this issue of veracity, it seems most probable
that Hübmaier spoke the truth, and Zwingli a slander.

by a widow named Bluntschli, who with her daughter Regula had been baptised by Aberli a week before.[1] Here Hübmaier had been lodged but three or four days when his presence in the city became known and he was arrested by order of the council, on the ground, as Zwingli puts it, "that he was hatching out some monstrosity"—though of this there was not the slightest proof, then or afterwards.

Some time before this, Hübmaier had rather indiscreetly written letters to the Zürich council, in which he had challenged Zwingli to a debate on the subject of baptism, and declared that he would confute the Zürich preacher out of his own writings. The council now took him at his word and summoned him to meet Zwingli. There were present also a number of the Swiss leaders, including Engelhard, Leo Juda, Sebastian Hofmeister, and Megander. Both Hübmaier and Zwingli have left accounts[2] of this debate and the subsequent

---

[1] They were fined for this : Aberli fifteen pounds for disobedience of the council's previous mandates, and five pounds in addition for each person baptised by him. The widow and her daughter were fined five pounds each. Egli, *Actensammlung*, No. 910.

[2] Hübmaier, in the Dialogue already cited. Zwingli's account is in two letters, one to his friend Capito, bearing date of January 1,

proceedings. Not only are these difficult to reconcile, but it is not always easy to reconcile Zwingli
with himself, as he has given two versions of the affair, differing in important particulars. In one letter
he says: "I met the fellow and rendered him mute as
a fish," but in the other he admits that Hübmaier
had a good deal to say for himself and that the
debate was protracted. Hübmaier, in the Dialogue
already referred to, so conducts the debate as to
make it appear that he won a triumphant victory—
that Zwingli was the one "rendered mute as a
fish." It is the old story; has there ever been a
religious debate since the world was, in which both
sides did not claim the victory?

But in this case we have also a quite impartial
testimony from a contemporary chronicle. In the
course of the debate Hübmaier attempted to make
good his promise of confuting Zwingli out of his
own mouth.

"In 1523 . . . I conferred with you in Graben
street upon the Scriptures relating to baptism; then and

1526, the other addressed to Peter Gynoræus, dated August 31,
1526. They are printed in full, in an English translation, in Jackson's *Huldreich Zwingli*, p. 249 *sq.* The originals are in Staehelin's
Briefe aus der Reformationzeit, p. 20, and Zwingli, *Op.*, VII., i.,
536.

there you said I was right in saying that children should
not be baptised before they were instructed in the faith;
this had been the custom previously, therefore such were
called catechumens. You promised to bring this out in
your ' Exposition' of the Articles, as you did in Article XVIII. on Confirmation. Any one who reads it
will find therein your opinion clearly expressed. Sebastian Ruckensperger of St. Gall . . . was present.
So you confessed in your book upon the unruly spirits,
that those who baptise infants could quote no clear word
of Scripture ordering them to baptise them. From this
learn, friend Zwingli, how your conversation, writing,
and preaching agree." [1]

This was carrying the war into Africa, surely, and
must have been most embarrassing to Zwingli,
especially as it was not only true, but could be
proved by witnesses as well as by his writings.

---

[1] Füsslin, *Beyträge*, p. 1, n. 54, pp. 252, 253. In one of his tracts
on baptism Hübmaier also asserts that he had similar confessions, in
their own handwriting, from other Swiss leaders. Œcolampadius
said : "Thus far we have found no passage in the Scriptures that
would move us to confess the baptism of infants." Leo Juda :
" We have no plain word of God about the baptism of infants."
Sebastian Hofmeister : "For the sake of the truth we have not
been ashamed to confess publicly before the Council in Schaffhausen
that our brother Zwingli is erring from the right way, and is not
proceeding according to the gospel, if he determines that little children should be baptised. I have certainly not allowed myself to be
compelled to baptise my children, and therefore you do what is exactly Christian when you introduce again now the true baptism of
Christ that had been so long neglected." He quotes Capito and
Bucer to similar effect. Hoschek, ii., 133 *sq.*

Nevertheless, then as always, the council gave the victory to Zwingli.

The formal hearing seems to have been held January 13, 1526, when (according to Zwingli) the council took the ground that Hübmaier should either depart from the city or recant his doctrine. The official record represents him as declaring that he accepted the validity of infant baptism and promised thereafter to abstain from rebaptising.[1] In the meantime (January 3rd) messengers had arrived from the Emperor and Ferdinand, demanding that Hübmaier be delivered to them for punishment, but twice the council had refused to grant this request. Zwingli boasts of this as an evidence of extreme liberality, and he is probably entitled to make much of the fact; but possibly it was not an exceptional liberality in this case, so much as the pursuance of the regular policy of the Swiss cantons. It may be conjectured that knowledge of these demands, and fear that he might be surrendered, had much to do with inducing Hübmaier to moderate his statements.

At this time he seems to have been treated with

---

[1] Egli, *Actensammlung*, p. 431.

no direct violence, and all the circumstances confirm the statement of Zwingli that he made an offer, of his own will, to recant his former opinions, and did so in his own words, not in any formulæ prescribed by the council. It was arranged that he should publicly read this recantation in the Minster of Our Lady, which was duly accomplished, after which a sermon or address was delivered by Zwingli. Then, to the consternation of all, Hübmaier arose, recanted his recantation, and went on to attack infant baptism, and to defend the baptism of believers only. He was violently interrupted, hurried away, and thrown into prison, where he was treated with great rigour for a month. He complains of this in his Dialogue: "Me, a sick man, just risen from a death-bed, hunted, exiled, and having lost everything I possessed, they required through the executioner to teach another faith." His wife was also cast into prison, without so much as a hearing.

A considerable number of other Anabaptists were also arrested and all were imprisoned together in the Water-tower, where they were ordered by the council to be kept on bread and water until they recanted.

9

" The imprisoned [says Hübmaier] were told that they would be kept in the prison until their death if they did not recant, so that they would behold neither sun nor moon, and that all together, the living and the dead, should remain in tha dark tower until no one remained alive, so that in this way all should die together, perishing and rotting by the stench."

It would be hard to believe that the people of Zürich would have tolerated such inhuman cruelty, or that the council were capable of inflicting it, if official records[1] did not fully confirm these statements.

It was while suffering this confinement, and expecting the worst, that Hübmaier composed his *Twelve Articles of Christian Belief*, which he printed a year later at Nikolsburg. These articles are set forth in the form of a prayer—possibly a reminiscence of the *Confessions* of Augustine—and perhaps none of Hübmaier's writings is so characteristic of the spirit of the man. Their comparative brevity makes it possible to quote these articles in full:

" [1.] I believe in God, Father Almighty, maker of heaven and earth, as my most precious Lord and most merciful Father, who for my sake hast created heaven and earth and all that in them is, and hast made me as

---

[1] Egli, *Actensammlung*, Nos. 934, 936, 937, 1338.

thy loved child from thy fatherly grace a lord over it and heir, to remain in it and live eternally.   Though I confess that we men, by the disobedience of Adam, lost this sonship rich in grace, this honour and heirship, nevertheless in thee as my most gracious Father I set all my comfort, hope and trust , and know surely and certainly that this fall will not be to me injurious or bring condemnation.

"[2.] I believe also in Jesus Christ, thine only begotten Son, our Lord, that he for my sake has expiated before thee for this fall, and made peace between thee and me, a poor sinner, and by his obedience obtained again for me the heirship.   Also he has, by his holy word sent, again given me power to become thy child in faith. I hope and trust him wholly that he will not let his saving and comforting name Jesus (for I believe he is Christ, true God and man) be lost on me, a miserable sinner, but that he will redeem me from all my sins.

"[3.] I believe and confess, my Lord Jesus Christ, that thou wast conceived by the Holy Spirit, without any human seed, born from Mary, the pure and ever chaste virgin, that thou mightest bring again to me and all believing men, and mightest obtain from thy Heavenly Father the grace of the Holy Spirit, which was withdrawn from me by reason of my sin.   I believe and trust that the Holy Spirit has come in me, and the power of the Most High God has, as with Mary, overshadowed my soul; that I may conceive the new man, and so in thy living, indestructible word and in the Spirit, be born again and see the kingdom of God.   For thou, Son of the living God, didst become man, in order that through thee we might become children of God.

"[4.] I believe and confess also that thou didst suffer

under Pontius Pilate, wast crucified, dead and buried, and all that because of my sins, in order that thou mightest redeem and ransom me from the eternal cross, pangs, suffering and death, by thy cross, suffering, anguish and need, pangs and bitter death, as well as by the pouring out of thy rose-red blood, in which thy greatest and highest love to us poor men is recognised. For thou hast changed for us thy heavy cross into a light yoke, thy bitter sufferings into imperishable joys, and thy death in the midst of anger into eternal life. Therefore I will praise and thank thee, my gracious Lord Jesus Christ, for ever and ever.

"[5.] I believe also and confess, O Christ, who hast mercy on me, that thou didst in spirit go and preach the gospel to the spirits that were in prison, that is, to the holy patriarchs, and didst proclaim to them the new and joyous tidings, to wit, that thou according to the prophesying of the holy prophets wast become man, sufferedst pangs and death, hadst paid and satisfied for the sins of all men as they for a long time had desired with great earnestness, devotion and fervent zeal, and powerfully leddest them accordingly out of the prison; and on the third day, united together again spirit, soul and body in the grave, and like a strong and powerful conqueror of death, hell and the devil, didst rise again from the dead for our sakes, so that all who believe in thee should not perish but in thee overcome sin, death, hell and devils, and obtain eternal life as thy brother and co-heir.

"[6.] I believe also and confess, my Lord Jesus Christ, that thou after those forty days in which thou didst walk on the earth for a testimony of thy joyous resurrection, didst ascend into heaven and sit down at

the right hand of thy Heavenly Father, in the same
power, glory and praise with the Father, who hath given
to thee all power over all his possessions, in heaven and
on earth. There thou sittest, mighty and strong, to help
all believers who set their trust, comfort and hope in
thee, and cry to thee in all their needs. Thou also
callest all those who are heavy laden to come unto thee
and thou wilt give them rest. Therefore, O Christ,
compassionate to me, there is no need to pray to thee in
this place or that, neither in bread nor wine, for thou art
found sitting at the right hand of thy Heavenly Father,
as the holy Stephen saw thee and prayed to thee. It is
also in vain to seek another advocate. Thou art and wilt
be the only one. He who believeth otherwise is in error.

"[7.] I believe and confess also that thence thou wilt
come to judge the quick and the dead on the day of the
last judgment, which will be to all godly men a specially
longed-for and joyous day. Then shall we see face to
face our God and Saviour, in his great glory and majesty
coming in the clouds of heaven. Then will be ended
our fleshly, sinful and godless life. Then will each one
receive the reward of his work; those who have done
good will enter into eternal life, but those who have
done evil into eternal fire. O my Lord Jesus Christ,
shorten the days and come down to us! Yet give us
grace and strength so to direct our lives in the meantime
that we may be worthy to hear then with joy thy gracious and sweet voice, when thou wilt say, 'Come, ye
blessed of my Father, inherit the kingdom prepared for
you from the foundation of the world; for I was hungry
and ye gave me food, I was thirsty and ye gave me
drink, I was a stranger and ye took me in, I was naked
and ye clothed me, I was sick and ye visited me, I was

in prison and ye came unto me. Verily I say to you, Whatsoever ye have done to one of the least of these my brethren, ye have done to me.' But the fearful and unbelieving, the excommunicated, unchaste, adulterers, drunkards, blasphemers, proud, envious, avaricious, robbers, bloodthirsty, sorcerers, idolaters, whoremongers, their part will be in the sea that burneth with fire and brimstone. From that deliver us at all times, O gracious and good Lord Jesus Christ.

" [8.] I believe also in the Holy Spirit, who proceedeth from the Father and the Son, and yet with them is the only and true God, who sanctifieth all things, and without him is nothing holy, in whom I set all my trust that he will teach me all truth, increase my faith and kindle the fire of love in my heart by his holy inspiration, and truly kindle it that it may burn in true, unfeigned and Christian love to God and my neighbour. For that I pray thee from the heart, my God, my Lord, my Comforter.

" [9.] I believe also and confess a holy Catholic Christian Church, which is the communion of saints, and a brotherhood of many pious and believing men, who unitedly confess one Lord, one God, one faith and one baptism; assembled, maintained and ruled on earth by the only living and divine word, altogether beautiful and without any spot, unerring, pure, without wrinkle and blameless. I also confess publicly that thou, my Lord Jesus Christ, by thy rose-red blood hast sanctified to thyself the Church, art her head and bridegroom, wilt also be with her to the end of the world. O my God, grant that I and all men believing in Christ may finally be found in this Church; also that we unitedly with her believe, teach and hold all that thou commandest us by thy word, and root out all things opposed that thou hast not planted; that we be not led into error by any views of men, institutions, or doctrine of the old Fathers, Popes, cardinals, universities, or old customs. O my Lord Jesus Christ, establish again the two bands, to wit, water-baptism and the Supper, with which thou hast externally girded and bound thy bride. For unless these two shall be again established and used according to thine institution and order, we have among us neither faith, love, church, oath, brotherly discipline, ban nor exclusion, without which things it will never be well in thy Church.

" [10.] I believe and confess also the remission of sins, so that this Christian Church has received keys, command and power from thee, O Christ, to open the gates of heaven for the sinner as often as he repenteth and is sorry for his sin, and receive him again into the holy assembly of believers in Christ, like the lost son and the repentant Corinthian. But when he, after the threefold brotherly reproof, will not abstain from sin, I firmly believe that this Church also hath power to exclude him and to hold him as a publican and heathen. Here I believe and confess openly, my Lord Jesus Christ, that whomsoever the Christian Church on earth thus looseth, he is certainly loosed and released from his sins in heaven. Again, whomsoever the Church bindeth and casteth out of her assembly on earth, he is bound before God in heaven and excluded from the Catholic Christian Church (out of which is no salvation), since Christ himself while he was yet on earth, hung at her side, gave and ordained for his spouse and beloved bride both keys.

" [11.] I believe also and confess a resurrection of the flesh, yea, even the body with which I am now surrounded, though it may be eaten by worms, drowned, frozen, or burned. Yea, and though my temporal honour, goods, body and life be taken from me, yet will I, at the day of the joyous resurrection of my flesh, first truly receive the true honour which avails before God, goods that pass not away, a body incapable of suffering, made clear and immortal, and eternal life. O my Mediator, Lord Jesus Christ, strengthen and hold me in thy faith!

" [12.] I believe and confess also an eternal life which thou, my Lord and God, wilt give to thy faithful and elect after this suffering life; that thou wilt endow them with sure, clear and joyous beholding of thy divine countenance, and satisfy them in all their desires with eternal rest, eternal peace and eternal salvation, which joy, delight and bliss no man can express or conceive here on earth. For no eye hath seen, no ear hath heard, and never hath entered into man's heart what God hath prepared for those who love him.

" O holy God, O mighty God, O immortal God, that is my belief, which I confess with heart and mouth and have witnessed before the Church in water-baptism. Faithfully, graciously, keep me in that till my end, I pray thee. And though I be driven from it by human fear and terror, by tyranny, pangs, sword, fire or water, yet hereby I cry to thee, O my merciful Father: Raise me up again by the grace of thy Holy Spirit, and let me not depart in death without this faith. This I pray thee from the bottom of my heart, through Jesus Christ, thy best-beloved Son, our Lord and Saviour. For in thee, O Father, I hope; let me not be put to shame in eternity. Amen." [1]

---

[1] This translation was made by the Rev. Professor Howard Osgood, D.D., of the Rochester Theological Seminary, but some

The closing paragraph of the above, like other words already quoted, clearly implies that Hübmaier was subjected to torture during his imprisonment at Zürich, and a statement of Faber's confirms this view of the case.[1] Nevertheless, Faber might have been wrong, and the admirers of Zwingli have been loath to admit the validity of the inference one would naturally draw from Hübmaier's words. The affair has been put beyond the possibility of doubt, however, by the publication of a letter previously unknown:

"The next day, [says Zwingli,] he was thrust back into prison and tortured. It is clear the man had become a sport of demons, so he recanted not frankly as he had promised; nay, he said he entertained no other opinions than those taught by me, execrated the error and obstinacy of the Catabaptists, repeated this three times when stretched upon the rack, and bewailed his misery and the wrath of God which in this affair was so unkind."[2]

----

changes have been made by the author of this biography, who therefore takes full responsibility for it, while thus making his acknowledgment of indebtedness to his former teacher and present much-valued friend.

[1] Quoted by Loserth, *Beilage*, No. 10.

[2] The callousness with which Zwingli records this treatment of his former friend is striking. There are other similar cases in his writings. For the letter, see Jackson, *Huldreich Zwingli*, p. 250.

By these gentle means he was "allured" (the grim pleasantry is Zwingli's) into making a more explicit recantation than before, which is still preserved in the archives of Zürich, and is believed by competent judges to be in his own handwriting. It bears no date, but is believed to belong to about the middle of March, and reads as follows:

" I Balthasar Huobmaier, of Fridberg, confess openly with this my handwriting, that I have not otherwise known or understood all Scriptures, which speak of water-baptism, than that one should first preach, after that believe, and thirdly be baptised, on which I have finally established myself. But now has been made known to me through Master Huldrich Zwingli the covenant of God made with Abraham and his seed, also circumcision as a covenant sign, which I could not disprove. Also it was put before me by others, as Master Leo [Juda], Doctor Bastian [Sebastian Hofmeister] and Miconien [Myconius], how love should be a judge and judger in all writings, which has gone very much to my heart; and also I have thought much of love, and have been finally moved to fall from my purpose, namely, that one should not baptise children, and that in the matter of rebaptism I have erred.

" 2. For the rest, it comes to me that I am under accusation, as if I rejected government and say that a Christian cannot sit in government [or] hold office—in which violence and injustice is done to me. I have always and everywhere said that a Christian may well sit in government, and that the more Christian he is, the

HULDREICH ZWINGLI.

FROM A MEZZOTINT BY R. HOUSTON.

more honourably would he rule.   This I have proved
with many writings, which I do not now remember.

"3. Again I am accused as if I would have made
all things common, which yet I have not done, but I have
called this a Christian community of goods: that when
one have and see his neighbour suffer, he should give
him alms, in order that the hungry, thirsty, naked and
imprisoned may be helped; and that the more a man
practice such works of mercy, the nearer he would be
to the spirit of Christianity.

"4. So also to baptism I have added nothing, have
not boasted any perception about it, neither have I been
the first who suffered himself to be baptised, but many
before me, even a quarter of a year.   Some likewise
suffered themselves to be baptised before me in Waldshut.   Likewise also particularly have I baptised no one
in the jurisdiction and districts of my Lords, the Zürich
Council—which has been given out about me untruth-
fully.

"5. Again, likewise I have never said that I am
without sin, or that I never could sin, but always and
everywhere have I confessed that I am a poor sinner,
conceived and born in sin, and shall always remain a
sinner till death.   May God not reckon to me such sin
of mine, to eternal condemnation.   Therefore, in such
things as I am accused of, no one should boast of my
name or use me as a cloak.

"6. Thirdly, since now Augustine and many others
after him even in our times have erred in baptism, therefore I beseech your wisdom for God's sake, wherever I
have herein embittered or injured anyone, that he may
forgive me, as we desire that God should forgive us our
sins.   May your wisdom also be pleased to remember

my great sickness, adversity, banishment and poverty, since I have no coat of my own to put on, thus unclad came I away. Also be pleased to remember the great wrath and fury which my adversaries have embraced against me, and be pleased therefore to look upon me in mercy for God's sake, that as much as lies in your wisdom I may not come or be delivered into the hands of my enemies, especially as I am an infirm man and in this infirm body cannot do without bodily care. So will I pray to God for your wisdom, and will never forget your Christian government my life long. Neither shall any evil be shown by me to your wisdom nor anybody else, either with words or works. This your wisdom may truly trust me." [1]

Except for the first paragraph, this is not a re-cantation, but an apology. The first paragraph is a guarded admission that he had previously been in error respecting infant baptism and rebaptism—an admission that Hübmaier should never have made, and the making of which must considerably modify the admiration that otherwise may justly be entertained for his character and conduct. It is only just, however, to remind ourselves that fortitude in the endurance of excruciating pain is not the gift of

[1] Staehelin (*Huldreich Zwingli*, i., 516) differs from Egli in holding that this is the original recantation of December or January, not the final document. It seems plain that Egli's view is sustained by the closing paragraph and its appeal for help, which was not likely to have been inserted in the first document. The original text is given in Egli's *Actensammlung*, No. 940.

every man.   Let him who is quite certain that his own fortitude would not give way under torture, cast the first stone at such men as have yielded their convictions on the rack.

It is certain that Hübmaier himself was deeply repentant in after years for this error.   In his *Short Apology* (*Op.* 13) he says:

" I may err—I am a man—but a heretic I cannot be, because I ask constantly for instruction in the word of God.   But never has any one come to me and pointed out a single word, but one single man and his followers —against his own previous preaching, word and print, whose name I spare for the sake of God's word—who against common justice and appeal in behalf of his own government, the confederacy, and also the Emperor, by capture, imprisonment, sufferings and the hangman, tried to teach me the faith.   But faith is a work of God and not of the heretics' tower, in which one sees neither sun nor moon, and lives on nothing but water and bread. But God be praised, who delivered me from this den of lions, where dead and living men lay side by side and perished.   O God, pardon me my weakness.   It is good for me (as David says) that thou hast humbled me."

Having obtained this recantation, such as it was and by such methods, the council decreed that Hübmaier should depart immediately from the country.   It was in fear of such a decision that the closing paragraph of the document was written.

Zwingli tells us that he and his friends interceded with the council, that this order should not be executed, since it would put Hübmaier in great peril, both from the other Swiss authorities and from the Emperor. Accordingly, he was suffered to remain for a time, under close surveillance, no doubt, until a favourable opportunity offered for sending him away so quietly that even the citizens of Zürich did not know of his departure. He made his way first to Constance, thence to Augsburg, and then, by what means we do not know,[1] to Nikolsburg, in Moravia, where he seems to have arrived not later than July, 1526. His brief visit by the way at Augsburg is chiefly noteworthy for his meeting there, for the first time, John Denck, whom he is supposed then and there to have won over to Anabaptism.

Excursus on the Act of Baptism among the Anabaptists

The baptism by Hübmaier of three hundred from a milkpail, according to the statement of a contemporary record, naturally suggests an inquiry as to the method

[1] From a letter of Œcolampadius it would appear that he stopped also for a time in the Austrian city of Steyer. A visit to Regensburg, as asserted by some, is possible; but Hoschek (i., 559) confounds with this visit (if it occurred) the circumstances, already narrated, of Hübmaier's first leaving that city.

of administering baptism practised by the Anabaptists. Affusion was evidently the method on this occasion, and there is no good reason to suppose that Hübmaier ever changed his practice. His clearest reference to the subject is contained in his tract *On the Christian Baptism of Believers*, in which he says: "To baptise in water is to pour outward water over the confessor of his sins, in accordance with the divine command, and to inscribe him in the number of sinners upon his own confession and acknowledgment." The first baptism among the Swiss Anabaptists was that of George Blaurock by Conrad Grebel, and it is said that Blaurock fell on his knees and Grebel baptised him—evidently an affusion or aspersion. The next recorded baptisms were performed by Blaurock and Mantz, and in each case it is said that it was done from a dipper or basin (Egli, *Actensammlung*, pp. 282– 284). These baptisms all occurred in late January or early February, 1525. But a few weeks later Conrad Grebel, at least, had obtained clearer light upon the subject. A contemporary chronicler say: "Wolfgang Uoliman [or Uliman, a native of St. Gall, and afterwards active among the Anabaptists there] met Conrad Grebel on the way to Schaffhausen, and in his company [or, by him, *bei ihnen*] was so highly instructed in Anabaptism that he would not be simply poured upon with water from a dish but entirely naked was pressed down and covered over in the Rhine." (Kessler, *Sabbata*, i., 262.) This is not merely a statement that Grebel immersed Uliman, which would be important, but also a testimony that, according to the writer's belief, such immersion was the result of complete instruction in Anabaptism—in other words, that immersion was the usual practice of the well-instructed Anabaptists.

This baptism of Uliman was before March 1, 1525. On Palm Sunday Grebel baptised a large number of people from St. Gall in the Sitter River—the only place near the city well adapted for immersion, and some two miles from the town. It would be silly to maintain that the people walked that distance to be sprinkled. This must be taken, therefore, as confirmation of the view that immersion was fast replacing affusion among the Swiss Anabaptists. The action of the Zürich Council on March 7, 1526, in making drowning the penalty of contumacious persistence in Anabaptism (Egli, *Actensammlung*, No. 936) shows a grim determination to "make the punishment fit the crime," which would be meaningless if immersion were not a general practice in the sect. That this is a correct interpretation of the decree, the words of Zwingli in his *Refutation of the Tricks of the Catabaptists*, sufficiently testify: "After that conference (the tenth, with the others, public or private) the most honourable senate [council] decreed that he should be drowned who rebaptised another "—the exact words are, *aquis mergere, qui merserit baptismo eum qui prius emerserat.* (Zwingli, *Op.*, iii., 364.) That the Swiss Anabaptists began with the practice of affusion, but soon generally adopted immersion, seems therefore to be the most probable conclusion from all the facts accessible.

Elsewhere we find definite proofs of immersion only among the Anabaptists of Augsburg, and in Poland, where the practice was introduced in 1575. It has been conjectured that Swiss Anabaptists fled to Poland and were influential in securing the adoption of immersion there, but documentary proof of this is wholly lacking. A conjecture rather more probable is that the Anabaptists of Poland, having before their eyes the practice of the Greek Church, which has never known any baptism other than immersion, were influenced by this example. The later Anabaptists known as Mennonites seem to have consistently practised affusion from the first—at least there is no case known to the contrary, except the congregation at Rhynsburg, which began to practice immersion in 1620.

10

CHAPTER V

HÜBMAIER AT NIKOLSBURG

1526–1528

IT is not difficult to conjecture why Hübmaier chose Nikolsburg as his next residence. Moravia was almost the only province in Europe where he could hope to find more than a temporary refuge. Not only did this region promise a comparatively safe haven, but it is probable that a large number of Anabaptists had already gone thither.[1] Here was not only safety, but the most fruitful field of labour known to him. That he should proceed at once to Moravia, and begin his labours with redoubled energy is precisely what we should expect of such a man. His activity would be stimulated,

---

[1] If they did not actually precede Hübmaier, they must have arrived in large numbers at about the same time, for a few months afterward they were estimated at twelve thousand (Loserth, p. 127). That these were all converts, and not in large part immigrants, is incredible.

no doubt, by memory of what he had experienced at Zürich, and especially by recollection that physical weakness and love of life had led him to deny the truth.

He must have felt that the lines had fallen to him in pleasant places. The Nikolsburg of to-day is a delightfully quaint town, of a pronounced mediæval flavour. It is out of the beaten track of globe-trotters, difficult of access, and hence seldom visited by the ordinary tourist. The old walls have disappeared, but the city has availed itself little of its liberty to straggle into the fields. The houses are grouped as of old about the steep, rocky hill, whose summit is occupied by the castle and the church— houses low and long, built flush with the street and entered from the street level, or at most by one or two rude stone steps; houses solidly built of stone, with red-tiled roofs, from which little, wicked-looking windows wink at the foreigner as he passes by. The bright and curious costumes of the peasants who throng the streets on a gala day are an added touch of mediævalism, for they are the same that have been worn for countless generations. Little but German is spoken in the town, and the

people are mostly devout Roman Catholics, though
a small and new Lutheran church stands on the
outskirts. No relics remain of the short-lived reformation here, and the name of Hübmaier has
completely faded from recollection. The historian
of the town, an antiquarian of some repute, had
never heard the name.

We know as yet from original sources too little
about the religious history of Moravia prior to
1526; but that the influence of Hus had been deeply
felt there is certain. There was a strong evangelical
party in the province before the arrival of Hübmaier, which had gained many adherents among
prelates, clergy, and noblemen, as well as among
the people at large. The Unitas Fratrum, though
originating in Bohemia, could almost claim Moravia
as the twin land of their birth, and later they became so identified with it as to bear, to this day,
the name Moravians. The political circumstances
were such as to favour an evangelical revival.
Since the twelfth century Moravia—a small terri-
tory of only 8,500 square miles, a little larger than
the State of Massachusetts—had been a Margravate
held by the younger sons of the kings of Bohemia,

A GENERAL VIEW OF MODERN NIKOLSBURG.

of whose crown it was a fief. But the royal power had always been weak, and Hübmaier's coming coincided with an interregnum. On August 29, 1526, Louis II. of Bohemia was defeated by the Turks at Mohacs, Hungary, and fell in the battle. As he left no heirs, in the following October the diet chose as king the Archduke Ferdinand, of Austria, who had married a sister of Louis and was in every way the most eligible prince. The choice was by no means a popular one, however, and it was some time before Ferdinand's royal authority was established. In the meantime, the Moravian nobles, always enjoying a large measure of independence, were absolute masters of the situation, and did as seemed to them good.

The people of Moravia were at this time mainly Germans, though there was among them a large proportion of that Czech (Slav) race which in early times had settled both this region and Bohemia. At the present day less than twenty per cent. of the Moravian people are Czechs, but it is probable that in the Reformation era the proportion was much larger. Evangelical views seem to have made progress equally among both peoples, but, if we may draw safe inference from the names that continually appear in the records, the Anabaptists were from the first and continued to be mostly Germans.

By the evangelical Christians of Moravia Hübmaier was kindly, even warmly, received. He became a guest in the home of Oswald Glaidt, who was then the coadjutor of the chief evangelical preacher, Hans Spitalmaier, both natives of Bavaria. This common nativity was an additional bond between them and Hübmaier, who praises both "because they bravely and faithfully held up the light of evangelical purity, and put it on the candlestick, so as he had known the like in no region." Glaidt was soon won to Anabaptist views by his eloquent and persuasive guest, and was baptised. Spitalmaier must have been gained at about the same time, for shortly after this we find him also a coworker with Hübmaier. A still more important convert was Martin Göschel, who had once been sub-bishop of Olmütz, and later provost of a nunnery at Kanitz. This latter position, with its large income, he attempted to hold in spite of his adoption and advocacy of evangelical doctrine, and he had only recently been ousted from it, resisting to the last.

But a yet greater triumph was to follow. Nikolsburg was in the domains of the barons of Lichtenstein, a Moravian noble family tracing its lineage back to the twelfth century, of which house there were then two brothers, Leonard and John. They had been well disposed towards evangelical doctrine, and it was due to their encouragement that the gospel had already made so great progress at Nikolsburg. They also soon came under the influence of Hübmaier, became convinced by his presentation of the truth, and were publicly baptised on confession of their faith.[1] Other noblemen of the region were well disposed to evangelical preaching, and from the fact that Hübmaier dedicated to them many of his treatises we may fairly infer that he expected at least their favour and protection, and was not without hopes of winning them also to his party. Such men were John of Brunnstein and Helfenstein, Governor-General of Moravia, to whom *The Reason Why Every Man should Receive Baptism*

---

[1] See the Anabaptist chronicles quoted by Beck, *Geschichts-Bücher*, p. 48.

was inscribed; Lord Arkleb of Boskowitz, Chancellor of Moravia, to whom was dedicated the treatise *On the Sword;* Lord Burian, of Kornitz, whose name heads *The Form of the Supper;* Frederick of Silesia, the patron of *The Second Book on the Will;* Jan Dubcansky, to whom the preface of *The Form of Baptism* is addressed in such terms as to make it certain that Hübmaier had great hopes of his adhesion to Anabaptism.

Here was a new experience indeed for the Anabaptists! Everywhere they had been despised, persecuted, counting themselves fortunate if barely permitted to live: here they not only found themselves tolerated, but saw their rulers actually embracing their faith, publicly avowing it, and using their wealth and power to promote the preaching of a pure gospel. The golden age seemed to have come for them—pity it should have endured for so short a time! Little more than a twelvemonth was Hübmaier permitted to carry on this work, but into that space he condensed the labours of many a lifetime. So great was the progress of the Anabaptists that within this single year not fewer than six thousand persons were added to them by baptism—some say double that number, but that seems hardly credible.

It must not be inferred, of course, that this was all the result of one man's labours. There were a multitude of other fervent preachers of the gospel; indeed, it is little exaggeration to say that every Anabaptist was an apostle and missionary. Hübmaier was, however, the acknowledged leader. In learning, in character, in eloquence, he was not less fitted for leadership than Luther or Zwingli; and had continued opportunity been offered him, there can be little doubt that he would have here accomplished that which would have left his name by the side of the greatest preachers and reformers of the age. If Luther had been crushed at Worms as Hus had been at Constance, we might now read as little of him as we do of Hübmaier.

Not only was he active as preacher and organiser, but his pen was incessantly busy. It was a fortunate circumstance for him that a printer of Zürich, Simprecht Sorg, surnamed Froschower,[1] had been compelled to flee from persecution, and had made

---

[1] This Froschower, or Froschauer, was the printer of Zwingli's early tracts, but had become an Anabaptist, and could no longer remain and conduct his business at Zürich.

his way to Nikolsburg, with the outfit of a printing establishment, and had arrived there at about the same time with himself. Froschower now became the regular publisher of Hübmaier's tracts, which flowed from the press in a steady stream. No fewer than seventeen pamphlets and treatises bear date of Nikolsburg, 1526 and 1527, though several of these we know to have been composed earlier. A few of these are quite brief, while others are booklets of some size. While we have no precise information as to the number of these publications issued and circulated, we know that it was very large, that they were read far and wide, and that they had a profound influence upon those into whose hands they fell. The greatest efforts were made to secure and destroy these pamphlets, and with measurable success, for only a few copies of each issue survive, in some cases a unique specimen only.

Of these Nikolsburg writings eleven are concerned with the Christian sacraments, or the ordinances of the Church, and no fewer than six of them with the ordinance of baptism; four are apologetic and polemic; while two are contributions to systematic theology.   Quotations have already been made from three of the first class of pamphlets (*Op.* 10, 17, 18) to give an idea of their nature and contents; and the passages that are of personal interest have been cited from one of the apologetic tracts (*Op.* 13).   The others are utilised in a similar manner in a later chapter of this book, on the teachings of Hübmaier.   Only a few general remarks, therefore, about this remarkable literary output of two years are in order here.

As a man of letters, Hübmaier deserves to be ranked along with Erasmus and Melanchthon,—as a man of letters, be it noted, not as a scholar.   He has no claim to be ranked among the first of the humanists—his taste was for theology rather than for the classics, and his learning was learning in the Scriptures.   There he was the peer of the best scholars of his age.   How thorough was his knowledge of the original tongues, especially of the Hebrew, we have no means of determining; but somehow, whether from originals or from translations, he had managed to acquire such a comprehensive and minute acquaintance with the Scriptures as would have made him a divine of mark in any age. And a ready memory kept these stores of knowledge ever at his command. He was never at a loss for a passage to support any contention of his own or to confute what he supposed to be an error of an adversary.

But while this mastery of the Scriptures is creditable to Hübmaier, and entitles him to a certain consideration as a theologian, it is not his chief distinction. It is his power of expression, his sense of literary form, his art of putting things, that sets him alongside of Erasmus. His style, considered as mere Latinity, is faulty enough—indeed, every college student now knows that the Latinity of the great Erasmus himself, loudly as it was praised by unscholarly contemporaries, was very bad measured by the classical standards. But as an instrument for expressing thought, Hübmaier's Latin demands no criticism, and his use of it shows him one who would have been a clever literary craftsman in any language. In this literary characteristic, he has a note of modernity found in comparatively few of the writers of his age.

The great bulk of Hübmaier's writing, however, is in his mother tongue, the German then spoken

in Bavaria. It differs somewhat, possibly for the
worse, from the German of Luther, but is unspeak-
ably better than the crabbed Swiss dialect in which
Zwingli wrote many of his books. In the best of
the tongues then spoken, Erasmus would have dis-
dained to write even an ordinary letter, to say
nothing of a book for the scholarly. But Hübmaier
did not write for the scholarly alone or chiefly; he
wrote for the common man, and he had the same
kind of power with the masses that Luther showed
in his address *To the Christian Nobility of the German Nation.* The tracts that poured forth from
the Nikolsburg press are among the best specimens
of religious literature produced by the sixteenth
century—strong, eloquent, persuasive, vital.

The ethical tone of Hübmaier's writings also
marks him for distinction among the writers of his
age. He is scrupulously fair to his adversaries—
always fair in intention, and usually fair in deed.
He never charges misconduct and heresy upon his
adversaries with that light-hearted carelessness of
fact which is characteristic of his age and of most
of its writers—of Luther and Zwingli, for example.
And the difference in tone between his controversial

writings and those of the period is marvellous. To read an average pamphlet of Luther's, written to confute some adversary,—*Wider Hans Wurst*, for instance, or *Contra Henricum Regem*,—and then to turn to any writing of Hübmaier's, is like escaping from the mephitic odours of a slum into a garden of spices. It is not merely that scurrilous abuse has been exchanged for courteous speech,— the whole atmosphere is different. There is a "sweet reasonableness" in Hübmaier's attitude toward men and truth, a confident belief that he is right, but a genuine willingness to be instructed, which is rare in any age and was unique in his. Of a brilliant English scholar it was said, as his fitting epitaph, "He died learning"; and of Hübmaier it may be said with equal truth that each year of his life saw him take a long stride forward, not only in knowledge of the truth, but in that love that is not easily provoked and thinketh no evil.

The success of Hübmaier's work was considerably marred, if not seriously hindered, by controversies among the brethren themselves. The fact has already been recognised that there were considerable differences among the Anabaptists from the first. One of the most fair-minded contemporary writers, Sebastian Franck, says of them that he had found no two who exactly agreed. But up to this time we may say of them, with some confidence, that if there was any tenet in addition to the baptism of believers on which they agreed it was the duty of non-resistance.[1] Many, but not all, drew from this the corollary that a Christian man could not lawfully be a magistrate, for the civil ruler must bear the sword and use it when necessary against evil-doers. This is especially true of the Swiss Anabaptists, with whom Hübmaier had been most closely allied.

But there was now coming into the Nikolsburg community a man who taught a contrary doctrine wherever he went. This was Hans Hut, a native of Franconia, and said to be of Waldensian descent, who, as early as 1521, had gotten himself into prison for refusing to have his babe baptised. On gaining his freedom, he went to Nürnberg, where he learned the trade of bookbinder and made the acquaintance of John Denck. A little later he was a

---

[1] The Schleitheim Confession is strong on this point, and Kessler's testimony is conclusive. *Sabbata*, i., p. 232.

bookseller at Wittenberg, and when the Peasants'
War broke out he made his way to Thomas Münzer
at Mühlhausen. Captured at the battle of Frankenhausen, where Münzer and his peasants were overthrown, he obtained his liberty by convincing his
captors that he was in the camp as a book-peddler
and not as a soldier. His plea may have been true,
but there is plenty of evidence in his subsequent
career that he had fully made his own the chiliastic and anarchistic principles of Münzer. To the
preaching of these he gave the rest of a stormy and
checkered life.

He joined Denck for a time in Augsburg, in the
spring of 1526, and was baptised by this Anabaptist
preacher, who had himself but a little before been
baptised by Hübmaier. Up to this time, though
opposed to the baptism of infants, Hut was not
definitely connected with the Anabaptists; henceforth his labours were confined to that sect—or,
more properly speaking, to one party among the
Anabaptists. There had always been certain of
these who rejected the tenet of non-resistance, to
this extent at least—that the godly might use the
sword against the ungodly, in setting up the king-

dom of God. In other words, there was always a chiliastic wing of Anabaptists, who believed that the kingdom of heaven comes not only with observation but by violence. By these Hut was speedily hailed as a prophet, and had no hesitation in proclaiming himself to be such. He was a man of striking appearance and powerful personality, nearly illiterate but a master of popular eloquence. While really ignorant of the Scriptures, he had that glib command of such texts as bore on his own favourite themes which often passes with those who know still less for wide and deep Biblical knowledge. Wherever such a man went, he was sure to be a firebrand.

Such he proved to be in Nikolsburg, where he made his appearance toward the close of the year 1526, or early in 1527. He proclaimed that the day of the Lord was at hand. He was the prophet sent by God to warn the ungodly that their overthrow was near. To the saints he announced that their mission was that of a chosen people—to root out the wicked who then ruled the world as the Israelites destroyed the people of Canaan. The time of the persecution of the saints was nearly at

II

an end; the two-edged sword of God's vengeance would soon be put in their hands. It was a curious feature of the teaching of these fanatical Anabaptists, that while they denied the right of the sword to magistrates and denounced all war as "carnal," they believed that when Christ should begin his millennial reign it would be not merely the right but the duty of his subjects to take up the sword and put the ungodly to slaughter.

Even before Hut's coming, a small party of fanatical Anabaptists had found refuge in Nikolsburg, holding views differing from his, but harmonising with them wondrous well—a remnant, perhaps, of Münzer's following, who escaped the slaughter of Mühlhausen and wandered from place to place until they reached Moravia. The leading spirit among these was Jacob Widemann, and his pet vagary was community of goods among Christian brethren as a cardinal principle of the gospel. He had taught an extreme form of non-resistance, insisting that Christians are forbidden to use the sword in self-defence or as magistrates, and, as a corollary to this, that Christians ought not to pay taxes, since these are used for the support of governments and the waging of war. He and his followers called taxes "blood money." Of the antecedents of Widemann — who was popularly known by the nickname of "One-eyed Jacob"— little is known, except the statement of an old chronicle that he came from the land of Ens (Salzburg), and had first made Hut's acquaintance at Augsburg.

Widemann and Hut speedily joined forces. Widemann and his adherents found little difficulty in grafting Hut's doctrine of the sword, as the exclusive perquisite of the saints, upon their previous tenet of non-resistance; while Hut and his followers were not slow to perceive that if the end of the age was at hand there was little use in private property. There was a natural affinity between the two parties — and, besides, they both found themselves confronted by the same formidable opponent, Hübmaier.

He was too well versed in the Scriptures, and too well ballasted with common sense, to be carried away by this fanaticism. He had never held to community of goods, though this charge had been falsely made against him, as well as against certain of the Swiss Anabaptists. But this was when Zwingli and his helpers were more anxious to discredit the Anabaptists than to discover and tell the precise truth about them; and Hübmaier had consistently denied the imputation. He was in favour of such community of goods, he said, as prevailed in the church at Jerusalem, when not one of them said that aught of the things which he possessed was his own, but sold their lands and houses that distribution might be made to those who had need. So, he held and taught, Christian believers should hold all property subject to the needs of the brotherhood, available for the assistance of needy brothers—a very different thing from what is generally meant by communism. Nor had he ever taught the extreme doctrine of non-resistance, forbidden Christians to be magistrates, or to pay their taxes. Above all, he had no chiliastic delusions, he had proclaimed no wild exegesis of the prophetic writings, he had not taught his followers to look for the immediate second coming of Christ and the setting up of his millennial kingdom.

It is not hard to understand the fascination that these teachings of Hut and Widemann had for a despised and down-trodden people. To have it apparently proved from Scripture that the time was at hand when Christ would appear in the heavens, set up his kingdom on earth and rule with his saints a thousand years, and that all enemies should be speedily put under his feet, was fitted to carry away the ignorant and simple-minded, and even some of sufficient learning to have known better. Or, if any have difficulty in comprehending how ideas so absurd (to them) should find so easy and so wide acceptance, let them recall the reception given to precisely similar teaching in one of the most intelligent communities of our own land, no longer ago than fifty years. William Miller and Hans Hut were theological twins, and there is a most instructive similarity in the character, reception, and results of their teaching. Like Miller, Hut was rash enough to set an exact day for the ending of the old order and the coming of the new kingdom—the second anniversary of the battle of Frankenhausen. When May 15, 1527, came and the world still stood, he was, again like Miller, quite undismayed by the failure of his prediction, and proceeded to make another with equally cheerful confidence, this time fixing the catastrophe for the day of the summer feast, Whitsunday, 1529. Many so completely believed him, in spite of his first failure, as to forsake their homes, sell their goods, and throng him from place to place, awaiting the great day of their Lord's coming.

Of Hut's preaching during this time, one choice specimen has been preserved:

"Then [shortly before the end of the age] all the godless will be destroyed, and that by true Christians; if their number [the true Christians] shall be sufficient, they will go from Germany to Switzerland, and to Hungary, and have no regard to princes and lords. Then some thousands of them shall assemble, and every one shall sell his goods and take the money with him, so as to be sure, meantime, of food; then they shall wait until the Turk comes.[1] If the Turk fails to strike down any of the princes, monks, priests, nobles, or knights, they will then be stricken and slain by the little company of true Christians. But if the godless shall march against the Turks, then the true Christians shall remain at home; but, if many of the princes or many of the lords remain at home too, and do not march against the Turks, they shall be struck down a little while afterwards. Then it will come to pass that the true Christians will have no one, but God alone, and God himself will be and remain their lord."[2]

---

[1] This and what follows is an allusion to an impending invasion of Austria by the Turks, which indeed happened, not in 1527, but two years later.   [2] Quoted by Hoschek, ii., 231, 232.

The schism thus produced among the Anabaptists and the disturbances caused by Hut's preaching became very serious. Some of Hübmaier's most prominent disciples were carried away by this fanaticism, including Oswald Glaidt and other preachers at Nikolsburg. Even Göschel seems to have gone over to Hut; of all the former evangelists, Spitalmaier is the only prominent one who is known to have stood by Hübmaier without wavering. Something was needful to be done to check the movement, and first of all a conference or disputation was tried. The leaders met in Bergen, but the discussion left them farther apart than before. Then the Lichtenstein nobles intervened, and summoned all the preachers to the castle at Nikolsburg, where the whole subject was thoroughly threshed out in their presence. By this time the Nikolsburg preachers had all seen more clearly whither Hut's teaching was tending, and they joined Hübmaier in defending the authority of civil government, its right to bear the sword, and the duty of Christians to pay taxes for its support. Whether the question of the community of goods was also discussed is not clear. Hut stoutly

maintained the teachings that he had been propa-
gating to be the truth and the plain sense of the
Scriptures, and utterly refused to yield. The result was that Lord Lichtenstein detained Hut as a
prisoner in the castle.[1]

As this action of Lichtenstein was apparently
approved by Hübmaier, the accusation was at once
brought against him, and has been repeated to this
day, that he thus proved himself an inconsistent
advocate of religious liberty, and was a persecutor
when he had the opportunity. The action of the
ruler, however, seems quite justified by the facts
as we know them. Hut was plainly teaching sedition and murder — sedition as a present duty,
murder as a duty in the near future. No principle
of religious liberty requires that a government shall
leave such a firebrand to go about in the community. There was so much excitement in the
city following this action of the Prince, and so
vehement charges were made against him for this
action, and the conduct of the other preachers was
so violently questioned, that Hübmaier was con-

---

[1] The insinuation of Hoschek (ii., 234), that the intention was
"perhaps to have burned him at the stake," is quite gratuitous.

strained to call the whole church together and make them a long oration on the matter. The other preachers stood by him, and eventually the church seem to have been satisfied that the proper course had been pursued. In the meantime Hut made good his escape from the castle. One suspects that the Prince was not averse to this solution of the matter; at any rate, some friendly hands let the preacher down with a rope over the walls by night.

Hut made his way back to the city of Augsburg, but this town had ceased to be a safe refuge for Anabaptists. Many were arrested and imprisoned, among them Hut, against whom the authorities had been previously warned by the council of Nürnberg. While imprisoned in the tower, he is said to have suffered severe tortures. His death was mysterious. He was found one day in his cell, badly burned and in a dying condition. An old chronicle says that the careless jailer left a light near the straw, which took fire. The enemies of the Anabaptists circulated a story that he attempted to escape by setting fire to his cell and was fatally burned in the attempt. It is impossible to

determine which account is true; but what seems
to be beyond question is that his dead or moribund
body was hastily taken into court and ordered
to be burned; and at sound of the alarum-bell, his
body was carried to the gibbet beyond the walls,
and there burnt to ashes.[1]

Widemann, as the less dangerous man of the two,
seems not to have been imprisoned or otherwise
troubled.   He continued to lead the party opposed
to Hübmaier, and, in spite of the latter's opposition, the sentiment in favour of community of
goods continued to grow in Nikolsburg, and ultimately this led to the division of the church and
the emigration of the communistic element, but not
during Hübmaier's lifetime.   A more immediate
result was the composition and printing of the
treatise *On the Sword*, in which Hübmaier set forth
his ideas on civil government with the utmost clearness, fulness, and frankness.

This was the last, and in some respects the most
important, of his Nikolsburg pamphlets.   It is a
less ambitious performance than his two treatises

---

[1] Newman, in his *History of Anti-Pedobaptism*, says December 7,
1527, but the Anabaptist chronicles make the year 1529.   Beck,
Geschichts-Bücher, p. 34, *cf.* p. 50.

on the *Freedom of the Will*, but it has a practical
value that does not always pertain to academic
discussions in theology. The existence of the
Nikolsburg church, and the permanence of the
reformation in Moravia were seriously threatened.
The division in the church pointed towards its
speedy disintegration, unless the strife provoked by
Hut and Widemann could be ended. What was
perhaps more serious was that, if the Moravian
nobles should become convinced that the majority
of Anabaptists sympathised with the fanatical
ravings of Hut, they would look upon the entire
sect as seditious and dangerous persons, to be sup-
pressed and even punished, rather than encouraged.
This was the charge that had everywhere been
brought against the Anabaptists by their enemies,
and at that day it was generally believed outside
of Moravia. Recent German investigators, like
Cornelius and Keller, have done much to free the
Anabaptists from these (in the main) undeserved
imputations. But still more recently, certain
English writers,[1] themselves advocates of modern

---

[1] Richard Heath, *Anabaptism*, from its Rise at Zwickau to its
Fall at Münster, 1521–1536 ; E. Belfort Bax, *Rise and Fall of the
Anabaptists*.

socialistic theories, have represented the whole Anabaptist movement as a splendid but unfortunate attempt to realise a complete socialistic programme,
a radical overturning of existing institutions, almost
an entire anticipation of the teachings of Lassalle
and Marx.

While the motives of the recent writers are far
more laudable than those of their predecessors, the
result is almost precisely the same. The contemporary writers wished to load the Anabaptists with
obloquy; their English historians wish to crown
the Anabaptists with honour, as the first to attempt
the application of a theory yet destined to be the
salvation of mankind; but in either case the Anabaptists are equally misrepresented, and the opinions of a few are attributed to the whole. The
misrepresentation is most serious when the violent
measures advocated by Hut and afterwards put in
practice at Münster are represented either as the
convictions of the majority or the legitimate consequences of the views prevalent in the body.

It was, therefore, to neutralise the effects of this
misrepresentation throughout Moravia, no less than
to win to sounder ideas concerning the teaching of

the Scriptures the erring Anabaptists themselves, that this treatise *On the Sword* was composed. As the entire document is given in the Appendix, it is necessary to do no more here than call attention to its chief characteristics, and briefly summarise the argument. And, first of all, it is worth while to note carefully its tone and temper. Hübmaier found himself in practically the same dilemma that confronted Luther a few years earlier, at the time of the peasants' revolt. The peasants appealed to Luther's writings as affording justification for their claims, if not for their deeds, and the Catholic writers hastened to charge upon him the moral responsibility of the revolt. If the princes and rulers of Germany had taken this view of the case, no doubt there would have been a speedy end of Luther's reformation. What did Luther do under these trying circumstances? He lost his head completely, and instead of trying by expostulation and argument from the Scriptures, for which he professed so great respect, to win the peasants from their errors and bring them back to their loyalty and obedience, he hastily composed and printed his pamphlet, *Against the Murdering and*

Robbing Bands of the Peasants.[1] The violence and
coarseness of the abuse that he poured upon the
peasants,—the justice of whose cause he had explicitly approved a short time before,[2]—his eager
advocacy of a policy of extermination by the
princes, the bloodthirsty exhortations to the nobles
to show no compassion, but to smite as long as
they could move a muscle, disgusted and discon-
certed his own friends and closest adherents. Ever
since that crisis, admirers of Luther have been compelled to apologise for and extenuate his conduct
as best they might. But Hübmaier makes no such
demands upon his biographer. His tractate, *On
the Sword*, is temperate in language and thoroughly
Christian in its tone. He said nothing for which
he need blush or we apologise. No contrast could
be greater.

In truth, we see Hübmaier here at his best as a con-
troversialist. The tractate shows great familiarity with
the Scriptures and clear understanding of their meaning,

[1] Luther's *German Works*, Erlangen ed., xxiv., 287 *sq.* Walch
ed., xvi., 91 *sq.* This appears in an English version in *Historical
Leaflets*, No. 4, edited by Henry C. Vedder, Crozer Theological
Seminary, 1901.

[2] Luther's *German Works*, Erlangen ed., xxiv., 257 *sq.* Walch
ed., xv., 58 *sq.* An English translation may be found in Michelet's
Life of Luther (Bohn ed.), pp. 161–180.

shrewd appreciation of both the strength and the weakness of his adversaries, good sense, tact and humour. He cites one after another the fifteen texts on which the opponents of magistracy chiefly relied: John xviii., 36; Matt. xxvi., 53, 54; Luke ix., 54, 55; xii., 13, 14; Matt. v., 40; 1 Cor. vi., 7, 8; Matt. xviii., 15–17; Matt. v., 38, 39, and Luke vi., 29; Eph. vi., 14–17; 2 Cor. x., 4, 5; Matt. v., 43–48; v., 21; Luke xxii., 25, 26; Rom. xii., 19, 20; Eph. iv., 15, and Col. i., 18. Each of these texts is subjected to a thorough and candid examination. Hübmaier here appears to great advantage as an interpreter of Scripture. His exegesis is thoroughly good; there is hardly a word that one would wish to see changed; and he points out, with equal kindness and distinctness, the errors of his brethren. These had been caused by a too rigid literalism of interpretation, and a refusal (or at least a failure) to compare Scripture with Scripture.

It is by this method clearly shown that Paul speaks of a twofold sword, the spiritual and the temporal. The former is the word of God, with which the Christian is to overcome his adversaries. The latter is borne by the magistrate, for the protection of the innocent and the punishment of the evil doer. Governments are of God; the magistrate is his minister. When Jesus forbade his followers to use the sword, he spoke to men who had no right to use it—they had not been elected or appointed for that purpose. He refused to be a judge —that was not his office—but he did not condemn those whose business it was to judge. He that takes the sword without authority shall perish by the sword, but not he that bears the sword according to God's command and order. A Christian ought to suffer wrong rather than bring a suit to right himself, but the magistrate and judge are bound to protect him from wrong and to redress his wrongs unasked. Excommunication and the sword have nothing in common: one is a spiritual penalty, to be imposed by the church; the other a physical penalty, to be inflicted by the magistrate. The magistrate does not hate an enemy when he punishes; his sword is a good rod and scourge of God. In short, the Scriptures, fairly interpreted throughout, do not condemn magistracy, but sustain it.

With the departure of Hut, the chiliastic excitement at Nikolsburg declined, and the teaching of the extreme doctrines against which this treatise was aimed ceased. How far Hübmaier's arguments were effectual in promoting a better understanding of the Scriptures among the Moravian Anabaptists can only be conjectured. Whether because of his success, or for other reasons, controversy regarding the sword rapidly decreased, and the only principle that remained as a cause of division from 1528 onward was the community of goods. On this matter Widemann successfully maintained his ground, with a following constantly increasing in numbers and weight. It is possible that if Hübmaier had continued his active labours a few years longer, he might have won a victory all along the line; but

VIEW OF NIKOLSBURG IN 1678.

FROM AN OLD PRINT.

the publication of this treatise, the preface of which is dated June 24, 1527, marks the close of his ministry at Nikolsburg. A few weeks later he was a prisoner, on his way to Vienna, where he was soon to meet his death.

12

CHAPTER VI

THE TEACHINGS OF HÜBMAIER

1524–1527

A PREACHER of the gospel and for the most part a writer on practical questions, not a speculative theologian, Hübmaier nevertheless held a well-reasoned system of theology. Of his writings that resemble a systematic statement of his beliefs, one [1] is no more than an amplification—it can hardly be called an exposition—of the Apostle's Creed, while the other [2] is a catechism. His only other writings that may be called theological, in the strict sense, are his two treatises on the Freedom of the Will. Elsewhere in his published works he frequently discussed theological questions, but in an incidental and fragmentary way, as might be expected of one whom choice and circumstances had

---

[1] *The Twelve Articles of Christian Belief, Op.* 18.
[2] *The Table of Christian Doctrine, Op.* 11.

combined to make preacher and reformer rather than thinker and doctor. He was not by any means a religious opportunist; he did not lack definite theological ideas because he restrained himself from giving them expression. To his apprehension, truth presented itself in sharp and clear outlines; it was a well-defined body; he did not refrain from systematic statement of doctrine because his ideas were hazy, or because he was indifferent, but because other matters seemed to him of more pressing importance. In times more quiet he would have given more attention to theology.

We shall not waste time, then, if we undertake to dissect out of Hübmaier's writings a skeleton of doctrine, which underlies all his teaching and gives it consistency, coherence, and firmness. And we shall do well to begin at the point where he himself began; for he was led to his clear views of Scripture truth, as we have seen, by the independent study of the Scriptures themselves. Prior to 1522 he had been content with the scholastic theology of which his old master and friend, Eck, continued to the last to be so ardent and eminent an exponent. The authority of the Fathers and great doctors of

the Church was sufficient for the master, but the
disciple was led by study of the Bible to the rejection of dogma and Fathers, and indeed to an
entirely different estimation of the Scriptures themselves.   As a Catholic he had always, in a vague
and careless and ignorant way, regarded these as
the foundation of the faith, but his personal acquaintance with them gave him a new apprehension
alike of their spiritual value and of their religious
authority.   Thenceforth, the rejection of all human
authority in religion, and of every usage of human
origin as well, and the substitution therefor of the
faith and order of the Scriptures, seemed to him
the only possible and defensible course for Christian
men to take.

" We should inquire of the Scriptures," he says in one
of his Dialogues,[1] " and not of the Church, for God will
have from us only his law, his will, not our wrong heads
or what seems good to us.   God is more concerned with
obedience to his will than with all our offerings and
self-invented church usages.   .   .   .   Thou knowest,
Zwingli, that the Holy Scripture is such a complete, com-
pacted, true, infallible, eternally immortal speech, that
the least letter or tittle of it cannot pass away."

---

[1] *A Conversation of Balthasar Hübmaier, Op.* 10.

And he will by no means admit that some things are essential and other things unessential:

> " For an earnest command demands an earnest obedience and following. ' Verily, verily, I say unto you,' Christ has not used such precious words for a matter that may be done or left undone, as each pious Christian can see for himself. But it is just the way of human wisdom to hold as of least weight that which God highly regards or commands." [1]

The most explicit and elaborate statement of this supremacy of the authority of Scripture is contained in the already quoted theses in which Hübmaier challenges his master Eck to debate.[2] But, after all, his belief on this subject is shown less by any of his formal declarations than by his constant attitude towards the Scriptures, which is one of reverence and obedience. His writings contain little but quotations from the Bible,—exegesis and exposition. His continual inquiry, as each point is discussed, is, What do the Scriptures say about this? And his treatment of the text is candid. His exegesis is nearly always right — modern scholarship finds little to quarrel with in his inter-

---

[1] *Ground and Reason, Op.* 16.
[2] *Supra*, p. 89 *sq.*

pretations — and even when he is wrong he is honestly, not perversely, wrong.   There are few writers in the history of the Church who have searched the Scriptures with a greater zeal to discover their teaching, or have come to the study with a more open mind, or who have bent fewer texts from their plain meaning to support a favourite theory.

The method of interpretation avowed and practised by Hübmaier is simple in the extreme.   It is to take a plain text in its plain meaning, applying to its exegesis the principles of grammar and ordinary common sense.   In only one case does he yield to the tendency to allegorise, and in that case his exegesis is worthy of reproduction as a curiosity, though it has no other value.   He is attempting to prove from Scripture that the fall of the body is irrecoverable and fatal, while that of the soul is half recoverable and innocuous, and he does it thus:

" Adam, the image (*figur*) of the soul, as Eve is the image of the body, would rather not have eaten of the fruit of the tree.   He was not tempted by the serpent, but Eve was tempted.   He knew that the speech of the serpent contradicted the word of God, and yet he chose to eat of the fruit against his own conscience (*gwissen*), so as not to grieve his rib and his body, Eve, but he himself would rather not have yielded.   Since he then obeyed Eve rather than God, he lost the knowledge of good and evil, so that he cannot will or choose the good, and cannot reject or renounce the evil.   Consequently nothing pleased him except that which pleased his Eve, that is, his body." [1]

Emphatic and absolute was his repudiation of the Romanist's contention that an infallible interpreter (the Church) is necessary, or else the Scriptures will lead men astray.   The Church is only the collected Fathers and doctors, and if these individually do not know the Scriptures they do not and cannot collectively know them.   "They well know," he says, "that a single woman—such as the pious Christian woman Argula von Stauff—knows more of the divine word than such red-capped ones will ever see and lay hold of."   The humblest believer is able to understand the Scriptures, so much at any rate as is necessary to salvation, and it is his duty to learn this by his own study of the word, not to take it at second-hand from anybody.   The possibility of error in thus interpreting the divine word is admitted, but this is due for the most part to the obscurity or brevity of certain passages.   The remedy

---

[1] *Freedom of the Will, Op.* 23.

is to recognise that Scripture can be interpreted only by Scripture. If we put beside these obscure or brief passages other passages on the same subject, and bind them together like wax candles, and light them all at once, then the clear and pure splendour of the Scriptures must shine forth.[1] In this way, the believer who surrenders himself to the guidance of the Spirit of God will be led into all the truth.

In Theology proper—the doctrine of God—Hübmaier was orthodox according to the standards of Nicæa and Chalcedon. There is no trace in his writings of the anti-Trinitarian theories taught by Denck and attributed to Hätzer.[2] He declares his belief in God, the Father Almighty, the highest good, all-wise and all-merciful — his wisdom and power shown in his creation and ruling of the world, his mercy in the sending of his only begotten Son. This Son, Jesus Christ, is true God and man, conceived of the Holy Ghost, born of Mary, the pure and ever chaste Virgin; and the Son of the living God thus became man that through him we might

---

[1] *Simple Explanation* of the words, " This is my Body." *Op.* 9.

[2] The book said to contain Hätzer's heretical views was burned by Capito, and it is impossible now to judge whether the accusation was just or not,

become children of God. After his passion and death, Jesus Christ rose from the dead, ascended into heaven, and sits at the right hand of his Father, "in the same power, glory and praise with the Father, as our only intercessor, mediator and propitiator before the Father. There he sits, mighty and strong, to help all believers who put their trust in him, and it is in vain to seek another Advocate."[1] This is the longest single passage in Hübmaier's writings on the subject of Christ's divinity, and he puts into it matters commonly discussed under the head of Soteriology, as well as those that immediately pertain to Christ's relation to the Father. Of the Holy Spirit he only says that he "proceeds from the Father and the Son, and yet with them is the only and true God, who sanctifies all things, and without him is nothing holy," and who teaches believers all truth.

The election of grace is not formally discussed in any writing, but is often touched upon in the treatises on the *Freedom of the Will*. There seems to be some confusion of ideas, however, and it is tolerably plain that the subject had not been

---

[1] *Twelve Articles, Op.* 18.

thought through with the thoroughness characteristic of the *Institutes* of Calvin. It is indeed only fair to bear in mind that until that wonderful theological treatise appeared, the Reformation theology had not become clear and consistent on this matter. Where even Melanchthon hesitated and stumbled, we need not be surprised that another's utterances should be equivocal. Hübmaier teaches that all things take place according to the will of God, but a distinction is drawn between the "benevolent" and the "permissive" will. The benevolent will of God is the will of his mercy—he wills all men to be saved; the permissive will is that those who will not hear Christ he leaves to the consequences of their refusal. If God has specially elected some to salvation, this is a secret decree, and it is vain for us to probe the divine secrets. It is blasphemous to maintain that men sin and are lost in fulfilment of a divine decree, and not of their own choice. This view he sustained by exposition of the Scriptures, and he did not shrink from those that seem opposed to his position:

"'God has mercy on whom he will have mercy, and whom he will he hardens' (Rom. ix., 18). These

words are the utterances of the almighty and secret will
of God, which is pledged to no one, nor anything, and
therefore he can without injustice have mercy on whom
he will, or condemn whom he will.   This will the schoolmen call the ' omnipotent ' will, a will that no one can
resist.   Yes, God has the power and the right to make
of us a vessel, either for honour or dishonour, without
our being able to reply and say, ' Why hast thou made
us so? '   Besides this will, however, we find another revealed will of God, according to which God wills that all
men should be redeemed and come to the knowledge of
the truth.   Christ himself has plainly made known this
will in the words, ' For God so loved the world that he
gave his only-begotten Son, that whosoever believes in
him might not perish, but have eternal life ' (John iii.,
16).   ' He suffered for our sins, and not for our sins
only, but for the sins of the whole world.   He is also
the true light, that lights every man that comes into the
world.   To them that received him he gave power to become sons of God.'   Therefore he has commanded us to
preach the gospel to every creature, that every one who
receives it, who believes and is baptised may be saved.
Hence it follows that according to his revealed will God
hardens, darkens or condemns no one and nobody, unless it be one who of his own will and wickedness will be
hardened, darkened and condemned, and that is those
people to whom Christ comes as to his own and they receive him not.   When, therefore, it is said in the Scriptures that no one can resist God's will, the reference is
not to the revealed, but to the secret will of God.   But
any one who does not observe this distinction gets into
many difficulties and errors.

    " The revealed will of God the schoolmen call the

'ordered' will, not as though the secret will were without order, for everything that God wills and does is right and good, but he himself is subject to no rule, but his will itself is the rule of all things. The schoolmen call that will ordered, because it is fulfilled according to the word of Scripture, in which he has revealed his will; and so we speak also of the 'secret' and 'revealed' will of God, not as though there were a double will in God, but the Scripture speaks so in order to accommodate itself to human weakness, that we may know that although God is almighty and can do all things by his power, yet he will not deal with us poor creatures according to his omnipotence, but according to his mercy, which he has shown by his Son. God wills that all men should be saved (1 Tim. ii., 4). Who then can resist the will of God ? 'Nay, but, O man, who art thou that repliest against God ? Shall the thing formed say to him who formed it, Why hast thou made me thus ?' (Rom. ix., 20). If then God wills that all men should be saved, it must be done according to his will, and therefore the question is whether we will or not.''[1]

It will not seem entirely inexplicable to one who has read carefully this extract, that Hübmaier should be claimed as an advocate of their theologies, with equal confidence, by both Arminians and Calvinists. In the tenet that afterwards became the shibboleth of Calvinism, an atonement limited to the elect, the sympathies of Hübmaier would cer-

---

[1] *Freedom of the Will, Op.* 23 ; Hoschek, ii., 154.

tainly seem to be plainly with the Arminians.   He
would, however, find himself in congenial company
among those who to-day call themselves "moderate" Calvinists.   One thing is certain, he was
not an antinomian:

"Grace comes to us, not from us, so that no one can
boast except of the merits of our Lord Jesus Christ.
Whoever maintains that God will have sin, does not
know what sin is.   If any one says, 'If God did not will
it, I would not sin,' I affirm, on the contrary, that God
does not will that we sin.   We set ourselves in opposition
to his revealed will.   We ought not to sin in order that
the mercy of God may be more richly displayed, but we
ought not to sin that we may not make ourselves unworthy of mercy, and expose ourselves to the penalties
of divine justice.[1]

". . . The people have learned only two things,
without bettering their lives: the first, in that they say,
'We believe, faith saves us'; the second, 'By ourselves
we can do no good.'   Now both are true.   But under
the cloak of these half-truths all wickedness, unfaithful-
ness and unrighteousness has won the upper hand, and
brotherly discipline in the meantime has grown more
cold in many than before in a thousand years.   Yea it is
true and is fulfilled, the common proverb: 'The older
the worse.'   'No better, but much worse.'   'The older
the colder.'   'The longer the world stands the worse it
is.'   This stroke we must suffer from the godless, but
it cries to God that we suffer this because of our own

---

[1] *Freedom of the Will, Op.* 23.

guilt. For we would all be Christians and evangelical by taking wives and eating flesh, never sacrificing, never fasting, by blasphemy, usury, lying, deceit, oppression, trickery, compulsion, driving, stealing, robbery, burning, playing, dancing, banqueting, idleness, whoring, adultery, seduction of girls, tyranny, strangling, killing. The lightness and freedom of the flesh sits on the topmost bench; on the uppermost seat the pride of this world reigns, sings and triumphs in all things. No Christian shines forth among all men. Brotherly love and faith is wholly extinguished, and all this, sad to say, takes place under the seeming of the gospel.

" For, as soon as you say to such evangelical people, ' It is written, brother, " Cease from evil and do good," ' he immediately answers, ' It is written, " We cannot do anything good." All things take place by the destiny of God and of necessity.' They mean by this that it is permitted them to sin. If you say further, ' It is written, " Those that do evil shall go into eternal fire," ' straightway a girdle made of fig-leaves is found to cover their crime, and they say, ' It is written, " Faith alone saves, and not our works." ' With such subtleties we are nevertheless good evangelicals, and know how to quote, flourish and bounce around in a masterly way with the holy Scriptures—as the friends of Job, yea as the devil (Matt. iv.)—for the defence of our freedom and the sauciness of the flesh." [1]

To comprehend Hübmaier's Anthropology, it is necessary to understand at the outset that he believes the Scriptures to teach clearly the trichoto-

---

[1] *On Brotherly Discipline,* *Op.* 21.

mous nature of man. Here for once he falls into an exegesis that is puerile. "And I pray God your whole spirit and soul and body be preserved blameless unto the coming of our Lord Jesus Christ" (1 Thess. v., 23) is his favourite text. And he does not hesitate to argue from this that the spirit is in different case from the body and soul since the fall, because the apostle says here "the whole spirit," but does not say "the whole soul" or "the whole body," for what has once fallen and been broken to pieces is no longer whole! It was not Hübmaier's fault but his misfortune that he was not a Greek scholar,[1] yet a glance at the Vulgate from which he generally quoted should have been quite sufficient to show the untenableness of such exegesis: *ut integer spiritus vester et anima et corpus sine querela in adventu Domini nostri Jesu Christi servetur*—this, equally with the Greek, should be rendered, "may your spirit and soul and body be preserved whole, without blame, at the coming of our Lord Jesus Christ."

This is a bad beginning, and what follows is not

---

[1] It is claimed in his behalf that he knew both Greek and Hebrew, but it is certain that he made little or no use of the original texts.

much better. Adam, says our author, was created
pure, and entirely free in the choice of good and
evil, but when he sinned he lost this freedom, not
only for himself, but for all his descendants. But
fully to understand what this implies, we need to
distinguish a threefold will: the will of the body,
the will of the soul, the will of the spirit. The
body became by Adam's sin corrupted, so that it
can do nothing but sin. The soul also participated
in this fall: it became so wounded and sick that it
cannot of itself choose the good and resist the evil.
The spirit participated in the effects of the fall,
since it is a prisoner in the corrupted body, but it
did not participate in the offence of Adam, for it
did not yield to the sin of disobedience. In his
catechism, where this question is of necessity more
briefly discussed, there is a summary of his fundamental doctrine regarding human nature that is
admirable in its point and clearness:

"To sum up then: God made us free in body, soul
and spirit. This freedom and goodness became, by the
disobedience of Adam, captive in the spirit, wounded in
the soul, and corrupted in the body. Hence, we are
conceived and born in sin, children of wrath. If we are
to become again free in spirit, sound in soul, uninjured

in body, in consequence of the fall, it must be through a new birth, without which, Christ says, we cannot enter the kingdom of God."[1]

It is evident that what Hübmaier sought was escape from the paralysing Augustinianism of Luther; and he attempted to work out a theory that should make a reality and not an empty form of the preaching of the gospel. This he believed he had secured by making the spirit an unwilling partner in the sin of Adam, and therefore exempted in a measure from the results of sin. Hence, while the will of the body and the will of the soul are no longer free, the will of the spirit is free. It is only so that deliverance from his sinful state is possible to man, through the hearing of the gospel, as he goes on to argue at length:

" 'But the natural man receives not the things of the Spirit of God, for they are foolishness to him, neither can he know them, because they are spiritually discerned. But he that is spiritual judgeth all things, yet he himself is judged by no man' (1 Cor. ii., 14, 15). Here you see, Christian reader, the perfection of the human spirit, since it judges all things, even the wounds of the soul. Likewise you see that the body and the soul are severely wounded, and that the spirit only has

---

[1] *Ein Christennliche Leertafel, Op.* 11.

13

preserved the hereditary righteousness in which it was
created from the beginning. In relation to man who is
redeemed by Christ, we find that the body is still
wretched, but that the spirit is joyful, willing and devoted to every good thing, yet the soul is sad and
troubled because it stands between the body and the
spirit and does not know which way to turn, as though
blind and not understanding heavenly things by natural
faculties. But when it is awakened by the word of God
from the Heavenly Father, and when it is encouraged
and led through much consolation, and is held by the
Son of God and enlightened by the Holy Spirit, it dis-
criminates between good and bad, has its lost freedom
again, can also freely and willingly obey the Spirit, and
will choose the good as once when it was in Paradise.

"All this the word of God effects in the soul. Therefore David exclaims: 'He sent his word and made them
whole' (Ps. cvii., 20). Therefore Christ says: 'If ye
continue in my word, ye are truly my disciples; and ye
will know the truth and the truth will make you free'
[John viii., 31, 32]. Therefore let every one who has
ears to hear, hear that we have become free again by the
word and truth sent to us from God through Christ. In
this way real health and liberty are restored to man again.
Now, too, the soul is free and can obey either the spirit
or the body, but if it obeys the body it becomes body,
if the spirit, spirit. Further, it can command the body,
and tame it to make it go into the fire for the sake of
Christ's name with the soul and spirit, though against its
own desire. And although we find in all our conduct
many weaknesses and imperfections, the soul is not
responsible for them, but the body, that is an evil
instrument and a vessel empty of all that is good.

" The commandment is given to the spirit as a help, a witness against sin; to the soul as a light to learn the way of piety, and to the body for the knowledge of sin. But when the body hears the law it is terrified, and from fright all the hair stands on end. The spirit is in a jubilee of joy, and the believing soul thanks God and praises him for giving him a light to its feet. However, if our spirit is to be free and our soul well, and the fall of the body harmless, all this must necessarily be accomplished through the new birth in Christ. If that is not accomplished, we cannot enter into the kingdom of God. According to the apostle, God creates us freely by the word of truth, that we may be the beginning of creation, that is, the first fruits of the creation, and in this word we are again free and sound, so that there is no longer anything worthy of condemnation in us. Christ has made the fall of Adam entirely harmless to us, and therefore no one should complain any more of Adam, and excuse his sins by his fall, as everything has been recovered for us that we lost by the sin of Adam. For Christ has merited by his Spirit that our spirit's prison (the body) does it no harm. By his soul he has merited for our soul, that it is enlightened by his divine word; and by his body for our body, that after the resurrection it shall be glorious and immortal. For this reason, whoever sins now himself bears the penalty of his sins, because he has himself to blame for them, and not Adam or Eve, body or sin, death or devil, for all that has been bound and vanquished in Christ."

This is the sum of the first book on the *Freedom of the Will*. In his second treatise on the subject Hübmaier goes at large into the exegesis of the

Scripture passages that bear on the subject, and makes plainer than before his desire to give reality to the preaching of the gospel. The doctrine taught by Luther and his followers was that in spiritual things the unregenerate man is wholly blind, unable to work the righteousness of God, and his will has become utterly hostile to God, so that he cannot by his own powers give any assistance or co-operation towards his own salvation. He is as a man in the rapids of Niagara, being swept towards destruction, not only unable to do anything to help himself, but unable even to grasp the rope thrown to him by a friendly hand,—nay, not even desiring to be saved, and must against his will be dragged ashore, kicking and struggling against his rescuer to the last. It was thought necessary to teach such a doctrine of the will in order to magnify the divine grace in man's salvation, and to represent man as having any power of co-operation was thought to be a minimising of God's grace and a bringing back again of the idea of salvation by works. But to Hübmaier it seemed clear that God's veracity and good faith were no less at stake in this matter than the might of his grace. For what purpose are all the invitations of the gospel, if man cannot possibly heed them?

"Only a foolish king could place a goal before his subjects and then say, 'Now run that you may get there,' when he already knows beforehand that they are bound in iron and that they cannot run. It were certainly a cunning God, who invites all men to the supper, and really offers his mercy to every one, if he after all did not wish the invited to come. It were a false God who should say in words, 'Come here,' and yet in secret in his heart should think, 'Sit yonder.' It would be an unfaithful God who should publicly offer grace to man, and should clothe him in new raiment, yet in secret take it away from him and prepare hell for him. Cursed be he who maintains that God has commanded us impossible things, for everything that is impossible to our strength is possible by the word which God has sent. . . . As the human eye is capable of seeing light, and yet cannot see it unless the light streams into the eye, likewise man has the power to see the light of faith through the word of God, yet he cannot see this light unless by the heavenly illumination it is borne into his soul. . . . Whoever denies the freedom of the human will, denies and rejects more than half of the Holy Scriptures."

From the passages already quoted, it will be seen that Hübmaier's theory regarding original sin is very nearly, if not exactly, that now called the realistic. When Adam fell the race fell, since the

race was potentially in him. The imputation of
Adam's sin to his posterity, that great subject of
quarrel among theologians, does not engage his
thought, nor does he go at any length into the
nature of sin itself, but what he does say is very
much to the point. He defines sin to be "every
motion or desire against the will of God, whether
in thought, word or deed," in which he evidently
comes nearer to the profound truth than those
modern theologians who would limit sin to conscious trangression of the law.

The group of doctrines usually treated by theologians under the head of Soteriology receives
scant attention in Hübmaier's writings. Not that
he had any doubt regarding any of them, but the
circumstances under which he wrote were such as
to call for no extended treatment. Of the atonement, for example, as the means of salvation, he
speaks definitely but once; and if his words were
literally interpreted they would show that he
was satisfied with the theory of satisfaction as
taught by Anselm, or possibly as developed by
Aquinas. As to the execution of the divine election, the means by which men are actually saved,

"effectual calling," he declares that this calling is twofold:

" LEONARD.—How does God call or draw men ?

" JOHN.—In two ways, inwardly and outwardly. The outward drawing takes place by the public proclamation of his holy gospel, which Christ commanded to be preached to every creature, and is now made known everywhere. The inward drawing is wrought by God, who enlightens the soul within, so that it understands the undeniable truth, and is so thoroughly convinced by the Spirit and the preached word, as to confess from the conscience that these things must be so, and cannot be otherwise." [1]

Of this calling through the word Hübmaier makes much in all his writings, believing evidently that it is the chief means by which God has appointed men to be saved.   Hence the importance, in his estimation, of the preaching of a "pure, true, clean gospel," words that flow from his pen so often as to become a sort of formula.

The result of this calling, of this hearing the word, is faith,

" a perception of the unspeakable mercy of God, of the gracious favour and good-will which he bears to us through his well-beloved Son, Jesus Christ, whom he

---

[1] *Table of Christian Doctrine, Op.* 11 ; Hoschek, ii., 266,

did not spare, but gave to death on account of our sin, that sin might be paid and we be reconciled with him, and be able to say to him with assurance of heart, Abba, Father, ' our Father, who art in heaven.' " (*Op.* 11.)

This faith is something more than mere belief; if genuine, "living," it will manifest itself by bringing forth the fruits of the Spirit. Faith is the human side of this transaction, and in consequence of faith, or in connection with it, the Spirit of God works a complete change in man's affections and will:

" I believe and trust that the Holy Spirit has come in me, and the power of the Most High God has, as with Mary, overshadowed my soul, that I may conceive the new man, and so in thy living, indestructible word and in the Spirit be born again and see the kingdom of God.[1]

" If we are to become again free in spirit . . . it must be through a new birth, without which, Christ says, we cannot enter the kingdom of God. ' Of his own will begat he us with the word of his power ' [James i., 18]. In him alone do we really get free and sound again. So Christ says, ' The truth will make you free indeed' [John viii., 32]." [2]

There is no mention of justification in Hübmaier's writings, even where we might fairly expect to find

---

[1] *Twelve Articles*, *Op.* 18.
[2] *Freedom of the Will*, Hoschek, ii., 265.

it,—in his catechism; and of course no distinction between justification and sanctification. This omission cannot be explained like many others; the importance that these doctrines assumed in the Reformation period, and the amount of attention given them by all writers, preclude any explanation, on grounds of lack of necessity, inadvertence, and the like, for their absence from the carefully elaborated and deliberately printed works of any man of the time. The omission must be deliberate, calculated, wilful. An omission of such character can be accounted for only on one ground, that Hübmaier was anxious to mark clearly his divergence from Luther in some matters that the latter reckoned cardinal in the Protestant theology. Beyond this we are utterly in the dark.

From his treatment of faith and regeneration Hübmaier passes naturally to the discussion of Ecclesiology, and, as we might expect from the circumstances that called forth his writings, this is the subject that receives by far the largest amount of space. Having heard the word, having believed in Christ, having been born again by the Spirit, one is fitted for the next step, which is to receive baptism.

The baptism of the Spirit is already his: it is fitting and natural, therefore, that he should have the baptism of water:

"Water baptism . . . is an external and public testimony of the inward baptism of the Spirit, set forth by receiving water. By this not only are sins confessed, but also faith in their pardon, by the death and resurrection of our Lord Jesus Christ, is declared before all men. Hereby also the recipient is externally marked, inscribed and incorporated into the fellowship of the churches, according to the ordinance of Christ. Publicly and orally he vows to God, by the strength of God the Father, Son, and Holy Spirit, that he will henceforth believe and live according to the divine word, and in case he should be negligent, that he will receive brotherly admonition, according to the order of Christ in Matt. xviii. Such are the genuine baptismal vows, which we have lost for a thousand years, Satan meanwhile crowding in with his monastic and priestly vows, and putting them in place of the holy.[1]

"The third error, that we have called the water of baptism, as well as the bread and wine of the altar, a sacrament, and have so regarded them; though not the water, bread or wine, but the vow of baptism or love-plight properly and rightly is a sacrament; which in Latin is an oath-plight and promise with joining of hands, which the baptised make to Christ, our invincible leader and head, that he will contend manfully under his flag and banner in Christian faith until death."[2]

---

[1] *Table of Christian Doctrine, Op.* 11 ; Hoschek, ii., 254.
[2] *Form for Baptising, Op.* 19.

But while thus careful to disclaim all sacramental efficacy for baptism, he will not admit that it is a mere negligible form:

" Read the history of the apostles and you will find that the Samaritans believed Philip and afterwards were baptised.   So also Simon and the chamberlain of Queen Candace believed and afterwards were baptised.   Paul believed and afterwards was baptised.   Cornelius and his household believed, received the Holy Spirit and afterwards were baptised with water.   Lydia, the seller of purple, and the jailor, believed and were baptised. Who would or can think that all these would have been baptised, if the order and earnest command of Christ had not moved and constrained them to it ?   Truly, they might indeed have said, ' We have believed the word of God, and we have in part received the Holy Spirit: what need have we of baptism?   Faith saves.'   Nay, not so, but he who believes is baptised and does not dispute, for he sees the order of Christ before his eyes and performs it, where water and a baptiser may be had; but when the two cannot be had, there faith is enough.   Take an example.   Had the chamberlain, sitting beside Philip and believing, died straightway before they came to the brook, he were no less saved before the baptism than afterwards.   This is the meaning of Christ when he says, ' He that believes and is baptised shall be saved, but he that believes not is condemned '; for no doubt many thousands have been saved who have not been baptised, for they could not obtain it.   But as the chamberlain had both the baptiser and the water together, he was bound by the command of Christ to be baptised.   Had he not done it, Christ would have held him as a despiser and transgressor of his words, and as such he would have been punished." [1]

But though he insists thus strenuously on belief before baptism, and on the duty of every believer to be "baptised rightly, according to the order of Christ, even though he be a hundred years old," he will not for a moment admit that he is rightly called an Anabaptist:

"I have never taught Anabaptism. I know of none, except that in Acts xix. But the right baptism of Christ, which is preceded by teaching and oral confession of faith, I teach, and say that infant baptism is a robbery of the right baptism of Christ, and a misuse of the high name of God, Father and Son and Holy Spirit, altogether opposed to the institution of Christ and to the customs of the apostles. [2]

"But since this oath [in the pledge of baptism] is made to Christ himself, who abides in eternity, the once baptised should not be rebaptised, as the Novatians and Hemerobaptists. Yet since the invented infant baptism is no baptism, those who have received water baptism according to the order of Christ cannot be charged with rebaptism, though in their childhood and in the blindness of their forefathers they were formerly bathed in water." [3]

---

[1] *Ground and Reason, Op.* 16.
[2] *Short Apology, Op.* 13.
[3] *Form for Baptising, Op.* 19.

According to the Scriptures baptism is in some way connected with the remission of sins. In some cases Hübmaier so states this connection as to permit the inference from his words that he would have agreed with Alexander Campbell and his followers. But it is evident, on reading farther, that this is merely an unguarded and careless expression of his belief. Elsewhere he defines more strictly what this connection is:

"Water baptism was given for the forgiveness of sins. Acts ii., 38; 1 Pet. iii., 21. It is all contained in the ninth and tenth articles of Christian belief, where we confess a universal Christian Church, a communion of saints and forgiveness of sins, which was the understanding and conclusion set forth by the Nicene Council, with these words, ' I confess one only baptism to the remission of sins.' Therefore, as much as one is concerned about communion with God the Father, Son and Holy Spirit, yea, also about communion with the heavenly host and with the whole Christian Church, also about the forgiveness of his sins, so much should he be concerned about water baptism, by which he enters and is incorporated in the universal Christian Church, out of which there is no salvation. Not that the remission of sins is to be ascribed to the water, but to the power of the keys which Christ by his word has given to his Spouse and unspotted bride, the Christian Church, in his bodily absence, and hung at her side when he said to her, ' Receive the Holy Spirit; whose sins ye loose they are

loosed, and whose sins ye retain they are retained.'
John xx., 22, 23.   Just so Christ speaks in another place
to the Church, 'Verily I say to you, Whatsoever ye bind
on earth shall be bound in heaven, and whatsoever ye
loose on earth shall be loosed in heaven.'   Matt. xviii.,
18.   Here one sees plainly that the universal Church has
the same power to loose or to bind sins now on earth
which Christ himself as a man aforetime bodily here on
earth had.   He who believes the word of God enters the
ark of Noah, which is a true figure of baptism, that out
of this ark he be not drowned in the flood of sin." [1]

By baptism, it is said in the last quotation, the
believer becomes incorporated in the Church.   That
naturally raises the question, What does Hübmaier
understand by the Church? in what sense or senses
does he use that word?   The answer to this question is not obscurely hinted at in the above paragraph, but it is well to see what are the more
explicit definitions:

". . . The people . . . have with public confession of Christian faith and with reception of water
baptism been inscribed, marked and incorporated with
the assembly of the universal Church, out of which is no
salvation, as there was none out of the ark of Noah.
Out of this people there has now become a separate and
outward church, and a new daughter born of her mother
—as the mother, that is, the universal Church, does the
will of her husband and spouse, who is Christ Jesus, the

[1] *Ground and Reason, Op.* 16.

Son of the living God, whose will he performed unto
death—in order that the will of God the Father by his
beloved Son, the mother and daughter, be maintained on
earth as it is in heaven." [1]

.   .   .   .

" LEONARD.—Seeing you have now assured the church
of your faith by your baptism, go on and tell us what is
the church.

" JOHN.—The Church is sometimes taken to include
all men who are congregated and united in one God, in
one Lord, in one faith and in one baptism, and confess
the faith with the mouth, wherever they may be on earth.
That is the universal Christian Church, the body and
communion of saints, that meets only in the Spirit of
God, which is named in the ninth article of the creed.
Sometimes the church is taken to include a particular
external congregation, parish or people, that belongs
under one pastor or bishop, and comes together bodily
for doctrine, baptism and the supper. The church as
daughter has equal power with the mother, the universal
Church, in binding and loosing upon earth, as long as she
uses the keys according to the command of Christ, her
spouse and husband.

" LEONARD.—What is the difference between these
two churches ?

" JOHN.—The particular church may err, as the papal
Church has erred in many things, but the universal
Church cannot err. She is without spot or wrinkle, is
ruled by the Holy Spirit, and Christ is with her to the
end of the world. God always keeps for himself seven
thousand who have not bowed their knees to the idol of
Baal.

---

[1] *Concerning Brotherly Discipline, Op.* 21.

"LEONARD.—Upon what is the Christian Church built?

"JOHN.—On the oral confession of faith that Jesus is the Christ, the Son of the living God. This external confession, and not faith alone, makes a church, for a church has power to bind or to loose, is external, is a body, while faith is eternal. Although faith alone justifies, it does not by itself save. Public confession must be present as we read plainly in Matt. xvi., 18: 'On this rock (to wit, the preceding confession) I will build my church.' See also Matt. x., 32; Luke xii., 8; Rom. x., 10."[1]

Christ has girded his bride, the Church, with two bands: the second of these is the Supper, which is the pledge of brotherly love and the memorial of Christ's sufferings. The bread and wine are real bread and wine: but they are also the body and blood of Christ, yet only in the sense of memorials. Hübmaier asserted an important difference between his teaching and Zwingli's, and reproached the latter for falsifying the Scriptures in saying "This is my body" is equivalent to "This signifies my body." Not even Luther is more emphatic in rejecting this exegesis of the Swiss reformer, and insisting that "is" must be taken in the plain sense of "is" and nothing else. But then he immediately argues away

---

[1] *Table of Christian Doctrine, Op.* 11 ; Hoschek, ii., 202.

that for which he has so valiantly contended, in a manner more creditable to his ingenuity than to his good sense and good faith.

"This is my body," he says, is immediately followed by "Do this in remembrance of me." It is a well-known rule that every subject must be understood by its predicate. Hence, "This is my body" must be taken to mean, This bread is the body of Christ that was crucified for us. But, as matter of fact, the bread was not crucified, did not die for us. Therefore the bread must be the body of Christ not in reality but in remembrance, for the words "in remembrance of me" qualify all the preceding words. Hence the breaking, distributing, and eating of the bread is not an actual breaking, distributing, and eating of the body of Christ, but a remembrance of his passion, an eating in faith that he did this for us.[1]

Whether Hübmaier's exegesis or Zwingli's is the better may be a fair question, but what is perfectly plain is that they reach exactly the same result. One cannot resist the conclusion that this difference between the two teachers amounted to just nothing

---

[1] *Simple Explanation, Op.* 15 ; Hoschek, ii., 134 *sq.*

14

at all, and that on Hübmaier's part it was nothing more than a survival of that subtle, hair-splitting method of debate learned by him in the universities, from which he never completely emancipated himself. He had no grounds, certainly, to condemn Zwingli, and he shows too much eagerness to find a cause of accusation against one who had indeed wronged him, but against whom he was not therefore permitted to seek vengeance in this way.

If the *Form of the Supper* which he published is to be construed literally, then Hübmaier was in favour of surrounding the service with much ritual; with its homilies and prescribed prayers it is extremely liturgical. The actual administration is, however, very simple:

" Now the priest takes the bread into his hand, breaks it, and gives it to those present, and says, ' The Lord Jesus the night on which he was betrayed, took bread, and when he had given thanks he broke it and said, " This is my body that is given for you, do this in remembrance of me." Take and eat this bread, brothers and sisters, in memory of the body of our Lord Jesus Christ, which he gave us when he died for us.' And when all have eaten, the priest takes the cup with the wine and says, with eyes lifted, ' God, to thee be the honour and praise.' Then he passes it to them and says, ' In like manner the Lord Jesus took the cup when

he had supped, saying, " This cup is a new covenant in
my blood; do this as oft as ye drink it in remembrance
of me." Therefore take the cup and drink out of it all
of you, in remembrance of the blood of our Lord Jesus
Christ, that was shed for us for the forgiveness of our
sins.' And when all have drunk the priest says, 'As oft
as ye eat this bread and drink this cup, ye do show forth
the Lord's death, till he come.'"

It is also clear that Hübmaier was what in these
days would be called a "close communionist"; that
is, he held that baptism should always precede the
communion, and as there was but one baptism, the
baptism of a believer, those who had received only
the so-called baptism bestowed on them in their
infancy were not entitled to come to the Lord's
table. This view he clearly sets forth in his *Form
for Baptising in Water:*

" Everywhere the supper of Christ has been held, and
men have communicated under both forms (as they call
it), and yet no baptism has preceded, against the clear
Scripture, which shows this order: first, preaching;
second, faith; third, confession; fourth, water baptism;
fifth, breaking of bread (Acts ii. and other places).
But Satan can well suffer it that one builds up something
to-day, and in a little time breaks it down again; for
thereby many people are so greatly weakened, mazed
and vexed, that they do not at all know what they should
believe and hold."

One of the characteristics of the Anabaptists generally was the importance they attached to discipline and the Ban, or excommunication. This may be seen in the Schleitheim Confession and many of their extant documents. Hübmaier does not differ from the general body in this respect; indeed, he would make this the doctrine of a standing or falling church. Again and again he uses language like this:

"Yea, God lives and himself testifies that I speak the truth: unless brotherly discipline be restored, received and used according to the earnest command of Christ, it is impossible that it can be right and well with Christians on earth. Although we all with all our might cry, write and hear the gospel, yet crying, labour and toil is in vain and unprofitable—even water baptism and the breaking of bread are in vain and to no purpose and without fruit —where brotherly discipline and Christian excommunication do not accompany them."

To this subject he has devoted two entire treatises, but the briefest statement of his views is in his catechism:

"LEONARD—What is fraternal discipline?
"JOHN—When one sees his brother sin, he should go to him in love and admonish him fraternally and privately to leave off such sin. If he does leave off, his soul is

won.   If he does not, then two or three witnesses should
be taken, and he may be admonished before them a
second time.   If he yields it is well; if not, the church
should hear it.   He is brought before her and admonished the third time.   If he leaves off his sin the church
has won his soul.

"LEONARD—Where does the church get its authority?

"JOHN—From Christ's command, given in Matt. xviii.
18; John xx., 23.

"LEONARD—By what right may one brother use his
authority over another?

"JOHN—By the baptismal vow, which subjects every
one to the church and all its members, according to the
word of Christ.

"LEONARD—Suppose the admonished sinner will not
correct his course?

"JOHN—Then the church has the power and right to
exclude and excommunicate him, as a perjurer and
apostate.

"LEONARD—What is excommunication?

"JOHN—It is exclusion and separation to such an extent that no fellowship is held with such a person by
Christians, whether in speaking, eating, drinking, grind-
ing, baking, or in any other way, but he is treated as a
heathen and a publican, that is, as an offensive, disorderly and venomous man, who is bound and delivered
over to Satan.   He is to be avoided and shunned, lest
the entire visible church be evil spoken of, disgraced
and dishonoured by his company, and corrupted by his
example, instead of being startled and made afraid by
his punishment, so that they will mortify their sins.
For as truly as God lives what the church admits or
excludes on earth is admitted or excluded above.

"LEONARD—What are grounds for exclusion?

"JOHN—Unwillingness to be reconciled with one's brother, or to abstain from sin.

"LEONARD—For what should we exclude?

"JOHN—Not for six shillings' worth of hazel nuts, as our papist friends have been wont to do, but on account of an offensive sin, and for the sake of the offender, that he may reflect, know himself and abstain from sin.

"LEONARD—If he abstains from the sin, avoids the paths by which he might again fall, and does better, what position is the church to take?

"JOHN—She is to receive him again with joy, as the father the prodigal son, and as Paul the Corinthian, opening heaven to him and welcoming him to the fellowship of Christ's supper."

On the question of singing hymns the Anabaptists were as much troubled and divided as some modern Presbyterian sects. Some opposed the use of anything but the psalms for this purpose, yet on the other hand some of the oldest Anabaptist compositions extant are hymns. Hübmaier took a moderate and sensible view of this, as of most practical questions.

"With singing and reading in the churches I am well contented (but not as they have hitherto been conducted), when it is with the spirit and from the heart and with understanding of the words and edification of the church as Paul teaches us (1 Cor xiv., 15; Col. iii.,

16; Eph. v., 19).   But otherwise God utterly rejects it
and will have none of our Baal cries (Mal. ii., 17; Ezek.
xxxiii., 31, 32).'' [1]

The Anabaptists were likewise greatly divided on
the question of the community of goods, some
holding it to be an inseparable part of church order
that the brethren should have all things in common, as in the church at Jerusalem.   In his writings
Hübmaier does not deal with this question, for he
does not appear to have been brought into personal
contact with Anabaptists who held this theory till
the closing months of his life.   There is no reason
to doubt that the explanation he made to the Zürich
council, already quoted in full, correctly represented
both his private views and his public teaching, not
only up to that time, but to the end of his life.
The fact that at Nikolsburg he found this doctrine
closely associated with Hut's chiliasm and denial of
the right of the sword, would not be likely to incline
him to its acceptance, to say the least.   We may,
without fear of hasty conclusion, set Hübmaier
down as a disbeliever in this doctrine as a necessary
part of Christianity.

---

[1] *Short Apology, Op.* 13.

As to eschatology, Hübmaier held precisely those beliefs that were then and are still reckoned orthodox. He taught the resurrection of the body, a final judgment, an everlasting life with God for the redeemed, and an eternal retribution for those dying in their wickedness. He treats all these points briefly and with reserve, but so as to make clear his full acceptance of them all, because he believed them to be taught in the Scriptures. There is not a trace of the restorationism found in the teachings of Denck. On one question about which some of the Anabaptists were more outspoken, he is inclined to make no positive pronouncement, namely, the fate of those dying in infancy. The Romanists and some Protestants settle this question easily, by saying that all infants who are baptised are saved, while others are lost. The Calvinist used to be ready with his answer, that all elect infants are saved, leaving it to be certainly inferred that non-elect infants are lost. Hübmaier will go no farther than the Scriptures go. He cannot find in these an explicit declaration that all infants are saved, therefore he will not assert it; nevertheless he makes it plain that he considers the salvation of all infants to be an

opinion wholly consonant with what the Scriptures
do say, and there he leaves the matter, trusting to
the love and mercy of God, and confident that He
will do right.   And what more can any one do who
founds his theology strictly on the Scriptures?

Of Hübmaier's teachings regarding liberty of
conscience, the relations of the religious and the
civil powers, and the like, enough has been said.
The question of oaths he discusses very slightly,
but here he must have disagreed positively with the
more austere Anabaptist groups.   If magistrates
and courts are according to the order of Christ,
judicial oaths can be no less so.   Nor need we linger
over the negative and polemic side of our author's
teachings, interesting though these frequently are,
and racy though his language often is.   Hübmaier
was frequently at his best in polemic writing.   He
is less abusive, less scurrilous, than the major part
of the writers of the period.   He could write against
an opponent without dipping his pen in gall and
vitriol, though he sometimes offends against a
modern sense of propriety in speaking of and to his
adversaries.

In spite of all that we have found in this man

that demands our reprobation, have we not found much more that has moved us to admiration? Notwithstanding his wavering at Zürich, does not Hübmaier seem to us to stand forth as one of the heroic figures of the Reformation age? He might have taken for his own, words that Addison has put into the mouth of his Cato:

" 'T is not in mortals to command success,
    But we 'll do more, Sempronius—we 'll deserve it."

CHAPTER VII

HÜBMAIER THE MARTYR

1527–1528

FROM the time of his election to the Margravate of Moravia (October, 1526), Ferdinand of Austria had been determined to make his authority as absolute in that province as in his own duchy of Austria. The Moravian nobles had long been accustomed to a semi-independence that they now resigned with great reluctance, but they could oppose no effective resistance to the force that Ferdinand could put into the field, and slowly, with an ill grace, they submitted. As there could be no open resistance, so there could be no flat disobedience—passive, sullen, disaffected if not disloyal, they obeyed when they must, and disobeyed when they dared.

Ferdinand was a loyal son of the Church, and was determined to suppress heresy everywhere in his domains. He was not ignorant of the fact that Moravia was, just then, the chief hotbed of heresy in Europe, and so soon as he could make his authority felt in the province he began to demand the co-operation of the nobles to suppress heresy and punish heretics. A general edict, bearing date August 28, 1527, required instant and strict enforcement of the decree of the Diet of Worms, and directed that special pains be taken by magistrates and governors to bring to punishment those who were practising rebaptism and denied the venerable sacrament of the altar.[1] Special edicts relating to affairs in Moravia were issued later, but this was the one under which the arrest and prosecution of Hübmaier occurred.

The terms of the edict make it plain that, among all the heretics, the Anabaptists were singled out for especial severity. The writings that Hübmaier had been so industriously composing and circulating were now read far beyond the bounds of Moravia, and the hereditary domains of Ferdinand were beginning to feel the result of the evangelical agita-

---

[1] Loserth, p. 171, from the State archives. *Cf.* Beck, *Geschichts-Bücher*, p. 60, n. 1.

tion. Not only Moravia, but the Tyrol, Salzburg, and even Austria itself were swarming with heretics. From many sources it may be gathered that genuine and not unreasonable apprehension was caused by the rapid spread of Anabaptism. All the interests of the Roman Church demanded its immediate and effective repression. And every Catholic ruler was apprehensive lest the progress of heresy should mean the weakening of his own authority—that revolt from the Church would only be the prelude to a revolt from civil authority.

It would not require much time for the authorities to learn that Nikolsburg was the storm-centre of this new movement, and that the leader there was the same pestilent fellow who had already given them so great trouble at Waldshut, and upon whom they had been most anxious to lay hands for three or four years past. Copies of certain writings of his had been transmitted to the Austrian Government, which thereupon proceeded to act with decision. Early in July, probably, the lords of Lichtenstein were commanded to come to Vienna and bring with them this heretic and rebel, long a fugitive from Austrian justice. The command was obeyed, and

Hübmaier and his wife were taken to Vienna and confined until arrangements could be made for their trial.[1]

A preliminary examination seems to have been given him at once, for Ferdinand wrote, July 22nd, to Freiburg a letter in which he said:

"Since Dr. Balthasar a long time ago was pastor in our city of Waldshut, and through his preaching and misleading doctrine mischief, ill-will, disturbance and rebellion greatly increased among the common people in our borderlands, the city of Waldshut all but fell away from us and our house. When the city of Waldshut was afterwards conquered, he fled and came into our Margravate of Moravia. On account of all this we have circumspectly lain in wait for him, until we brought him to our royal prison here in Vienna, and have confined him in prison, and had him examined, yet without torture, on the enclosed list of questions. Now you were very active during the said disturbance at Waldshut, and that of the peasants, and know much about this business of the Doctor's, and no doubt remember it well. Since, therefore, the affair does not admit of postponement, we command you, speedily and without delay, to give thorough and diligent examination to the list of questions,

---

[1] Of the three different, and even conflicting, accounts in Anabaptist chronicles of the period, the above is the most probable. Hoschek simply gives the various accounts (ii., 253) without attempting to reconcile them or decide between them; while Loserth (p. 173) gives the above, but does not hint that there is any conflict on this point. See Beck, *Geschichts-Bücher*, pp. 52, 53.

with reference to the late hearing; also that you learn by thorough inquiry whatever else you can concerning all that is herein included, and give us your counsel regarding the same, that we may know in future how to perform our whole duty in the uprooting of evil, and by punishment to make so much the better example for others.[1]

After this preliminary examination, which is distinctly stated to have been held in the royal prison at Vienna, Hübmaier and his wife were sent elsewhere for several months.

The place of their confinement is said by all the contemporary authorities to have been the castle of Greisenstein, or Grätzenstein or Greutzenstain, but there has been and is dispute as to the identification of this spot. Beck and Loserth think that the castle of Kreutzenstein is meant, on the ground that it is known to have been used in the sixteenth century as a State prison. Others have generally identified the place with Greifenstein, a castle still in possession of the Lichtenstein family, a few miles from Vienna on the Danube. This identification' seems the more probable, and suggests that Hübmaier may have been left in the custody of his noble

---

[1] Quoted by Loserth (p. 174) from the State archives at Innsbruck.

friends for a time, who, though powerless to protect him, might be able to alleviate his confinement somewhat.

In our ignorance of all the facts, the lords of Lichtenstein necessarily lie under the odious suspicion of having surrendered their chief preacher with altogether too much alacrity, for it does not appear that they made any attempt whatever to save him. It is possible, even probable, that it required all their power and social standing to secure their own immunity from prosecution. But the suspicion may, after all, do them an injustice. Much was made in the preliminary accusation, and throughout the process, of Hübmaier's alleged disloyal conduct at Waldshut. It was no uncommon thing, in those days, to arrest a man on a charge of sedition and condemn him for heresy, or *vice versa*. It may well be the case that the demand sent to Nikolsburg for the surrender of Hübmaier specified sedition as the chief offence—it may even have been the only offence then named.[1]

The circumstances all confirm this hypothesis.

---

[1] So Loserth (p. 173), who says persecution for heresy did not begin in Moravia until March, 1528.

CASTLE GREIFENSTEIN, AS IT APPEARS NOW.

If the charge were sedition and not heresy, it is difficult to see on what decent pretext the lords of Lichtenstein could have declined to surrender for trial one whose offence was alleged to be flagrant. Had a question been raised at this time concerning the religious beliefs and teaching of Hübmaier, the barons might have been expected to make some protest at least, if not to resist forcibly. For their preacher was no greater heretic than themselves— no worse in belief, though perhaps more influential, than the other evangelical preachers. But it seems beyond question that not only the Lichtensteins, but also the other evangelical preachers of Nikolsburg, were not accused at this time. Indeed, they were treated with a lenity that would be most surprising, were it not so apparent that the immediate object of wrath was Hübmaier, and that Austria was willing to let the general persecution of the Anabaptists slumber until this arch-heretic had been dispatched.

But if everything thus points towards treason as the charge on which Hübmaier was surrendered, it is certain that when once Austria got her claws on him the charge of heresy was also raised and pressed. This was apparent in the preliminary examination given him at Vienna, before he was. sent to Greisenstein, and his imprisonment there weighed heavily on his health and spirits. Hübmaier was not a man of great fortitude, as he had already shown at Zürich, and it is more than probable that the ardour of his labours at Nikolsburg, following the hardships he had previously experienced, had left him with a small stock of physical strength. In his bodily weakness, his soul began to quail at the prospect of torture and death, and he bethought him of expedients by which his life might again be saved. The intervention of his old schoolmate and friend, John Faber, now vicar-general of the Bishop of Constance, occurred to him as the thing most likely to be helpful. Accordingly he urgently requested the favour of an interview with Faber, and the request was granted. Faber hastened to Greisenstein, moved in part possibly by affection for his old school-fellow, but still more by hope of winning to the truth a heretic so distinguished. He took with him no books but the Bible, and had a long interview—or rather, a series of interviews—with Hübmaier, of which he has left

a full account.   It is open to suspicion in some particulars, but in the main bears the impress of truth.

Faber reached Greisenstein December 14th, and
in his visit to his former friend was accompanied by
Lord Mark of Leopoldsdorf and Ambrozius Salzer,
rector of the Vienna gymnasium—neither of whom,
however, seems to have taken any part in the discussion.   Faber began with a long address, in which
he expressed the sincere love he had never ceased
to cherish for the comrade of his school-days, and
promised his aid in any way that he could render
it.   But above all he was anxious to convince his
friend of his errors, and lead him back to the truth.
To this Hübmaier is said to have replied:

"Although I certainly know that I shall have to die,
and that I have deserved the penalties that await me, yet
I do not wish that the poor people, who have received
their doctrine from me, should remain in error on my
account.   Whatever I have either written or taught
hitherto was not for my own advantage, but simply from
the conviction that the Spirit of God was leading me to
do it, and at this moment there is no man in the world
whom I would rather see or hear than you.   Hence I
have often thought, when I heard you speak of the
articles of my faith, how I could bring it about for you
to instruct me, and if I were found in error, to lead me
out of it; and for this reason I must now tender my

humblest thanks to his Royal Grace for sending you to
me, and as far as my strength permits, if God hears my
deepest prayers, I will show myself thankful for this
favour.   Besides, be assured that I will obey no one in
the whole world so gladly as you alone.   One thing I
ask, that my errors be refuted by passages of Holy
Scripture, so that I may not be pressed to act contrary
to my conscience." [1]

They differed at the very beginning, however, on
the use and interpretation of the Scriptures, Faber
urging the usual Catholic saying that the Scriptures
are infallible only when interpreted by an infallible
Church.   But Hübmaier contended that any believer, led by the Holy Spirit, can discern the true
sense of Scripture, at least so far as all things necessary to salvation are concerned.   Obscure passages
did not demand an authoritative interpreter, but
only that they be compared with other passages less
obscure; and thus the meaning of the text might
be authoritatively obtained.   When they went on
to the chief tenets of the Anabaptists, agreement
was still less possible.   Faber could not convince
Hübmaier from the Scriptures that infants should
be baptised, nor that there is any change in the
elements in the eucharist, nor that the mass is a

---

[1] Quoted by Hoschek, ii., 255.

sacrifice for sins.　On other questions that were debated, if we may believe the account of Faber, Hübmaier was more tractable, and suffered himself to be understood as holding nothing that could be called heretical regarding intercession of the saints, the Virgin Mary, purgatory, fasts, justification by faith, free will, and the like.

The interview closed with this exhortation from Faber: "What I have said, I have said with a good, sincere purpose.　Now see to it, and take care of yourself for your own good."　To which Hübmaier's final reply was, "Everything that you have said I certainly accept with thanks, and your presence at this place is dearer than that of any one else in the whole world.　I will consider everything in a becoming way, and whatever I find to be true in my conscience I will publish in a separate work dedicated to his Royal Grace.　Be yourself, I pray, a faithful defender and intercessor for me in this matter." [1]

These conversations were protracted through several days, and were of such interest to both parties that at least once the debate continued until

---

[1] Hoschek, ii., 259.

two o'clock in the morning, and was resumed again at six o'clock! Their conclusion left Hübmaier in a decidedly more hopeful state—there seemed to him now a fair prospect that his life might be saved. He had made considerable concessions, it is true, but he doubtless persuaded himself that they were not of great moment and did not really compromise his integrity. On the main questions of the supreme authority of Scripture, the baptism of believers only, the rejection of transubstantiation, he could congratulate himself that he had stood firm. His ambiguous statements about what Melanchthon later called *adiaphora*, he probably believed to be of slight importance.

As a result of this conference and debate Hübmaier sent from his prison to Ferdinand, under date of January 3, 1528, a formal statement (*Rechenschaft*) of his beliefs, a document that has been called by some of his biographers a recantation. The following summary of these articles, mostly in the words of the author, will show how far this title is justified by the contents:

"1. Faith alone is not enough for salvation. We must

prove faith with works of love toward God and our neighbour.

"2. Since mere faith does not suffice for salvation, good works must also be added to it.

"3. Whoso permits his faith to stand by itself and does not prove it by good works, he changes Christian liberty into liberty of the flesh. [This condemns Luther's doctrine.]

"4. In this miserable and dangerous life, it is most necessary to impress unceasingly on the people the fear of God, that in all their works they should keep God before their eyes.

"5. A man should take care of all his thoughts, words and acts, according to the plumb-line of the divine word, so that he can always preserve a good conscience towards God.

"6. All things do not come to pass of necessity.

"7. He who denies the free will of men and calls it an empty claim, is nothing in himself, nicknames God a tyrant, charges him with injustice, and gives the wicked excuse to remain in their sins.

"8. To avoid evil works and repent of our sins is the doctrine of the whole gospel.

"9. The blessed Virgin Mary is, and always was, pure and unspotted.

"10. Mary is the mother of God.

"11. Christ was truly God.

"12. Original sin is not only an infirmity or defect, as some write, but a condemnable sin, if we are not in Christ and live according to the flesh. It is the mother and root of all sins.

"13. I know in the Scripture no ground for a special purgatory, outside of heaven and hell.

"14. Although Christ has given us many signs to know when the day of his coming is at our door, yet no one knows this day save God alone. I have firmly withstood John Hut and his followers, because they have named a specific time for the last day, namely, next Whitsunday, and have preached this to the people and led them astray [exhorting them] to sell house and goods, to leave wife and child, and have misled the simple to leave their work and run after them,—an error that has sprung from a gross misunderstanding of the Scripture.

"15. The prayers of Christ's faithful ones are advantageous.

"16. Concerning confession I have hitherto preached that the Scriptures teach three kinds of confession: one before God, another before the man whom we have wronged, and the third before the Church through acknowledgment of sins.

"17. The Church is an external assembling and community of believers in one Lord, one faith and one baptism.

"18. Whoever preserves his virginity, has a precious jewel. Aged widows should be received into the Church.

"19. Fasts ought to be observed.

"20. Sundays should be observed. Certain holidays — such as Christmas, Easter, Whitsunday — I am well contented [to observe], but not so large a number, as I disputed more than twenty years ago at Freiburg, *De non multiplicandis festis*.

"21. On the fast days one should eat no meat.

"22. The ten commandments should be frequently taught to the people in these troublous days. I have taught this in my catechism, where I have set down the ten commandments as the first beginning of a Christian life.

"23. Excommunication is a necessary medicine in Christianity.

"24. The intercessions of the saints in our behalf are not in vain.

"25, 26. Most illustrious, most mighty king, most gracious lord, I am strongly opposed to the teaching of John Hut and his followers regarding baptism and the sacrament, and shall oppose them in teaching and writings all my life so far as God gives me power. For I can say, on the ground of the divine word and with good conscience, that he has perverted both articles. I have no doubt that I should, with God's help, soon abolish his baptism and supper. I have taught nothing concerning baptism, save that it should be public confession with the mouth of Christian faith, also a renunciation one must make of the devil and all his works. Therefore the baptism I taught and Hut's baptism are as far asunder as heaven and hell. Also as to the supper, I trust in God I shall not bear his burden.

" But also, your royal majesty, see, further, that I am not stiff-necked and self-willed, since I offer to defer to the next [general] Council [of the Church] the two articles I have taught and others pertaining to faith, and as to these will gladly submit myself to the Church; and will in the meantime permit these articles to remain in abeyance, and as to the others will so show and conduct myself that your royal majesty will hereafter receive a special pleasure that I have laboured well and faithfully. But if your royal majesty will not await a council, then I beg to defend these articles with the Holy Scriptures before your majesty's honourable councillors and the university. Your majesty may then be judge. I would gladly so hold myself that I may remain safe before God in my conscience and can stand with my soul before the last judgment. I will also earnestly pray God day and night, that he will of his divine grace give me to know means and way through which your royal majesty and the whole of Christendom may come to Christian welfare and peace. God, who is with me in my distress, will hear me; and if your royal majesty should be well pleasing, I would gladly draw up and write an ordinance of Christian government, whereby with God's grace and the help of their imperial and royal majesties, we could come right soon to peace and unity.

"27. Respect and honour should be paid to the authority of magistrates and laws, as set forth in the book *On the Sword;* and all conspirators and rebels are to be condemned.

"Wherefore, O most mighty and most gracious king, I pray, by God and his mercy, that your royal majesty— as the merciful lord of Austria, of whom always and everywhere this praise and title of the Merciful has been written, and especially since Dr. John Faber, and Master Max Beckh, bishop in Austria, and Master Salzer, rector of the University of Vienna, have shown me so great grace and favour—may show grace and mercy to me, an imprisoned and afflicted man, who now lies in great sickness, cold and trouble. For with God's help I will so conduct, order and hold myself that your royal majesty shall have pleasure therefrom. The people I will with great earnestness and utmost diligence urge to devotion, fear of God and obedience, wherein I would always bring them. Your royal majesty and his brother need have no doubt regarding my pledge; my Yea shall be

Yea, and so it will be found at the last day.   So help me
God.   Amen.'' [1]

On all but two points, baptism and the Lord's
Supper, Hübmaier thus indicated his willingness to
conform to the teachings of the Catholic Church.
Faber adds in his statement that his friend denied
that it was an article of faith that the body and
blood of Christ are in the sacrament of the altar.
If this statement is correct, it only shows that
Hübmaier's strong point was not the history of the
Church and its doctrines, which is abundantly
shown by all his writings.   His strength lay in his
knowledge of the teaching of the Scriptures, and
his ability to quote these freely in support of his
contentions.   Arguing from the Scriptures he was
a Samson in controversy; when he began to speak
of the Fathers and history he became as other men
—and weaker than many.

Precisely what he expected to accomplish by
composing such a statement and appeal as the foregoing, it is difficult to conjecture.   He can hardly

---

[1] In the less important articles abridged, but for the most part in
Hübmaier's own words, as preserved in MS. in the archives of the
Ministry of Justice, discovered by Beck, and first printed by Loserth,
pp. 176–180.   A similar abstract, less full and correct, in Hoschek,
ii., 504, 505.

have had a serious expectation of saving his life, even by a complete recantation. If he became reconciled to the Roman Church, and so escaped burning as a heretic, there remained the charge of treason, for which his head must answer. After all the provocation the Austrian Government had received from him, now that it had him safely in its power it was little likely to permit him to escape. If Hübmaier could not see this clearly, he must have been blind indeed. Yet the only rational explanation of this strange affair seems to be that in his suffering and despair he clutched at the vain hope of mercy, and now once more (as formerly at Zürich) was prepared to deny much that he had taught, if not all, to save his life. Though he still holds to his belief about the sacraments, his profession of willingness to submit to the decision of an Ecumenical Council even in this makes one suspect that a promise of release would have drawn from him a still further concession.

Hübmaier's conduct in these closing months of his life is far from heroic. The praise of unswerving constancy to the truth cannot be awarded him. It is impossible not to draw a parallel between him and a more famous man of this period, Archbishop Cranmer. Their cases were strikingly similar, for both had been guilty of acts of rebellion and treason, as well as the advocacy of heresy. They were alike also in possessing more moral than physical courage —or perhaps it was only fortitude in which they were really deficient. Men differ greatly in their capacity to endure excruciating physical pain, and no one who has not had the experience can be quite certain how he would himself behave under torture. Savonarola is still a third example, and an eminent one, of failure to bear, as well as the average man, this cruel test; but the world has pardoned him this one defect in an otherwise heroic character. It has done the same in the case of Cranmer, rightly judging that his fortitude in the supreme hour out-weighs and all but obliterates his earlier shameful defection.

Shall the world do less in the case of Hübmaier? Should we not see in him one in whom the spirit was willing and only the flesh weak? He recanted no more of his former opinions, certainly, than did Savonarola and Cranmer, if as much. He cannot be proved to have denied anything that he had held to be fundamental in the teachings of the Scriptures.

As to his political conduct, he had always maintained that to be blameless, and he never admitted himself to have been guilty of treason or sedition, even in hope of saving his life.   And in the end, as to Cranmer and Savonarola, strength was given him to meet his doom with a constancy and calm fortitude that moved the admiration of all beholders.

Ferdinand was very far indeed from being moved by any feelings of pity or clemency towards Hübmaier or any of the Anabaptists.   On the contrary, it could not have been long after the reception of the above appeal—supposing that he ever really saw or heard of it—that he began to prod his officials, and require them to show more zeal in the prosecution of such heretics as they already had in prison, and to search actively for others.   Accordingly, on March 4th, his regent for Lower Austria sent an apology to the King, in which he recounted what had been accomplished, in spite of great difficulties, towards the detection and punishment of the heretics.   The following paragraph from this document especially concerns us:

" As to the case of Dr. Balthasar Hübmaier, through the bishop and several judicious theologians we have made ample arrangements that he shall be dealt with according to the command of your majesty. That we have forwarded no report concerning his trial for so long a time is the fault of his fickleness. For though Hübmaier promised the bishop and the other doctors opposed to him, in the hearing that has taken place, to recant his teaching and belief, and to send such recantation to the bishop within a specified time, he has not yet kept his pledge, but has presented only an ambiguous statement (*eine halbe Meinung*), and no completely valid recantation. Wherefore the bishop was prevailed upon—against our earnest solicitation, according to your majesty's command for dealing with Hübmaier—to let him set down in writing his reasons for sustaining his doctrine concerning rebaptism and the venerable sacrament. With the composition of this writing Hübmaier has busied himself up to last Saturday, the last of February. So soon as it comes to us through the bishop, we shall forward it to your royal majesty, and it ought to be already in your majesty's hands." [1]

From this it appears that this final statement was finished February 29th. A few days elapsed for transmission of it to the King, and then the order came that Hübmaier should be brought back to Vienna. He arrived about March 3rd, and the final

[1] Nothing further is known of this last writing of Hübmaier's, except that it could have contained no recantation. Further search may discover it among the Austrian archives. The document from which the above extract is taken was found by Dr. Beck in the archives of the Ministry of Justice, and is given by Loserth, p. 183.

process began. Few details are known, but it is
certain that he suffered on the rack, and possibly
other tortures were applied. On this occasion,
however, he remained firm; he could not be induced
to retract his teachings regarding baptism and the
eucharist. His double condemnation followed, as a
matter of course. His friend, Dr. Faber, published
immediately after his death a little pamphlet called
the *Reason Why the Patron and First Beginner of
the Anabaptists, Doctor Balthasar Huebmayr, was
Burned at Vienna on the 10th of March, 1528.* In
this is given, apparently from official sources, the
record of the final condemnation, as follows:

" First, Dr. Balthasar Hubmayer has confessed that at
Waldshut he preached rebellion against the government,
which does not tend to peace, but is contrary to God,
right and his conscience, whence arose much perversity
and revolt against the government and great shedding of
blood.

" Again, he has confessed how from Waldshut he had
given counsel and written a letter to his royal majesty,
which served better to promote rebellion than obedience.

" Again, he has also confessed that while at the aforesaid Waldshut he went into their houses and said to them
that their cause was just, whether it should turn out that
they died or recovered; he had also counselled and
helped them to swear a league, to oppose all that would

WIEN.

VIENNA IN THE FIRST HALF OF THE SEVENTEENTH CENTURY.

not abide by the doctrine that he preached, in which he confessedly acted contrary to God and his conscience and the government.

"Again, he has also confessed that he enlarged and expounded the articles of the peasants, which were sent to him from the camp, and that he imagined such as received the same to be Christian and reasonable. He confesses also that in this he erred and did wrong.

"Again, he has also confessed how it happened that many of the magistracy of the city of Waldshut went to Lauffenberg. There also Hans Müller, the architect, in place of the mayor, permitted the community to be called together in the council house, and he announced to them the decision of the Diet that according to the will of his royal majesty the city should be overwhelmed and the citizens should be punished, and advised all who would not suffer such things to withdraw from the city until affairs should be better. Upon that Dr. Balthazar publicly took leave of everybody, and went home and said he would not be in the report. Thereafter early in the morning he went out of the city, came by himself to Zürich, and was there imprisoned on account of the second baptism, since the same was opposed to Zwingli, to whom the people of Zürich adhere. He was also at Zürich racked on account of anabaptism, and compelled to testify who had led him into such baptism, and why he had baptised in their jurisdiction. Therefore he made a public recantation of his opposition to infant baptism.

"Again, he also confessed that he had so preached, and added counsel and deed, in order that he could thereby live a good life and be his own master! In all of which he confesses that he did wrong. Also their

16

reason and object was to have no government, but only from their own number to draw out and elect one.

"Again, the aforesaid Doctor Balthasar confesses that he does not at all believe in the sacrament of the altar nor in infant baptism.

"Therefore, Doctor Balthasar, on account of this crime and condemned heresy is condemned to the fire." [1]

Though urged to confess to a priest and receive the last rites of the Church before his death, Hübmaier steadfastly refused. On March 10th, he was led forth to his death, his wife (of whom it is related that "she was hardened in the same heresy, more constant than her husband") exhorting him to fortitude. The story that he was borne through the streets to his execution on a cart, while his flesh was torn by red-hot pincers, does not rest on the best authority. We have the testimony of an eye-witness [2] to his end, and the details are self-evidencing. As he was led to the place of execution, he from time to time repeated for his own consolation verses of Scripture, and remained to the last "fixed like an immovable rock in his heresy." He was accompanied by an armed troop, and a large crowd, and

---

[1] Loserth, *Beilage*, No. 10.

[2] Stephan Sprügel, dean of the philosophical faculty in the University of Vienna. Quoted by Loserth, pp. 185-187.

as he came to the pile of fagots he lifted up his voice
and cried in the Swiss dialect:

"O gracious God, forgive my sins in my great
torment. O Father, I give thee thanks that thou
wilt to-day take me out of this vale of tears. With
joy I desire to die and come to thee. O Lamb, O
Lamb, that takest away the sins of the world! O
God, into thy hands I commit my spirit."

To the people he said, "O dear brothers, if I have
injured any, in word or deed, may he forgive me
for the sake of my merciful God. I forgive all
those that have done me harm."

While his clothes were being removed: "From
thee also, O Lord, were the clothes stripped. My
clothes will I gladly leave here, only preserve my
spirit and my soul, I beseech thee." Then he
added in Latin: "O Lord, into thy hands I commit
my spirit," and spoke no more in Latin.

As they rubbed sulphur and gunpowder into his
beard, which he wore rather long, he said, "Oh salt
me well, salt me well." And raising his head, he
called out: "O dear brothers, pray God that he
will forgive me my guilt in this my death. I will
die in the Christian faith."

When the wood was kindled and he saw the fire, he said with a loud voice: "O my Heavenly Father, O my gracious God!" As his hair and beard burned he cried out, "O Jesus, Jesus!"

And then, overwhelmed with smoke, he breathed out his soul. The one who relates his death, no friendly and sympathetic observer, adds that he felt more joy than pain in thus witnessing his faith with his life. Three days later his devoted wife, with a great stone tied to her neck, constant to the very last in testifying to her faith, was thrown into the waters of the Danube.

CHAPTER VIII

THE SUPPRESSION OF THE MORAVIAN ANABAPTISTS

HÜBMAIER'S death was popularly likened to that of John Hus, and like the Bohemian leader, he was regarded as an innocent martyr—we have the word of his friend Faber for that. The evangelical Christians mourned the loss of a man of light and leading; Catholics rejoiced that one of their most formidable opponents had been for ever silenced. The testimonies borne to the rank of Hübmaier as an evangelical leader, praises of his learning and eloquence, are numerous, emphatic, and convincing. Kessler spoke of him as "the αρχικαταβαπτιστα of Nikolsburg," and he probably imagined that to be Greek, and to mean "chief Anabaptist." Vadian, the burgomaster of St. Gall, says that he was *eloquentissimum sane et humanissimum virum* (assuredly a very eloquent and cultivated man). Bullinger describes him as *wohl beredet*

und ziemlich belesen gewesen aber eines unstäten Ge-
müts, mit dem er hin und her fiel (a man of good
repute and become tolerably well read, but of an
unstable disposition, through which he was much
misled).[1]

As to the estimate of him by the Roman Church,
the letter of Faber, written to two of his friends on
the very day of Hübmaier's martyrdom, is a good
example:

" As to Vienna, I can give you no news, except this
one item: we must henceforth fight the plague of the
Anabaptists. You already know how, after the destruction of one of their heads, numerous others straightway
grow up! So their Dr. Balthazar, who has been a long
time in prison because of his heretical doctrines, has
now suffered the death penalty. We ought to hope that
a large part of the heretics will vanish from the earth, so
soon as an example has been made of the man who was
the head of the Anabaptists and the inspirer of other
criminals." [2]

This is, to be sure, but the opinion of one cleric;
but the Roman Church showed its official estimate

---

[1] One of the Anabaptist chronicles speaks of him as *in Latenische
Grichischer und Hebräischer sprach wol erfaren.* Beck, *Geschichts-
Bücher*, p. 52. But we have seen reason to conclude that his ac-
quirements in Greek and Hebrew were limited.

[2] Quoted by Loserth, p. 157.

THE TOWER OF THE CASTLE AT NÜRNBERG, IN WHICH ANABAPTISTS
WERE IMPRISONED.

of the importance of this heretic, and the dangerous quality of his influence, by putting his writings on the Index, along with those of Luther and Zwingli, as the most pestilent literature produced by the Reformation.[1]

It would be useless to deny that the death of such a man was a heavy blow to the Anabaptist cause in Moravia, and to the Nikolsburg church in particular, but it was by no means fatal. Lord Leonhardt Lichtenstein and his brother were permitted in due time to return to their estates, and apparently continued their connection with the Anabaptists. It is certain that they could not be induced to do anything to persecute the brethren, even if they partially withdrew from them. But the death of Hübmaier was the signal for active measures to be undertaken against all Anabaptists by Ferdinand's Government, which the Moravian nobles might do nothing actively to help, but which, on the other

---

[1] In the *Index Librorum Prohibitorum*, drawn up in 1619 for the Spanish Inquisition by Archbishop Bernhard of Sandoval, he is named four times : Balthasar Pacimontanus, Balthasar Hubmaier, Balthasar Hilcmerus, Balthasar Isubmarus. His name stands fourth among the *hereticorum capita aut duces*, preceded only by those of Luther, Zwingli, and Calvin. Schwenckfeld is the only other heretic named.

hand, they dared not openly oppose. At the same time, they did what they could to discourage the more extreme and fanatical among the Anabaptists, and thus lessen the pretext for severe measures against them; though we do not again read of so energetic proceedings as the imprisonment of Hans Hut in the Nikolsburg Castle.

As the danger of a Turkish invasion became more pressing, in the summer of 1528 it became more and more a practical question among the Nikolsburg brethren whether a Christian man could lawfully take up arms in self-defence, or pay a war-tax for defence against this foe. The party that had agreed with Hübmaier became known as the *Schwertler*, or men of the sword; while their opponents were named the *Stäbler*, or men of the staff, *i. e.*, of peace and non-resistance. Jacob Widemann was the leader of the *Stäbler*, and gradually the idea of community of goods became even more important in their eyes than opposition to the sword. It was at length with them the doctrine of a standing or falling Church, since they were firmly convinced that a true Christian brotherhood could exist on no other basis. Peace was not so much disturbed among the Nikolsburg brethren as made impossible, unless all would adopt the views of Widemann and make their practice conform thereto.

Lord Lichtenstein used every effort to induce greater moderation on the part of the *Stäbler*, and to restore unity in the brotherhood. He seems finally to have intimated that this faction must either be less contentious or leave his domains, and so they chose to leave. According to the chronicle, he rode with them to the boundary, drank a parting glass with them, and wished them Godspeed. They went their way to Austerlitz,—a town about thirty miles to the north, near Brünn, the capital of the province,—in later years the scene of one of Napoleon's great victories. Here they established themselves.

The proprietors of Austerlitz were ready to welcome them and to afford them entire liberty. It is even said that waggons were sent to meet them at the boundary, where they had been dismissed by Lord Lichtenstein, and to help them on their way. They were given permission to build houses and to live their lives in their own way; and the

experiment of an Anabaptist community was forthwith begun. For some years they suffered no interference, and so the experiment was conducted
under most favourable conditions. The nobles
were glad to encourage them, for population was
sparse, labour was scarce, and apart from their religious notions the Anabaptists were known to be
settlers of the most desirable sort, sober and industrious. The Austerlitz colony did not long remain
the sole Anabaptist community: a colony soon
went forth and settled at Auspitz, nearly midway
between Nikolsburg and Austerlitz, and gradually
others "swarmed," until there are said to have
been by 1536 no fewer than eighty-six settlements,
mostly numbering several hundred persons each,
one being as large as two thousand. And in every
case these communities seem to have enjoyed a
uniform, steady prosperity.

Socialistic ideas often found advocates during the
Reformation period, but here in Moravia was the
most conspicuous, if not the only, instance of a
practical experiment in the working out of these
ideas. Jacob Huter is credited with the chief part
in the organisation of these Moravian communities,

for Widemann, though a born agitator and a
would-be despot, proved himself to have no real
gifts of leadership and organisation.   Huter came
to Moravia from the Tyrol soon after the establishment of the Austerlitz community, and for the next
seven years spent much of his time there, perman-
ently impressing his ideas of organisation on the
communities.

The unit of all these communities was the "household," consisting in most cases of several hundred
souls, all occupying a common building.   Over each
of these groups was a general superintendent,
the "householder."   The community idea was
carried into all the details of living: the household
had a common kitchen, a common bakehouse, a
common brewhouse, a common schoolhouse, a
common lying-in room, a common nursery, a common sick-room, and an order of "sisters" were
nurses of the children and the sick.   There was also
a common dining-room, but in other respects each
family lived its own separate life.[1]   Clothing and

---

[1] This "household" is an anticipation of the phalanstery of Four-
rier, so complete in its details as almost to justify a suspicion that
some account of these Moravian communities had become known to
the French economist.

bed-linen and such personal effects were treated as individual property, but all else was owned in common. There must necessarily have been much interference with personal liberty under such a system. For example, marriage outside of the community was strictly forbidden and was punished by instant expulsion. The young sisters who manifested some reluctance to marrying the only eligible suitors were virtually compelled to matrimony.

Economically the experiment was successful—as to that the testimony is ample and unanimous. There were no drones allowed in these busy hives, and there was no poverty. The socialist ideal of equal effort by all, and equal sharing by all in the fruits of labour, was fully realised. Industry and frugality, together with good management, had their reward, and the communities without exception became prosperous, not to say rich. It cannot be safely argued from this fact, however, that a general socialistic organisation of a nation would be economically successful; for these were a picked people in more respects than one, with much less than their due proportion of the aged and disabled and incorrigibly lazy, and far more than their proportion of able and willing workers.

Primarily these communities were agricultural. Their fields were the best cultivated and bore the largest crops in all the region. Moravia was then as now celebrated for its breed of horses, and those sent to market from these communities were esteemed the best and brought the highest prices. Men from these households were sought by the landowners of the region as managers of their farms, stables, vineyards, mills. But though primarily agricultural, the communities were skilled in the handicrafts also, and in a little time gained almost a monopoly of certain manufactures—as tailors, smiths, weavers, they had no superiors. The knives, scythes, shoes, stockings, bolting-cloths, handkerchiefs, and similar wares sent forth from these centres of industry were highly esteemed and eagerly bought. They were known to be honest goods, at fair prices.

Ecclesiastically, these communities differed from any others called Anabaptists. They had a chief pastor or bishop, an officer not found among others

of the sect, and perhaps adopted from the Bohemian Brethren.   Under this head there were in each
community "ministers of the word" (generally, not
necessarily, a plural eldership) and "ministers of
necessities," or deacons.   One of the ministers of
the word was usually the "householder."   Nobody
might preach until he had been called to this office
by the vote of the community, even though he had
been an honoured preacher elsewhere, and this rule
was rigidly enforced.   The preacher was a man of
much authority among them—indeed, he might
easily become, and in too many cases actually was,
a despot.

But though economically prosperous, these communities cannot be regarded as in other respects
a satisfactory realisation of the Anabaptist ideal.
Nor did they realise their own ideal of a perfect
brotherhood: in proportion as the community prospered, the spirit of real brotherly love declined.
Nowhere among Anabaptists, seldom anywhere
among Christian people, has a more unlovely spirit
developed.   The selfish domineering of the "householder" preachers; the strife between those who
wished to be preachers and those who, already

occupying that office, refused to share their power
with others; the murmurings and bickerings and
jealousies among the members; the harsh intolerance shown to those who failed to abide by the
community rules; the unchristian severity with
which the excluded were treated—these and such-
like things have seldom been paralleled, and they
are the harder to forgive since they were done in
the name of a more perfect Christian brotherhood.
All Anabaptists seem disposed to a reckless use of
the "ban," but these communities alone would, in
Christ's name, expel an erring brother and leave
him to starve, rather than give him food or drink.
Their Roman Catholic persecutors were not more
cruel to these "brothers" than they were to each
other.

The success of these socialistic Anabaptists, and
the shelter given to them in Moravia for some years,
led to a great immigration of the brethren from the
surrounding regions. Historians, not too favour-
ably inclined towards the sect, estimate the total
membership of these groups as high as seventy
thousand.[1] The noble landowners were glad to

---

[1] Hast, *Geschichte der Wiedertäufer*, p. 212.

encourage their coming, for never had they been able to obtain labourers so satisfactory on their estates. Moravia was in that day, as in our own, one of the most fertile provinces of Austria, and it was experiencing a great access of prosperity in the growth of these Anabaptist communities. The testimony to the sober, law-abiding character of the people composing them is unbroken by any accusation of offence, even from their bitterest foes, save the form of religion that they professed and practised. This, however, was a continual offence, and the wonder is that they were unmolested so long.

The downfall of the communities began in 1535. By that time Ferdinand was sufficiently freed from his various embarrassments, chiefly immediate fear of the Turk, to permit him to give serious attention to matters never long absent from his thoughts—first among them the clearing of his dominions of all heretics. A fierce persecution was begun in the Tyrol, that ended in the martyrdom of Jacob Huter at Innsbruck, February 24, 1536, and the destruction or scattering of his followers. A simultaneous attempt was made to eject the Anabaptists from

A ROOM IN THE TOWER AT NÜRNBERG.

Moravia. A royal edict issued by Ferdinand in the spring of 1535 says:

"It is a well-known fact that in the Netherlands the Anabaptists, committed to prison and held in subjection, have in the sequel begun to rebel against authority. Accordingly, neither Lutherans nor Zwinglians, nor, in fine, any sect, will suffer among them these heretics; it is, therefore, the will and intention of his Majesty not to suffer them any more in Moravia." [1]

Against their own wishes probably, against their own interests certainly, the Moravian nobles yielded to the royal command, and the Diet issued an order for the banishment of all Anabaptists. There was the less disposition to resist the royal policy, doubtless, because of the excesses that the Anabaptists were now committing at Münster. True, these people in Moravia had shown no such lawless and violent tendencies, but were they not also Anabaptists? And what might they not do if they had the opportunity? The argument was, at any rate, sufficiently plausible to silence objections and quiet tender consciences, if such there were among the persecuting party.

---

[1] Quoted by Heath, *Anabaptists*, p. 75. Similar edicts, of various dates, are given in the chronicles. Beck, *Geschichts-Bücher*, p. 177 *et al.*

The landlords, who had hitherto given these groups willing harbourage, were now obliged to withdraw their protection and give notice to the "households" to leave their domains at once. Vainly did the innocent victims protest against this injustice; the utmost concession they could obtain was permission to take with them their movable property. The decree was executed by military force, pitilessly, and these unfortunate people were compelled to abandon the homes they had built, even the harvests they had sown, and find refuge where they might, in a region where every Government declared them outlaws. The dense forests of Moravia, the valleys in the mountains of Bohemia, gave them temporary hiding.

But, though scattered, they did not scatter in panic or disorder; there was a wise method in their flitting. They broke up into little groups, preserving their organisation, and wherever one of these groups settled, there was the nucleus of a new community. For a considerable time, therefore, though the persecution caused great personal distress and yet greater financial loss to the "households," it had little or no effect in diminishing their numbers.

In fact, according to their chronicles, their numbers actually increased under the stress of this trial. Their meekness and patience in bearing this great injustice doubtless had due effect on the people, and won converts from those who might otherwise have been untouched.

In spite of the general spirit of meekness shown by them, there was one spirited protest against this cruel and unjust treatment. This took the form of a letter to Johann von Lipa, Marshal of Moravia, who had before this been one of their protectors, and had protested against the royal decree so long as protest was of any avail; and who now found himself in the hateful predicament of being compelled to enforce a decree of banishment against a people with whom at heart he sympathised. This protest, though probably from the pen of Huter, is written in the name of the entire brotherhood, and is the only official apology of the Anabaptists of this period.

"We brethren, who love God and his word, the true witnesses of our Lord Jesus Christ, banished from many countries for the name of God and for the cause of divine truth, and have come hither to the land of Moravia, having assembled together and abode under your jurisdiction, through the favour and protection of the Most High God, to whom alone be praise and honour and laud for ever: we beg you to know, honoured ruler of Moravia, that your officers have come to us and have delivered your message and command, as indeed is well known to you. Already we have given a verbal answer, and now we reply in writing: viz., that we have forsaken the world, an unholy life, and all iniquity. We believe in Almighty God, and in his Son our Lord Jesus Christ, who will protect us henceforth and forever in every peril, and to whom we have devoted our entire selves, our life, and all that we possess, to keep his commandments, and to forsake all unrighteousness and sin. Therefore we are persecuted and despised by the whole world, and robbed of all our property, as was done aforetime to the holy prophets, and even to Christ himself. By King Ferdinand, the prince of darkness, that cruel tyrant and enemy of divine truth and righteousness, many of our brethren have been slaughtered and put to death without mercy, our property seized, our fields and homes laid waste, ourselves driven into exile, and most fearfully persecuted.

"After these things we came into Moravia, and for some time have dwelt here in quietness and tranquillity, under your protection. We have injured no one, we have occupied ourselves in heavy toil, which all men can testify. Notwithstanding, with your permission, we are driven by force from our possessions and our homes. We are now in the desert, in woods, and under the open canopy of heaven; but this we patiently endure, and praise God that we are counted worthy to suffer for his name. Yet for your sakes we grieve that you should thus so wickedly deal with the children of God. The righteous are called to suffer; but alas! woe, woe to all those who without reason persecute us for the cause of divine truth, and inflict upon us so many and so great injuries, and drive us from them as dogs and brute beasts! Their destruction, punishment, and condemnation draw near, and will come upon them in terror and dismay, both in this life and in that which is to come. For God will require at their hands the innocent blood which they have shed, and will terribly vindicate his saints according to the words of the prophets.

" And now that you have with violence bidden us forthwith to depart into exile, let this be our answer: We know not any place where we may securely live; nor can we longer dare remain here for hunger and fear. If we turn to the territories of this or that sovereign, everywhere we find an enemy. If we go forward, we fall into the jaws of tyrants and robbers, like sheep before the ravening wolf and the raging lion. With us are many widows, and babes in their cradle, whose parents that most cruel tyrant and enemy of divine righteousness, Ferdinand, gave to the slaughter, and whose property he seized. These widows and orphans and sick children, committed to our charge by God, and whom the Almighty has commanded us to feed, to clothe, to cherish, and to supply all their need, who cannot journey with us, nor, unless otherwise provided for, can long live—these we dare not abandon. We may not overthrow God's law to observe man's law, although it cost gold, and body and life. On their account we cannot depart; but rather than they should suffer injury we will endure any extremity, even to the shedding of our blood.

" Besides, here we have houses and farms, the property that we have gained by the sweat of our brow, which in the sight of God and men are our just possession: to sell them we need time and delay. Of this property we have urgent need in order to support our wives, widows, orphans and children, of whom we have a great number, lest they die of hunger. Now we lie in the broad forest, and if God will, without hurt. Let but our own be restored to us, and we will live as we have hitherto done, in peace and tranquillity. We desire to molest no one; not to prejudice our foes, not even King Ferdinand. Our manner of life, our customs and conversation, are known everywhere to all. Rather than wrong any man of a single penny, we would suffer the loss of a hundred gulden; and sooner than strike our enemy with the hand, much less with the spear, or sword, or halbert, as the world does, we would die and surrender life. We carry no weapon, neither spear nor gun, as is clear as the open day; and they who say that we have gone forth by thousands to fight, they lie and impiously traduce us to our rulers. We complain of this injury before God and man, and grieve greatly that the number of the virtuous is so small. We would that all the world were as we are, and that we could bring and convert all men to the same belief; then should all war and unrighteousness have an end.

We answer further: that if driven from this land there remains no refuge for us, unless God shall show us some special place whither to flee. We cannot go. This land, and all that is therein, belongs to the God of heaven; and if we were to give a promise to depart, perhaps we should not be able to keep it; for we are in the hand of God, who does with us what he wills. By him we were brought hither, and peradventure he would have us dwell here and not elsewhere, to try our faith

and our constancy by persecutions and adversity.   But
if it should appear to be his will that we depart hence,
since we are persecuted and driven away, then, even
without your command, not tardily but with alacrity, we
will go whither God shall send us.   Day and night we
pray unto him that he will guide our steps to the place
where he would have us dwell.   We cannot and dare not
withstand his holy will; nor is it possible for you, however
much you may strive.   Grant us but a brief space: peradventure our heavenly Father will make known to us
his will, whether we are to remain here, or whither we
must go.   If this be done, you shall see that no difficulty,
however great it may be, shall deter us from the path.

   " Woe, woe, unto you, O ye Moravian rulers, who have
sworn to that cruel tyrant and enemy of God's truth,
Ferdinand, to drive away his pious and faithful servants!
Woe, we say to you! who fear more that frail and mortal
man than the living, omnipotent and eternal God, and
chase from you, suddenly and inhumanely, the children
of God, the afflicted widow, the desolate orphan, and
scatter them abroad.   Not with impunity will you do
this; your oaths will not excuse you, or afford you any
subterfuge.   The same punishment and torments that
Pilate endured will overtake you: who, unwilling to
crucify the Lord, yet from fear of Cæsar adjudged him
to death.   God, by the mouth of the prophet, proclaims
that he will fearfully and terribly avenge the shedding of
innocent blood, and will not pass by such as fear not to
pollute and contaminate their hands therewith.   Therefore great slaughter, much misery and anguish, sorrow,
and adversity, yea, everlasting groaning, pain and torment, are daily appointed you.   The Most High will
lift his hand against you, now and eternally.   This we

announce to you in the name of our Lord Jesus Christ, for verily it will not tarry, and shortly you shall see that we have told you nothing but the truth of God, in the name of our Lord Jesus Christ, and are witnesses against you, and against all who set at nought his commandments. We beseech you to forsake iniquity, and to turn to the living God with weeping and lamentation, that you may escape all these woes.

"We earnestly entreat you, submissively and with prayers, that you take in good part all these our words. For we testify and speak what we know, and have learned to be true in the sight of God, and from that true Christian affection which we follow after before God and men. Farewell." [1]

The fierceness of this persecution soon declined, since there was no adequate local sentiment to sustain it, but it was again renewed in 1547, and from this time to Ferdinand's death, in 1564, was a period of suffering known in the Anabaptist literature as "the time of the great persecution." The reign of Maximilian II. (1564–1576) and the first half of his successor's reign (Rudolf II., 1576–1612) was a time of comparative freedom from molestation, and is called in the chronicles "the good time

---

[1] This document is given by Ott, *Annales Anabaptistici*, pp. 75–78, and in several other collections of Anabaptist documents. There can be no doubt of its genuineness. The above translation, with some changes, is from the *Martyrology* of the Hanserd Knollys Society, i., 149–153.

of the church." Once more their communities flourished, under the protection of the Moravian nobles, who successfully withstood the occasional demands of Austria's rulers that the Anabaptists should be driven out of the land.

In the meantime Nikolsburg had continued to be, in some sort, the headquarters of the Anabaptists. The House of Lichtenstein had not ceased to grant them countenance and protection, so far as possible, nor is there any hint that Lord Leonhardt ever withdrew from the body. There does not seem to have been any radical change in the attitude of the House towards the brethren during the lifetime of his son, Christopher, though it is not known that the latter was a member of the body. The Lichtensteins, and for the most part the other Moravian nobles, pretty uniformly returned a *non possumus* to all their monarch's edicts of persecution; and, if they did not openly protest, their capacity for passive resistance was practically unlimited. Unless the Austrian Government was prepared to send soldiers into Moravia, little could be done towards the dispersal of the Anabaptists.

But with the death of Christopher von Lichten-

stein, in 1572, a marked change came over Nikolsburg. He left no heir,[1] and the estates, therefore,
reverted to the Crown; and in 1576 the Emperor
sold them to Adam von Dietrichstein, whose descendants, subsequently raised to princely rank,
still hold them. The new lord of Nikolsburg belonged to a distinguished Romanist family, one of
whom was later Bishop of Olmütz and a Cardinal.
It was not to be expected that a man of such antecedents, known himself to be an ardent Catholic,
should tolerate in his domains those who were so
much despised and contemned by the Church as

---

[1] A younger branch of the family remained Protestant through the
sixteenth century, in spite of the severe persecutions to which all
were subject who resisted the Roman Church. About 1604, Count
Charles Lichtenstein became a convert to the Catholic faith, and
was rewarded by being raised to the rank of Prince in 1608, and in
1621 was made Regent of Bohemia. The family has ever since remained one of the most distinguished and powerful in Austria, and
possesses large estates in various parts of the Empire. Only a few
miles from Nikolsburg are the castles of Feldsburg and Eisgrub,
still owned by Prince Liechtenstein (to use the modern orthography),
the latter situated in the midst of a magnificent park of over a hundred square miles. The family has in recent years risen to royal
rank, for since 1866 Liechtenstein has been an independent princi-
pality—one of the smallest kingdoms in Europe, with an area of
only sixty-five square miles and a population not exceeding ten
thousand souls, situated between the Tyrol and Switzerland. But a
king is a king, even if his kingdom is no larger than a pocket-hand-
kerchief!

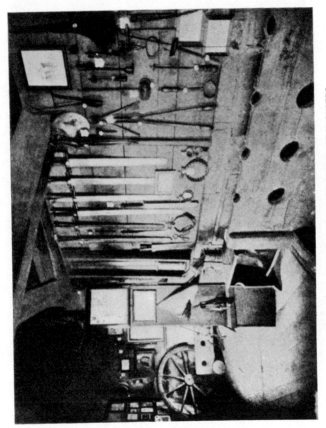

INSTRUMENTS OF TORTURE AT THE TOWER OF NURNBERG.

the Anabaptists. Lord Adam proceeded to enforce his faith with energy and to root out of the town and the surrounding country all who were suspected of heresy.

There were at this time in Nikolsburg and adjacent towns 3720 persons known or reputed to be Anabaptists. A historian of the period records the success of Dietrichstein's efforts to purify the region. Nikolsburg had been the refuge of all sorts of pernicious heretics, who had so flourished as to give the town a bad name everywhere. It had passed into a proverb: "He is from Nikolsburg, therefore he is an Anabaptist." Dietrichstein brought to pass in a few years so great a change that it might be said with equal truth: "He is from Nikolsburg, therefore he is a Roman Catholic and Jesuit Christian." [1]

This is, however, the usual and perhaps pardonable exaggeration of the eulogist. The new lord, like the proverbial new broom, swept clean—as clean as he could—but he did not accomplish so complete an alteration in the character of Nikolsburg

---

[1] Christopher Erhard, in *Sampt angetruckten Gespräch*, Ingolstadt, 1586, p. 31. Quoted by Loserth, *Communismus*, p. 55.

as the partial historian represents. His successors were less given to the policy of "Thorough," and the Anabaptist chronicles contain proofs in plenty that these repressive measures were only partially effective. No longer could the brethren be said to flourish in Moravia, but they still endured. The seventeenth century, however, was to witness their all but complete destruction. The Jesuits had obtained the ear of the Austrian Court, and had established their emissaries in important ecclesiastical posts throughout Moravia. The motive power for steady persecution was thus supplied; against their persistent malignity and sleepless vigilance no heretics might long stand.

In 1623 a new royal decree for the persecution of Anabaptists was issued through Cardinal Dietrichstein, and from this time forward there was little intermission of severity. Prince Liechtenstein, now a Roman Catholic and Marshal of Moravia, was active in the work, which was part of the reactionary policy of the Thirty Years' War wherever the Austrian and Imperial power extended. In this terrific persecution many thousands perished—there is no adequate and trustworthy record of the number. A list in one of the chronicles, drawn up about 1581, gives the number of martyrs among the brethren up to that time as 2169, but this is only a small fraction of the number who lost their lives for the truth's sake before the persecution was ended. Another chronicle thus describes their sufferings:

"Some were torn to pieces on the rack, some were burned to ashes and powder, some were roasted on pillars, some were torn with red-hot tongs, some were shut up in houses and burned in masses, some were hanged on trees, some were executed with the sword, some were plunged in the water, many had gags put into their mouths so that they could not speak and were thus led away to death. Like sheep and lambs, crowds of them were led away to be slaughtered and butchered. Others were starved or allowed to rot in noisome prisons. Many had holes burned through their backs and were left in this condition. Like owls and bitterns they dared not go abroad by day, but lived and crouched in rocks and caverns, in wild forests, in caves and pits. Many were hunted down with hounds and catchpoles."

By means of such measures, the number of Anabaptists in Moravia was sensibly decreased; most of the brotherhood who survived these fiery trials found a home elsewhere. The depopulation of the country, owing mainly to these persecutions, was so frightful that the Diet passed a special statute giving to every man in Moravia the extraordinary privilege of taking two wives, that the country might be repeopled![1]   Nevertheless, even so a remnant of the brethren survived and continued to live in the province, in ever-diminishing numbers, for at least a century longer.   Some found refuge in Bohemia and Hungary, where a few colonies are said to survive until this day.   One group made their way into southern Russia, where they remained until 1874, when they emigrated in a body to South Dakota, and there, in several communities, they seem to be renewing their former prosperity. Even in Moravia itself it is doubtful when they became entirely extinct, for traces of them were found by Dr. Beck as late as the year 1815; but no community is known to exist there now.[2]

In the sequel, therefore, we see the almost complete destruction of the fabric that Hübmaier and his associates reared with so great effort and at so costly sacrifice.   The traces of them and their

---

[1] *Encyclopedia Britannica*, art. " Moravia," historical sketch.

[2] It has not been thought necessary to give authorities for most of the several statements of this chapter.   The materials are derived, about equally, from Loserth's continuation of his biography of Hübmaier, *Der Communismus der Mährischen Wiedertäufer*, Wien, 1894, and Beck's *Geschichts-Bücher*.

labours disappeared as utterly as the wake of a vessel in the ocean.   Shall we, therefore, declare that they lived and laboured in vain?   Did such as Hübmaier give their lives for naught ?   Not so.   Hübmaier's contribution to the gradual progress of the truth, to the slow emancipation of man, to the final triumph of religious and civil liberty, was not only considerable but lasting.   His name, his example, and his teachings were long cherished by the brotherhood; and when his name and example had faded from recollection, his teachings lived on.   In an age of credulity and superstition he stood for the gospel proclaimed by the Apostles.   Among people groaning under the exactions of an effete feudalism and oppressed by despotic and selfish princes, he advocated justice and mercy on the part of rulers, sobriety and obedience on the part of subjects.   At a time when intolerance and persecution were universal, his was the voice of one crying in the wilderness for restoration of the God-given right of every man to study the Scriptures for himself, and to follow whithersoever they might lead.

"TRUTH IS IMMORTAL"

FACSIMILE OF HÜBMAIER'S FIRST APPEAL TO THE COUNCIL OF SCHAFFHAUSEN.

ORIGINAL IN THE SCHAFFHAUSEN ARCHIVES.

APPENDIX

ON THE SWORD

A Christian exposition of the Scriptures, earnestly announced by certain brothers as against magistracy (that is, that Christians should not sit in judgment, nor bear the sword).

*To the noble and Christian Lords, Arekleb of Boz-
kowitz and Tzernehor of Trebitz, Chancellor of
the Margravate of Moravia, my gracious Lords,
Grace and peace in God.*

*Noble, gracious Lord, your Grace well knows that all
those who in these last perilous times hold dear and
preach the holy gospel, must not only be deprived of
goods, but be tortured in body, yea, must even be wounded
in honour (which to men is the most precious jewel on
earth) and be oppressed by the godless. Even the
weapons of the hellish Satan are here, through which
he attempts without cessation to oppress, blot out and
burden evangelical teaching and truth. Yet he will
not succeed, his head must be bruised. Especially
also must it be charged now by such servants of the
devil, that all Christian preachers are rioters, seducers,
and heretics, since they repudiate magistracy and
teach disloyal doctrines. And yet this is not a cause
for wonder. The same thing also happened to Christ,
although he openly preached, "Render to Cæsar the
things that are Cæsar's" (when he paid the tribute for
himself and for Peter). Notwithstanding, he was compelled to suffer back-breaking pains by liars, since he
was reported a rioter and accused as a disturber of the
people, whom he had forbidden to give the tribute-
money to the Emperor. When the like now happens
to us, what difference does it make? The servant is*

275

not more than his lord, and the disciple is not more than his master. If they have persecuted the master of the house, much more will they do it to us. But that your Grace may learn and know, what from the beginning I have always and everywhere held concerning the magistracy, how I also openly preached in the pulpit at Waldshut and elsewhere,[1] as well as wrote and frequently taught (without any boast be it said) and how much I suffered for it from my opponents, who falsely charged many other things against me;—I have composed a small book in which your Grace may learn thoroughly my opinion, and elucidated in general all writings which my antagonists have hitherto with much zeal charged to forbid magistracy among Christians. Such a tract your Grace will receive graciously from me, and briefly note my sentiments concerning Christian magistracy in the contents of the writings. Since I always, in this and my other teachings and deeds, desire justice and right, if I err I will gladly permit myself to be banished and punished, as is just. But, according to the Scripture, let them bear witness against the evil; but if I err not, wherefore do they smite me, wherefore do they brand me? For though my enemies (of whom I have as many as the old scaly serpent) are never willing to let me be justly judged, I am not so. If my God and Lord must suffer that they do offence and violence to his word, I must also suffer, yet (God be praised) not as an evil-doer. Let every one judge as he

---

[1] I have more earnestly held with the Scripture concerning the pious magistracy, than any preacher within twenty miles. But I have also charged tyrants with their crime, whence arises their envy, hatred and enmity.—Marginal note by Hübmaier.

desires to be judged by the Lord. Well! since it is the will of God, on account of our sins, therefore I must and will, even against my will, fashion my will. Herewith, your Grace and my especially gracious Lord, I give myself submissively in all service for all time. Your Grace, farewell in Christ Jesus.

Given at Nicolspurg on the 24th day of June, 1527.

Your Grace's obedient

Balthasar Huebmör of Fridberg.

ON THE SWORD

Christ says to Pilate, " My kingdom is not of this world ; if it were of this world my servants would doubtless fight for me, that I should not be delivered to the Jews."—John xviii., 36.

From this Scripture many brothers say, "A Christian may not bear the sword, since the kingdom of Christ is not of this world." *Answer :* If these people would use their eyes aright, they would say a very different thing, namely, that our kingdom should not be of this world. But with sorrow we lament before God that it is of this world, as we testify when we offer the Lord's Prayer, " Father, thy kingdom come." For we are in the kingdom of the world, which is a kingdom of sin, death and hell. But Father, help thou us out of this kingdom; we stick in it clear over ears, and shall not be freed from it till the end; it clings to us even in death. Lord, forgive us this evil, and help us home into thy kingdom! Yet such brothers must see and confess the truth, that our kingdom is of this world, which should cause us heartfelt sorrow. But Christ alone could say with truth, " My kingdom is not of this world," since he was conceived and born without sin, a lamb without blemish, in whom is no deceit, but without sin and any spot. He alone with truth might also say, " The prince of this

279

world has come, and has found nothing in me," which we here on earth can nevermore speak with truth. For as often as the prince, the devil, comes he finds in us wicked lust, wicked desire, wicked longing. Whence also St. Paul, now filled with the Holy Ghost, yet calls himself a sinner [Rom. vii., 15–25]. Therefore all pious and godly Christians must confess themselves unholy even till death, whatever we may do of ourselves.

THE SECOND PASSAGE

Jesus says to Peter: "Put up thy sword in its place, for he who taketh the sword shall perish by the sword. Or thinkest thou that I could not pray to my Father, and he would send me more than twelve legions of angels? But how would the Scripture be fulfilled, that it must be thus?"—Matt. xxvi., 53, 54.

Mark here well, pious Christian, the word of Christ, so will you have an answer to the accusation of the brothers. First Christ says, "Put your sword into its place," he does not forbid you to bear it. You are not in authority; it is not your appointed place, nor are you yet called or elected thereto. "For who takes the sword shall perish with the sword." The sword means those who act without election, disorderly, and of their own authority. But no one shall take the sword himself, except one who has been elected and appointed thereto; for so he does not take it of himself, but it has been brought to him and given him. Now he may say, "I have not taken the sword. I would rather go unemployed, since I am myself not very stern. But since I am chosen thereto, I pray God that he will give me grace and wisdom that I may bear it and rule according to his word and will." So Solomon prayed and was given great wisdom by God to bear the sword well. Besides, do you hear this: Christ said to Peter, " Put up thy sword in its sheath." He did not say, Put it away, throw it from thee. For Christ blames him because he seeks it first, and not because he has it at his side—otherwise he would have blamed him long before, if that were wrong.

It follows further: " Who takes the sword shall perish by the sword," that is, he is brought under the judgment of the sword. Though he may not wish it, he will always be judged by the sword for his fault. Do you mark here how Christ sanctions the sword, that they shall punish with it, and suppress self-constituted authority and wickedness? And that they shall do who are elected for the purpose, whoever they are. Hence it is evident that if men are pious, good and orderly, they will bear the sword for the protection of the innocent, according to the will of God, and for a terror to evil-doers, according as God has appointed and ordained.

In the third place, Christ said to his disciples, when they asked him wherefore he was going to Jerusalem when the Jews had wished before to stone him: "Are there not twelve hours in the day?" As if he had said, They will not kill me until the twelfth hour comes, that is, the one ordained of God for my death, which Christ also calls the hour of darkness. But when the same twelfth hour was come, Christ said to his disciples, near the Mount of Olives, " Sleep on and take your rest. The hour is here that I should be given to death, in order that the Scripture might be fulfilled." Mark, Peter hears that the appointed and fore-ordained hour of God had come, yet he would oppose, and draws the sword of his own authority. That was the greatest [error]. Therefore Christ speaks: There is no use in protecting and guarding me further. The hour foreseen

by God is here, and even if there were twelve legions of
angels here they might not help me against the will of my
Heavenly Father. Therefore put up [thy sword]; it is
useless. I have already said to you, the hour is here;
the Scripture shall and must be fulfilled.

From that every Christian learns that one should not
cease to protect and guard all pious and innocent men,
so long as he does not certainly know that even now the
hour of their death is here. But when the hour comes,
whether you know it or not, you can no longer protect
and guard them. Therefore the magistrate is bound by
his soul's salvation to protect and guard all innocent and
peaceful men, until a certain voice of God comes and is
heard to say, Now shalt thou no longer protect this man
—as Abraham also heard a voice that he should slay his
son, contrary to the commandment, Thou shalt not kill.
Therefore the magistrate is also bound to rescue and release all oppressed and persecuted men, widows, orphans,
whether known or strangers, without any respect of persons, according to the will and most earnest command of
God (Is. i., 17; Jer. xxi., 12; xxii., 3; Rom. xiii., 1;
and many other passages) until they are called by God
to something else, which they will not need to wait for
long. Therefore God has hung the sword at their side
and given it to his disciples.

THE THIRD PASSAGE

"Lord, wilt thou that we command that fire from heaven fall and
consume them, as Elijah did. But Jesus turned to them and rebuked
them, and said, Ye know not what spirit ye are of. The Son of
man is come not to destroy men's lives, but to save them."—Luke
ix., 54, 55.

Here my brothers make a great outcry, as if the devil
were there, and say, "Now you see, Balthasar, that

Christ did not wish to punish with fire. And so we
ought not to do it, nor should we use fire, water, sword
or gallows." *Answer:* Look further, dear brothers,
where Christ comes to the end, [and see] what was the
authority and command given him by God. Consider
also therewith what is the power of superiors. Do that
and you shall already have an answer. Christ is come,
as he himself says, not to judge men, condemn them
or punish them with fire, water or the sword. He did not
become man for that. But his command and authority
was to make men hold with the word; that power he had
received when he became man. So he says himself
(Luke xii., 14), "Who has made me a judge between
you and your brother?" As if he had said, You may
find another judge. I am not here for that purpose, that
I should seize another power and command over you.
On the contrary, the power and authority of the magistrate is given by God, that he should protect and guard
the pious, and punish the wicked and destroy them;
therefore has he hung the sword at their side, and since
it is at their side they must use it. Now God always
punishes the wicked, perhaps with hail, rain or sickness,
and also through certain men who have been appointed
and chosen thereto. Wherefore Paul calls the magistrate
a "minister" of God. For what God might do of himself he often wills to do through his creatures, as through
his instrument.

Yes, and although the devil, Nebuchadnezzar and
many other wicked men are also called in Scripture
servants of God, still it is far otherwise with an orderly
government, when according to the command of God it
punishes the wicked for the good of the pious and innocent. But the devil and his crew do nothing for the

good or peace of men, but everything to their injury and hurt, in an envious and vindictive spirit. But the government has a special sympathy with all those who have transgressed; it wishes from the heart that it had not happened; while the devil and his followers wish that all men were unfortunate. ˙ Do you see, then, brothers, how far separated from one another are these two kinds of servants, the devil and orderly government? How also Christ wished to exercise his power on earth? Even so ought we to exercise our power and calling, whether in government or in obedience, for we must give an account for it to God at the last day.

THE FOURTH PASSAGE

" One of the people spoke to the Lord, Master, say to my brother that he divide the inheritance with me. But he said to him, Man, who appointed me a judge or divider over you ?"—Luke xii., 13, 14.

Here these brothers of mine cry out to Heaven, but too noisily, and say, " Hearest thou, Fridberger? Christ will not be a judge or divider. Judgment and court are forbidden by Christ; therefore the upright Christian should not be a judge, nor sit in the court nor bear the sword, for Christ did not wish to be a judge or divider between the two brothers." *Answer :* Hold up on your crying, dear brothers, you do not know the Scripture, therefore you are wrong and do not know what you are crying. Christ says, Man, who has appointed me a judge or divider over you? That is not my office; it belongs to another. Mark that: Christ does not condemn the office of judge, since it is not to be condemned, as will shortly follow. But he shows this, that no one should undertake to be a judge who has not been appointed and chosen thereto. Thence comes the election of burgo-masters, mayors, judges, all of whom Christ permits to remain, if with God and a good conscience they rule well over temporal and corporeal affairs. But he was not willing himself to assume it; he did not become man for that purpose, and he was not appointed thereto. In like manner also, no one should use the sword, until he is regularly elected for that purpose, or called in some other way by God, as Moses, between the Israelites and Egyptians [Ex. iii., 10], Abraham for the deliverance of his brother Lot [Gen. xiv., 14–17], and Phinehas against the unclean [Num. xxv., 7–9].

THE FIFTH PASSAGE

" If any man wisheth to bring thee before the court, and take thy coat from thee, let him have thy cloak also."—Matt. v., 40.

THE SIXTH PASSAGE

" It is already a defect among you that you have law-suits with each other. Wherefore do you not much rather let yourselves be wronged? Wherefore do you not much rather suffer wrong and be defrauded? But you do injustice and defraud, and such things to your brothers."—1 Cor. vi., 7, 8.

These two passages are announced by the brothers in so lofty and anxious a way, as if they believed they ought to offer themselves to the fire—a Christian may not be a judge. Well, we will search the Scriptures, thus we shall find a good answer. Suits, quarrels, complaints and wranglings before council or court, if one seeks them himself, are not right, as the aforesaid two passages very clearly show. But that, when the parties wish to go to law, a Christian may not without sin be a judge or decide justly between them, is not declared in the sixth chapter

of Paul's first letter to the Corinthians.   For Paul writes:
"How does any among you, if he has a complaint against
another, go to law before the unrighteous, and not before
the saints? (that is, before Christians).   Do ye not know
that the saints will judge the world?   If then the world
will be judged by you, are ye not good enough to judge
trifles?   Know ye not that ye will judge the angels, how
much more temporal affairs?   If now ye have law-suits
over affairs, name the most despised in the church and
set the same to judge.   To your shame I say that.   Is
it so indeed that there is no wise man among you, or not
a single one who can judge between brother and brother,
but a brother permits himself to go to law with another,
even before the unbelievers? "

Hear Paul now, dear brothers, and see.   If Christians
wish to go to law over affairs, that is, over temporal goods,
which is quite wrong, they should yet seek to be judged
by a Christian and not by an unbeliever.   Mark here,
brothers, you have skipped over that.   If Christians wish
to go to law and not to be at peace with each other, they
sin yet more, yea, they doubly sin, if they take their case
before an unbelieving judge and not before a Christian.
Therefore Paul mocks the Corinthians and says, " If ye
will go to law, ye should choose the most despised among
you to judge."   He says that to them for their shame,
since it is reasonable that they should be ashamed if they
had not among them any pious and wise Christians, who
might decide justly between them, but must run for an
unbelieving judge.

Now a blind man can see, that a Christian may properly and with a good conscience sit in court and council, and judge and decide about temporal cases; although
the wranglers and disputants sin, yet they sin more if

they take their cases before the unbelieving judge. If a Christian therefore may and should in the power of the divine word, be a judge with the mouth, he may also be a protector with the hand of him who wins the suit, and punish the unjust. For whoso shall judge righteousness ought not to hesitate to execute and fulfil punishment against the malicious. Who soles a shoe, if he dare not put it on? See, dear brothers, that councils, courts, and law are not wrong.

Thus also the judge may and should be a Christian, although the contending parties sin, because they do not much rather permit themselves to suffer wrong. Therefore a Christian may also, according to the ordinance of God, bear the sword, in the place of God, against the evil-doer and punish him. Though he is for the sake of the evil, he is also ordained by God for the protection and defence of the pious (Rom. xiii., 3, 4). Thus will the Scripture be true where it says: " You have an office not of men but of God; what you judge he decrees above you. Therefore shall the fear of God be with you, and you shall act with diligence, for God cannot see nor forgive iniquity " (2 Chron. xix., 6, 7). This Scripture is given to us as well as to the ancients, since it pertains to brotherly love. Do you say, Well, but is it not our duty not to go to law? *Answer:* Yes. We ought not to do anything wrong. Therefore it is always the duty of every Christian, should he ever be appointed a judge, to administer justice to citizens and foreigners. That must follow, or the Scripture must be broken to pieces, which no man can ever accomplish.

THE SEVENTH PASSAGE

" If thy brother sin against thee, go and rebuke him between thee and him alone. If he heareth thee, thou hast won thy brother. If he heareth thee not, take with thee one or two, so that all things may be established from the mouth of two or three witnesses. If he will not hear, tell it to the church. If he will not hear the church, hold him as a heathen and publican."—Matt. xviii., 15–17.

From this passage the brothers raise a grievous outcry against me and say: "If a magistrate were allowable among Christians, then the Christian excommunication would come to nothing and be disused. For when one punishes the evil-doer with the sword, the church may not use the ban." *Answer :* Excommunication and punishment with the sword are two very different commands given by God. The first is promised and given to the church by Christ (Matt. x., 14; xviii., 18; John xx., 23), for the admission of the pious into their fellowship and the exclusion of the unworthy, to use according to its will. So, whatsoever sins of men the Christian church forgives on earth, the same are surely forgiven also in heaven; and what sins are not forgiven here on earth the same are not remitted in heaven.

Since Christ delivered, entrusted and committed to his bride, the Christian church, his command to loose and bind in his bodily absence, as he had received it from his Father, therefore the Christian church may and shall in the meantime teach the people all that Christ has commanded her to teach. Also she has the authority and power to sign all men with the water-baptism, if they are willing to receive, believe, and order their lives by such doctrine, and to inscribe and receive them in her holy fellowship. For all that she rules and governs on earth, the same is done, performed, delivered and finished in heaven also. At some distant day this Christ, her Bridegroom, will come again in corporeal and visible form, in his glory and majesty, and will take again in person his

kingdom, until he shall deliver it up to his Heavenly
Father, as Paul writes (1 Cor. xv., 24), until God shall
be all in all. Even that is the secret [mystery] in Christ
and his Church, according to the contents of the letter
to the Ephesians, chapter v.

The other command relates to the external and temporal authority and government, which originally was
given by God to Adam after his fall, when he said to
Eve, " Under the man's authority shalt thou be, and
he shall rule over thee " (Gen. iii., 16). If now Adam
was set in authority over his Eve, then he received
authority over all flesh that should be borne by Eve in
pain. In like manner also God entrusted the sword to
certain other god-fearing men, for example, to Abraham,
Moses, Joshua, Gideon and Samuel. After that the
wickedness of men increased and became overflowing,
yea, the bulk of it became rampant. The people at one
time demanded from Samuel a king and abandoned God.
The same king, at the command of God, Samuel gave
them; and they thereby became bound to endure the
royal authority and subjection that the king exercised
thereafter, for their sins, since they had despised and
abandoned God and had earnestly demanded from Samuel and not from God a king, like the other nations.
Such subjection and burden we must and shall now day
by day suffer, endure and bear, obediently and willingly;
also give and render tribute to whom tribute belongs, tax
to whom tax belongs, fear to whom fear belongs, honour
to whom honour belongs.

And for this our sins are to blame, as the sins of Eve
that she must bring forth in pain, and as the sins of
Adam, that he must eat his bread in the sweat of his
face. For if we were pleased to be obedient to God and

19

pious, there would be against us no law, sword, fire, stocks or gallows. But since we have continually sinned, it must and will be so, and neither rebellion nor anything else can deliver us therefrom. For God's word is Yea and not Nay. But if we heap disobedience upon disobedience, and increase sins with sins, in his wrath God will give us kings, and children for princes, yea, he will let the effeminate rule over us, and if we try to escape Rehoboam we shall run into the hands of Jeroboam. All this befalls us because of our sins, according to the common and true proverb, "Like people, like king." "A stork gobbles up the frogs, who were not willing to recognise and receive as king the harmless log."

Wherefore, it is most necessary, O pious Christians, with greatest diligence and most earnest devotion to pray Almighty God for a pious, just and Christian government on earth, under which we may live a peaceful and quiet life, in all godliness and honesty. When God gives us such, we ought to receive it with special thankfulness. If he does not give, it is certain that we are not worthy of another and better, because of our sins. Of this case the Bible in the Old Testament gives us many histories as examples.

See now, dear brothers, that these two offices and commands, of the ban and the secular sword, are not opposed to each other, since they are both from God. For the Christian ban frequently has place and authority, as for example in many spiritual offences against which the sword may by no means be used, when according to the occasion of the sin there should be punishment. That Christ teaches us very clearly, when he says to the adulterous woman: "Woman, hath none condemned

thee?'' She says, ''No one, Lord.'' He answers,
'' Neither will I condemn thee. Go, and sin no more.''
Mark: Christ says, Woman hath no one condemned
thee? As if he would have said, If condemnation had
fallen on thee, according to the law of God announced
for adultery, I should say nothing to the judge, for it is
the commandment of God my Father, that they shall
stone the adulterer. But since no one has condemned
thee, neither will I condemn thee, for it is not my office.
I have not been appointed a judge but a Saviour.
Therefore go hence and sin no more. That is my
office, to forgive sins and to command that men walk no
more in sins. Hear then, dear brothers, how Christ so
properly exercises his own office, and lets the judicial
office stand at its own value. So must the Church also
do with its ban, and the government with its sword, and
neither usurp the other's office.

THE EIGHTH PASSAGE

" Ye have heard that it hath been said, Eye for eye and tooth for
tooth. But I say to you, Resist not evil, but if one give thee a
blow on thy right cheek, turn the other also."—Matt. v., 38, 39 ;
Luke vi., 29.

This Scripture is cited by the brothers as proudly as if
they meant that according to it magistrates must unbuckle the sword if they wish to be Christians. But
make room, don't be in too much hurry, dear friends,
and hear, you who wish to handle the Scriptures aright.
'' You have heard it hath been said (in the Old Testament, that is to say), Eye for eye and tooth for tooth.''
Therefore, when one comes and accuses another before
the judge, that he has struck out an eye or tooth (that
such charges were allowed to the ancients you will find

in the fifth book of Moses, in the first chapter)[1] the
judge must hear the complaint and testimony, and ad-
judge eye for eye and tooth for tooth, according to the
law of God. But in the New Testament it is not to be
done in that way, but if one smites thee on the right
cheek, do not complain of him, run for no judge, ask no
vengeance, as it was permitted to them of old, but turn
the other also. For to complain is always forbidden to
Christians, as you have heard in 1 Cor. vi., 7. If now
you suffer and do not injure, you do the business right,
for so has Christ specially taught each one to do. But
the magistrate is not therefore to unbuckle the sword.
Nay, he is much more commanded (if such mischief or
injury should happen among themselves or other people)
to protect the pious and punish the wicked with the
sword,—for that he is appointed a servant of God, to
the good for peace, to the evil for fear. Therein he
does the will of God.

Likewise, although the two contestants about worldly
goods sin before the judge, the Christian judge does not
sin when he judges the quarrel justly. So even if no one
makes a complaint, but the magistrate knows that one
has done another violence and wrong, he should none
the less perform his commanded office, and pronounce
just judgment and punish the offender. For so he bears
not the sword in vain. Thus there is a higher standard
[*staffel*, position] in the New Testament than in the Old,
that he who is injured and damaged does not complain,
and yet the magistrate punishes. In the Old Testament
the injured complains and the judge punishes. See,
dear brothers, how the thirteenth chapter of Romans

---

[1] The reference is to Deut. i., 16–18, but Ex. xxi., 24, and Lev.
xxiv., 20, are more to the point.—TR.

must correspond with the afore-mentioned word of Christ; for, if we put the two passages together one goes well with the other.

THE NINTH PASSAGE

" So stand now, your loins girt with the girdle of truth, and having put on the breastplate of righteousness, and your feet shod with the preparation of the gospel of peace ; in addition to all, having grasped the shield of faith, with which ye will be able to quench all the fiery darts of the evil one ; and take up the helmet of salvation, and the sword of the Spirit, which is the word of God."—Eph. vi., 14–17.

THE TENTH PASSAGE

" The weapons of our knighthood are not carnal, but mighty before God to the destruction of strongholds, wherewith we destroy the device and every high thing that lifts itself against the knowledge of God."—2 Cor. x., 4, 5.

But here the brothers run up and cry very greatly: " There, you see what the harness and weapon of the Christian should be, not made of iron or long wood; but the gospel, the gospel, faith, faith, the word of God, the word of God, shall be our sword and weapon. Paul forsooth is able to scour our harness, to furbish up well our Christian weapons; other preparations are all of the devil." *Answer :* Stop running, dear brothers, and mark what I will say in entire peace. First, I find it thus in the Scriptures. Paul speaks to us in these words to the Ephesians of one sword, and of another to the Romans, ch. xiii. Now tell me, whether here and there one sword or two are written about? You cannot say with truth, dear brothers, that he has written of one sword. For to the Ephesians and Corinthians Paul speaks of a spiritual sword, and says himself, " It is the word of God, with which one shall destroy that which lifts itself against the knowledge of God." So again he writes to the Romans of a temporal sword, which one bears at his side, with which he frightens the evil-doer, who cannot be frightened or punished with the word of God. Now if there are two swords, of which one belongs to the soul, the other to the body, you must let them both remain in their worthiness, dear brothers.[1]

In the second place, I beg, for the love of God, that you will read eleven lines before that passage from the Ephesians that you quote. Then you will certainly see and hear that Paul there describes the harness, sword and preparation, which we are to use against the devil, for the protection of the soul, and not the sword that men use against evil men, here upon earth, such as do harm to the innocent in goods, body and life. Now go on to read, and the truth will be disclosed to you from the lesson, when the text says: " Finally, my brethren, make yourselves strong in the Lord, and in the might of his strength. Put on the armour of God, that ye may be able to stand against the wily assaults of the devil. For we have not to do battle with flesh and blood, but with princes and authorities, with the world-rulers of the darkness in this world, with the spirits of wickedness under heaven," etc.

Mark here, dear friends; if your hearts were right, you would say, There are two kinds of swords in the Scriptures; one spiritual, which we are to use against the wily assaults of the devil, as Christ has commanded us against Satan (Matt. iv., 1–11). That is the word of God. Yes, of that sword Paul speaks here to the Ephesians and Corinthians whàt Christ himself says, " I

---

[1] The meaning plainly is, you must let each remain in its proper place. —Tr.

have not come to send peace but a sword " (Matt. x., 34). Besides there is a temporal sword, which is borne for the protection of the pious, and for the frightening of the wicked here on earth. With that the magistrate is girded, that he may with it preserve the peace of the land, and it will also be called a spiritual sword when it is used according to the will of God. These two swords are not opposed to each other.

Thirdly, inasmuch as Paul teaches that we should pray for the government, that under it we may live a peaceable and quiet life with each other in all godliness and honesty, I ask one question of you all, brothers, in a lump: Would a believing or an unbelieving magistrate be wise and skilful to preserve his people in such a peaceful, quiet, godly and honest life? You must, must, must always confess that a Christian magistrate will strive much more earnestly to do it than one who is not a Christian, who has at heart neither Christ, God, nor godliness, but only thinks how he may remain in his power, pomp and ceremony. You have examples of David, Hezekiah, and Josiah, as contrasted with Saul, Jeroboam and Rehoboam. Therefore get thee behind us Satan, and cease to mislead simple men; under thine appearance of great patience and spirituality, we know thee by thine old conceit.

THE ELEVENTH PASSAGE

" Ye have heard that it hath been said, Thou shalt love thy neighbour and hate thine enemy, but I say unto you, Love your enemy, speak well of those who speak ill of you, do well to them that hate you, pray for those who injure and persecute you, that you may be children of your Father in Heaven. For he letteth his sun shine upon the evil and the good, and giveth rain to the just and the unjust. For if ye love those that love you, what have you for a reward? Do not the publicans also the same? and if ye act friendly to your brothers who do likewise to you, do not the publicans so also? Therefore you shall be perfect, like as your Father in Heaven is perfect."—Matt. v., 43–48.

Here the brothers once more cry out murder on the magistrate, and say, "See there, the magistrate that a Christian is willing to be does not smite the wicked with the sword, but has love for his enemy, does him good and prays for him." *Answer:* Well now, let us take these words of Christ for ourselves and weigh them, and we shall not err. Christ says, "You have heard that it hath been said, Thou shalt love thy neighbour and hate thine enemy." Mark there precisely who is an enemy, namely, he whom one hates and envies. But now a Christian should hate or envy nobody, but should have love for all; therefore a Christian magistrate has no enemy, for he hates and envies no one. For what he does with the sword he does not perform out of hatred or envy, but according to the command of God. Therefore to punish the wicked is not to hate, envy or act the enemy. For in that case even God were moved by hatred, envy and enmity, which he is not, since when he wills to punish the wicked he does not do it out of envy or hate, but justice.

Therefore a just and Christian magistrate does not hate him whom he punishes; he is sorrowful of heart that he rules over people deserving of such punishment. Yea, what he does he does according to the ordinance and earnest command of God, who has appointed him a servant and has hung the sword at his side for the administration of justice. Therefore at the last day he must give an exact account of how he has used the sword. For the sword is nothing else than a good rod and scourge of God, which he [the magistrate] is called to use against the wicked. Now what God calls good is good, and if he calls thee to slay thy son, it would be a good work. When therefore God wills to do many things through his creatures, as his instruments, which he might accomplish alone and without them, he yet wills so to use us as that we serve each other, and do not go idle, but each one fulfils his own duty to which God has called him. One shall preach, another shall protect him, a third shall till the field, a fourth shall do his work in some other way, so that we shall all eat our bread in the sweat of our faces. Verily, verily, he who rules in a just and Christian way has to sweat enough—he does not go idle.

Now we see again plainly how the above-mentioned word of Christ and the sword so completely agree; wherefore one dare not, for the sake of brotherly love, ungird the sword. Yea, and if I am a Christian and rightly disposed, if I fall into a sin I shall wish and pray that the magistrate may punish me quickly, that I may no more heap sin on sin. Whence it follows that the magistrate may and should punish, not alone from justice, but from the love that he bears to the evil-doer (not to his evil deed); for it is good and profitable to the sinner that a millstone be at once hanged about his neck, and he be drowned in the water (Matt. xviii., 6).

THE TWELFTH PASSAGE

" Ye have heard that it was said to them of old, Thou shalt not kill, but he who kills shall be in danger of the judgment."—Matt. v., 21.

Why is it now, dear brethren, that you cry out to Heaven and shout overloud, " It stands written, ' Thou shalt not kill, Thou shalt not kill.' " Now we have also the command in the Old Testament, plain and clear, that we nevertheless shall kill.   Do you say, "Yes, but God commanded them"? then I reply, God has also commanded that the magistrate shall kill and degrade the turbulent.   He has for that girded them with the sword, and not in vain, as Paul writes to the Romans. Do you now ask, pious Christian, how "kill" and "do not kill" agree with each other?   *Answer :* completely:

As be chaste and be married, Matt. xix., 3–12.

As have a wife and have one not, 1 Cor. vii., 25–30.

As a testimony is true and is not true, John v., 31, 32; viii., 14.

As have all things and have nothing, 2 Cor. vi., 10.

As to be rich and to be poor, *ib.*

As to preach the gospel to every creature, and yet not cast pearls before swine, Matt. xxviii., 19; vii., 6.

As to love father and mother and to hate them, Ex. xx., 12; Luke xiv., 26.

As to see God and not see him, Gen. xxxii., 30; John i., 18.

As all men shall be saved, and those who do not believe shall be condemned, John i., 7–12.

As to swear by the name of God and not to swear, Deut. vi., 13; Matt. v., 34.

As not to sin and yet to have sin, 1 John i., 8; iii., 6.

As to sell all things that we have and give to the poor, and yet to give of our superfluity that we come not to poverty, Matt. xix., 21; 2 Cor. viii., 13–15.

As to be poor, and happy to give to him that takes, Matt. v., 42.

As Christ to be always with us to the end of the world, and yet not to have him always among us, Matt. xxviii., 20; John xvi., 7.

As God punishes the wickedness of the father on the son, to the third and fourth generation, and yet the son does not bear the wickedness of the father, Ex. xx., 5; Ezek. xviii., 17.

As we should not do good works before men, and yet should do good works that men may see them, Matt. v., 16; vi., 1.

As we do not know the mind of God, and yet he has revealed unto us the secret of his will, Rom. xi., 33; 1 Cor. ii., 7–10.

As ask of God all things and receive them, also ask and yet not receive them, Matt. vii., 7; James iv., 2.

As beat the swords into ploughshares and the spears into pruning hooks, and beat the ploughshares into swords and the pruning hooks into spears, Isa. ii., 4; Joel iii., 10.

As we shall not judge and yet judge, and set those inferior to us to judge, Luke vi., 37; 1 Cor. vi., 2–4.

As Abraham was justified by faith, and yet by works, Rom. iv., 3; James ii., 21; Heb. xi., 8.

As to please our neighbour, and yet not to please men, Rom. xv., 2; Gal. i., 10.

As to hate evil, and yet bless those that persecute us. Matt. xviii., 21; Rom. xii., 9.

As we shall become children, and yet shall not be children, Matt. xix., 14; 1 Cor. xiii., 11; Eph. iv., 14.

As God wills all men to be saved, and yet whom he will he pities, and whom he will he hardens, 1 Tim. ii., 4; Rom. ix., 18.

As the yoke of Christ is sweet, and yet impossible to men, Matt. xi., 20; xix., 26.

As the angels desire to see the face of God, and yet if his glory appears we shall be satisfied, 1 Pet. i., 12; Ps. xvi.,11.

As the judgment of God is good, and yet God has given a judgment that is not good, Rom. vii., 12.

As that the king should not have many wives, and yet Rehoboam had fourteen, Abijah as many, David also many, and Solomon 700, besides 300 concubines, Deut. xvii., 17; 2 Chron. xi., 21; xiii., 21; 1 Kings xi., 3.

As God will not keep his anger forever, and yet the condemned must go into everlasting fire, Ps. ciii., 9; Matt. xxv., 46.

As that there is no law given for the righteous, and yet Christ has given us a new commandment, 1 Tim. i., 9; John xiii., 34.

As God does not tempt, and yet God did tempt Abraham, James i., 13; Gen. xxii., 1.

As the Father and Christ are one, and yet the Father is more than Christ, John x., 18, 30; xiv., 6–12.

And many similar passages, which appear to be opposed to each other, as the wings of the Cherubim, and yet all alike come to a head in Christ. Therefore one should split the claws of Scripture and repeat it well, before he eats (that is believes), or he will eat death therefrom, and through half-truth and half-judgment will wander widely, widely from the whole truth, and go seriously astray. A comparison: Christ says, " This is my body, which is given for you; this do in remembrance of me." That is now a whole truth. Who now judges from this a half truth, says that the bread is the body of Christ and errs. But he who judges the whole truth, says that the bread is the body of Christ, which is given for us, but not bodily, in itself, or substantially, but retained in remembrance according to the command given by Christ at the last supper; and that is the whole truth and nothing else is. He who understands that can also see that " kill " and " kill not " may be entirely true and consistent with each other.

Now then we will take the word of Christ for ourselves, and see whether the magistrate is forbidden to kill. Christ says, " Thou shalt not kill," and he goes on to the roots of killing and says, " But I say to you, he who is angry with his brother is in danger of the judgment. But he who says to his brother, ' Raca,' is in danger of the council. But he who says, ' Thou fool ' is in danger of hell fire." Reading that in addition, dear brothers, you shall more clearly see what killing Christ has forbidden, namely, the killing that goes with wrath, ridicule, and abuse. But the magistrate (I speak of the true magistrate) does not kill from wrath, is not moved by words of ridicule and abuse, but [acts] according to the commandment of God, who has earnestly commanded him to slay the wicked and to keep the pious in peace.

Wherefore now the magistrate may kill the evil-doer, and in doing this he is guiltless according to the ordinance of God, and himself cannot be judged. And I, or any other required and summoned thereto, am guiltless in helping him; and whoso withstands him withstands the ordinance of Christ and himself will incur the eternal judgment. Do not believe me here, dear brothers, but believe Paul, that you will find yourselves safe. Therefore those whom we call hangmen were in the Old Testament pious, honourable, and brave men, and were called prefects, that is, executors of the ordinance and law of God. Since it is honourable to the judge to condemn with the mouth the guilty, how can it be wrong to kill the same with the sword and fulfil the word of the judge, since the executor of the law strikes or kills with

the sword none whom the judge had not commanded
him? We read that Solomon commanded the honourable
Benaiah to kill Shimei, Adonijah, and Joab (1 K. ii.).
Saul commanded Doeg to kill the priests (1 Sam. xxii.,
18), and David ordered his servant to slay the slayer of
Saul (2 Sam. i., 15). Since neither the judge nor the
executioner kill the evil-doer, but the law of God, therefore are the judge, magistrate and executioner called
in the Scripture servants of God and not murderers.
God judges, condemns and kills through them, and not
they themselves. Whence it follows, they who would
not kill the evil-doer but let him live, even murder and
sin against the command, "Thou shalt not kill." For
he who does not protect the pious kills him. and is guilty
of his death, as well as he who does not feed the hungry.

THE THIRTEENTH PASSAGE

"The kings of this world," says Christ, "lord it, and those in
authority are called 'Gracious lords.'[1] But you not so."—Luke
xxii., 25, 26.

What great maxim you make there, and especially of
the words, "but you not so" I cannot satisfactorily tell.
But I take pity on you as before. For you have not well
seen either the preceding or the following words, for if
you did you would understand them right and we should
soon come to agreement. Well, then, we will begin this
passage three lines farther back, and the meaning will
then appear plain. Thus reads the text: "There arose
a contention among the disciples, which of them should
be ruler," who should have the authority in external and
carnal things, since the secular authority is over flesh and

[1] Our English version has it "benefactors."

body and over temporal things, but not over the soul. To him according to the divine order the sword is entrusted, not that he may fight, war, strive and tyrannise with it, but to defend the wise, protect the widow, maintain the pious, and to tolerate all who are distressed or persecuted by force. This is the duty of the magistrate, as God himself many times in the Scriptures declares it, which may not take place without blood and killing, wherefore God has hung the sword at his side, and not a fox's tail.

THE LAST PASSAGE A SANCTION OF MAGISTRACY AMONG CHRISTIANS

Let every man be subject to the magistrate and power, for there is no power apart from God. But the power everywhere is ordained by God; so that he who sets himself against the power strives against the ordinance of God. But he who strives will receive condemnation of himself. For the rulers do not make the good work fear but the evil. Wilt thou not fear? then do good, so shalt thou have praise from the same. But if thou doest evil, then fear, for authority bears not the sword in vain. He is God's servant, a judge for punishment over him that does evil. So you are obliged to submit, not alone because of the punishment, but because of conscience; wherefore you must also give tribute, for they are God's servants who provide such protection. (Rom. xiii., 1–6.) This passage alone, dear brothers, is enough to sanction the magistracy against all the gates of hell. When Paul says plainly, " Let every one be submissive to the magistrate," whether he is a believer or unbeliever, you ought always to be submissive and obedient. He gives as a reason, " For there is no power but of God." Wherefore this obedience is the duty of all who are not against God, since God has not ordained the magistrate against himself. Now the magistrate will punish the wicked, as he is bound to do by his own soul's salvation; and if he is not able to do this alone, when he summons his subjects by bell or gun, by letter or any other way, they are bound by their soul's salvation also to stand by their prince and help him, so that according to the will of God the wicked may be slain and uprooted.

Nevertheless, the subjects should carefully test the spirit of their ruler, whether he is not incited by haughtiness, pride, intoxication, envy, hatred, or his own profit, rather than by love of the common weal and the peace of society. When that is the case, he does not bear the sword according to the ordinance of God. But if you know that the ruler is punishing the evil only, so that the pious may remain in peace and uninjured, then help, counsel, stand by him, as often and as stoutly as you are able; thus you fulfil the ordinance of God and do his work, and not a work of men.

But if a ruler should be childish or foolish, yea, even entirely unfit to rule, one may with reason then escape from him and choose another, since on account of a wicked ruler God has often punished a whole land. But if it may not well be done, reasonably and peaceably and without great shame and rebellion, he should be suffered as one whom God has given us in his anger, and wills (since we are worthy of no better) thus to chastise us for our sins.

He then who will not aid the magistrate to seek out the widows and orphans and other oppressed, and to punish the outragers and ravishers of the land, contends against the ordinance of God and will come to the judgment, since he acts contrary to the command and ordinance of God, who wills that the pious should be protected and the wicked punished. But if you are obedient, you should know that you have rendered such obedience, not to the magistrate or to man, but to God himself, and have become a peculiar servant of God, just as the magistrate himself is nothing but a servant of God. For that the magistrate has power and authority to put to death the wicked, Paul plainly testifies when he says, " The power does not bear the sword in vain." If the magistrate has no authority to kill, why has he the sword at his side? He then bears it in vain, which Paul will not suffer. He adds also explicitly, " The power is a servant of God." Where are they then that say, " A Christian may not bear the sword "? If a Christian may not be a servant of God, if he may not obey the command of God without sin, then were God not good. He has made an ordinance which a Christian may not fulfil without sin— that is blasphemy!

Accordingly, I counsel you with true love, brothers, turn back, take heed to yourselves. You have stumbled badly, and under the cloak of spirituality and humility have devised much mischief against God and brotherly love. All affairs remain more peaceful where one sees a Christian ruler and his subjects agree in a manly, brotherly, and Christian fashion, and many a tyrant would cease his striving and urging against God and all reason, and sheathe his sword according to the command of God. Yet if God wills that we should suffer, his will cannot be hindered by our protection.

To sum up: no one can deny that to protect the pious and punish the wicked is the strict command of God,

20

which stands to the judgment day. Examine the Scriptures, Christian reader, Is. i., Jer. xxi, xxii., Ps. lxi., Mi. vi., Na. iii., Prov. iii., Zach. vii., Habakkuk throughout. This command binds the ruler up to the present day, as well as those five centuries ago. For Christ says to you, " Thou shalt obey the secular king and call the ruler gracious Lord. Not only so, but the greatest among you shall be as the least, and the foremost as the servant." If one is conscious that Christ here commands those who would preach his gospel to serve, they ought not to undertake any foreign office, nor entangle themselves with secular business, as hitherto our Pope and bishops have become the first and last in all secular business—yea, even in the business of war. So that when two cocks in Germany or Italy have pecked at one another in a scrimmage, the Pope and his cardinals have taken sides with one of them.[1] This Christ cannot suffer, and so he says that the preachers of his gospel must be free of secular affairs, as also Paul writes to Timothy. (2 Tim. ii.)

In the second place: the text clearly points out that each of the disciples desired the pre-eminence, and they were quarrelling which among them should be greatest. Jesus could not see such a quarrel. It belongs to no Christian, out of lust for authority, to contend to be a ruler, but much rather to flee it. For if there is a frightful post to be found, outside of the sphere of the preacher, it is the post of magistrate and secular ruler. Christ speaks to this effect: " The kings of this world lord it and are called Gracious Lord." [Luke xxii., 25.] But

---

[1] The Pope has forbidden conflict between two men, and yet he has put eighty thousand men in the field and made them fight, and added his benediction and indulgence.—Marginal note by Hübmaier.

a Christian, if he is in authority, does not lord it. He does not desire to be called Gracious Lord, or Sir; but he considers that he is a servant of God, and is diligent in performing the ordinance of God, according to which he protects the pious and punishes the wicked. He exalts himself above none, but takes well to heart the word of Christ that the foremost shall be as a servant. Do you see, brothers, that here Christ himself points out how the oldest shall recognise and hold himself to be the youngest and the foremost to be a servant?—therefore there must always be, among Christians old and young, masters and servants, or he has given us this rule to no purpose. So, dear brothers, make no patchwork of the Scripture, but putting the foregoing and following words together in one entire judgment, you will then come to a complete understanding of the Scriptures, and you will see how the text does not forbid the magistracy to the Christian, but teaches one not to quarrel, war and fight for it, nor conquer land and people with the sword and force. That is against God. Also we should not greatly desire to be saluted as Lords, like secular kings, princes and lords. For the magistracy is not lordship and knighthood, but service according to the ordinance of God.

THE FOURTEENTH PASSAGE

" Avenge not yourselves, beloved, but give place to the wrath [of God] ; for it is written, Vengeance is mine, I will repay, saith the Lord. So, if thine enemy hunger feed him, if he thirst give him drink."—Rom. xii., 19.

Whoever has attended to the tenth and eleventh passages above cited will easily answer. For as the Christian ruler has no enemy, he hates no one; therefore he desires

vengeance on none. But he must do whatever he does
according to the command of God, who wills through
him, as his work testifies, to punish the wicked and
dangerous people. He does this, not in wrath, but with
sorrowful heart. But vengeance follows wrath; so, if one
wishes to avenge himself because of his own wrath, that
is here forbidden. Since vengeance is God's, he will repay the evil. (Deut. xxxii., Heb. x., Prov. xxv.) Paul
gives the reason for this, from the twelfth chapter to the
thirteenth: we should not avenge ourselves, because God
has ordained the magistracy for vengeance, as his servants, whose duty is to protect, to punish, to avenge.

THE FIFTEENTH PASSAGE

"Christ is our head and we are his members."—Eph. i., 4, 5;
Col. i., 2.

Here I must indulge myself, for they cry out at me:
"Do you not see that our head, Christ, has not striven
or fought? Therefore we must not strive, but patiently
go to death." First, dear brothers, I fear you do not
know what divine or Christlike means, for there is a great
difference between them. As to that, if we look at ourselves as we are by nature, Christ is not our head and
we are not his members. While he is righteous and
truthful, we are wicked and full of lies. Christ is a
child of grace, we are children of wrath. Christ never
did any sin, we are conceived and born in sins. Do you
see how as members we agree with the head?

Second, that Paul nevertheless calls us members of
Christ pertains to faith. That is said so many times.
If we know ourselves, that we ought to be members of
Christ, and yet are not, we confess ourselves guilty and

pray God for pardon through Christ Jesus. Through having done this, we firmly believe that God has forgiven us our sins. Now by faith we have become members of Christ, not in nature, that is, in will and works. So far as flesh is concerned, that cannot be obedient to the command of God, but by faith power is given us to become children of God, after the spirit and soul, and to will and work good—though still all our works according to the flesh are blameworthy, evil, and worthless, and not at all righteous in the sight of God.

Third, since we now know that only by faith are we children of God and members of Christ, we have not all one duty. So that one should take the lead in teaching, another protects, a third tills the earth, a fourth makes shoes and clothes. Yet these works all proceed from faith, and are done for the benefit of our neighbour. Paul also writes further: "Wherefore you must needs be in subjection, not only because of the wrath, but also for conscience' sake." [Rom. xiii., 5.] What does that mean? It is this: the secular power is ordained of God for the peace of society—even if there were no Scripture about it to make us obedient to the government, our own conscience and knowledge tell us that. We should help, protect, defend the government, and pay service and taxes, so that we may remain in worldly peace with one another; for to have peace in this world is not contrary to a Christian life. Otherwise Paul would never have taught us through Timothy to pray for kings, princes, and governors; but to keep peace with all men, as much as in us lies, that is right and Christian. (1 Tim. ii., Rom. ii.) But if God pleases to send us the exact contrary, we must receive it with patience. Do you see now, dear brothers, that your own conscience compels you to recognise that it is wise and helpful to punish the wicked and protect the good? That is called, in good German, "a general land-peace." So, says Paul, to further and preserve this peace we must pay taxes, customs and tribute.

Here mark you, dear brothers, if government is so unchristian that a Christian may not bear the sword, wherefore do we help and preserve it with our taxes? If we are not under obligation to prevent wrong to our neighbour as well as to ourselves, why do we choose a magistrate? Or are those in the magistracy not our neighbours? If we desire to live in peace under a heathen government, why not much more under a Christian? Since we are under a Christian government, the ordinance of God should appeal much more to our hearts than under a heathen. To what conclusion does that lead, dear brothers?

But Paul takes us farther and says: "The power is a servant of God," who shall use his protecting power for the good of our neighbour and the preservation of a general land-peace. Where is it written then that a Christian may not be such a servant of God as fulfils the command of. God to the good of all men? Or that he may not undertake such a divine work (as Paul himself calls it) according to the ordinance of God? God surely wills that we should share his grace with all, until we come to the real prohibition of his Holy Word; and that we should remain and persist in the same, through Jesus Christ our Lord. The peace of God be with you all. Amen.

TRUTH IS IMMORTAL

A FORGOTTEN HYMN OF HÜBMAIER'S

Much of the earliest Anabaptist literature is in the form of hymns, often crude in expression and halting in metre, but full of spiritual fervour. It would be surprising if so fertile a writer as Hübmaier had contributed nothing to this sort of literature; and still stranger, if he did write hymns, that none of them should be preserved. As a matter of fact, several of the old Anabaptist documents contain a hymn that is attributed to Hübmaier. It is not unknown, being printed in full, but anonymously, in Wackernagel's great collection,[1] vol. iii., p. 126 *sq*. The title there given is, "Ein preiss lied göttlichs worts" (A song in praise of God's word). As to the authorship, the editor contents himself with remarking that the hymn has been attributed without satisfactory reason to Erasmus Alber. Beck, Hoschek, and Loserth agree that the hymn is undoubtedly Hübmaier's. The text is herewith reprinted from Wackernagel, with a metrical translation, in which the attempt has been made to follow the original as closely as the exigencies of English versification would admit—at any rate, to represent fairly the spirit of the original.

[1] *Das Deutsche Kirchenlied*, three vols., Leipzig, 1870.

Frewt euch, frewt euch in diser zeyt,
jr werden Christen alle!
Wann yetz in allen landen weyt
Gots wort her dringt mit schalle.

   Est ist kein man, ders weren kan,
das habt ir wol vernummen,
Dann Gottes wort bleybt ewig stan
den bösen als den frummen.

Adam, Adam, du alter greysz,
wie hat es dir ergangen?
Nach deynem fall im Paradeysz
hast du von Got empfangen

   Sein Götlich wort genummen an,
vnd bist dadurch erhalten,
Dann Gottes wort bleybt ewig stan
den jungen als den alten.

Noe, Noe, du Gottes man!
Got hat dich auszerkoren,
Das du seyn wort hast gnummen an,
hat er zu dir geschworen,

   Mit wasser nit ertrincken lan,
wolt von seim zorn abweichen,
Dann Gottes wort bleybt ewig stan
den armen als den reichen.

Abraham, Abraham geb gut bescheyd:
er glaubet Got, seim Herren,
Das ward jm zelt zur grechtigkeyt,
seyn samen wolt er meren.

   Also hat Gott den allen than,
die seinem wort vertrawen,
Dann Gottes wort bleybt ewig stan
den die darauff thünd bawen.

Rejoice, rejoice, ye Christians all,
   And break forth into singing!
Since far and wide on every side
   The word of God is ringing.
And well we know, no human foe
   Our souls from Christ can sever;
For to the base, and men of grace,
   God's word stands sure for ever.

O Adam, Adam, first of men,
   What future did fate send you?
After your fall in Paradise
   How did your God befriend you ?
His holy word from him you heard,
   That word which faileth never,
To tend'rest age, to hoary sage,
   God's word stands sure for ever.

O Noah, Noah, man of God,
   Thy God hath thee selected
And sworn to thee an oath, since thou
   His word hast not rejected:
" With flood again to drown all men
   My wrath shall hasten never " ;
To swollen pelf, to want itself,
   God's word stands sure for ever.

And Abraham believed his God,
   And so, for his devotion,
His faith became his righteousness,
   His seed like sands of ocean.
Thus has God done for every one,
   Who trust him perish never;
To every one who builds thereon
   God's word stands sure for ever.

Loth, Loth, ein frumm Gotförchtig man,
Got thet jm zwen Engel senden,
Hiesz jn ausz Sodom zihen than
und solt sich nicht vmbwenden:
   Alsbald hüb Gott zu regnen an
mit schwefel und mit feüre,
Dann Gottes wort bleybt ewig stan,
kumbt vns allen zu steüre.

David, David, ein küng und herr,
ein man nach Gottes willen,
Hat angenummen Gottes leer,
darumb seyn wort erfüllet:
   Ausz seinem stamm Got globet an,
wolt er geboren werden,
Dann Gottes wort bleybt ewig stan
jm himel vnd auff erden.

Jesus Christus, Marie son,
vom heyligen geyst empfangen,
Was all Propheten gsaget hon
ist als an jm ergangen:
   Das hat Got als durch jn gethan,
vnd spricht " den solt jr hören! "
Dann Gottes wort bleybt ewig stan,
den sol wir loben vnd ehren.

Nun hört, nun hört vnd mercket mit fleysz
was vns fürter beschreiben
Im Testament auff newe weisz,
darinn sie thün verleiben,
   Was vormals ye gesaget ward
von Christo vnserm herren:
Dann Gottes wort bleybt ewig stan
vnd wirt sich allzeyt meren.

And Lot, devout, God-fearing man,
   Two angels came to find him,
And lead him out from Sodom safe,
   Nor should he look behind him.
God's fiery flood therein withstood
   No living thing whatever;
All men, like Lot, must pay their scot,
   God's word stands sure for ever.

O David, David, king and lord,
   A man of God's own choosing,
God's truth he hid within his heart
   Beyond all fear of losing.
From David's seed Christ should proceed,
   He swore who changeth never;
In heaven and on earth the same
   God's word stands sure for ever.

Jesus the Christ, of Mary born
   And of the Holy Spirit,
What all the prophets promisèd
   We shall in him inherit.
" Hear him," the call of God to all,
   To save us his endeavour;
To him all praise and honour raise—
   God's word stands sure for ever.

Now hear, now hear, and mark with care
   What else for us is written,
And learn from his new Covenant
   What more to do we 're bidden.
And what of old has been foretold
   Of Christ our Lord and Saviour;
To latest hour, in vaster power,
   God's word stands sure for ever.

Mattheus Leui Euangelist,
ein man vom Zoll berüffen,
Der erste Cantzler worden ist,
lernet allein zu suchen
    Disen Heilandt, der selber spricht
"kumpt, jr betrübten alle!"
Dann Gottes wort bleybt ewig stan
mit pracht vnd grossem schalle.

Marcus, Marcus der ander ist,
der auch reichlich auszpreytet
Mirackel grosz von disem Christ,
damit er hat geleytet
    Zum glauben bracht, das der allein
gerecht vnd frumm thüt machen,   ·
Dann Gottes wort bleybt ewig stan,
sie waynen oder lachen.

Lucas auch in die ordnung tritt,
grosz wunderthatt vns zeyget,
Zu schreiben ausz ist er der drit,
wie hoch vns Gott sey geneyget,
    Das er vns schickt von hymel herab
·seyn Son freundtlich lest locken,
Dann Gottes wort bleybt ewig stan,
wer das nicht glaubt, müsz pocken.

Johannes, Johannes, der Jüngling schon,
ist auch der vierdte worden,
Das Wort er fürt in gleichem thon,
lert vns den Christen orden
    Mit glaub vnd lieb beweysen recht
vnd sunst anders nicht suchen,
Dann Gottes wort bleybt ewig stan,
es hilfft kein scharrn noch puchen.

Matthew, the first evangelist,
   From Roman service taken,
Has now become chief counsellor
   And has his sins forsaken;
Hears Jesus call, who says to all,
   " Follow with best endeavour."
In ample fame, always the same,
   God's word stands sure for ever.

And Mark, yes, Mark, the second is,
   And richly he has taught us
The knowledge of that mighty power
   Wherewith our Lord has brought us
To faith in God, to which is owed
   All goodness whatsoever;
For all men's tears, for all men's jeers,
   God's word stands sure for ever.

Luke also follows in the train
   And tells the gospel story:
The wondrous works of Christ, and how
   From heaven the God of glory
To men undone has sent his Son
   That men might perish never;
Believe we must, or bite the dust,
   God's word stands sure for ever.

And John, the fourth evangelist,
   A youth of wondrous beauty,
Reveals to us the Word divine
   And teaches us our duty.
With faith and love your calling prove
   And seek no other lever;
It gives no aid to hoe or spade,
   But God's word stands for ever.

Saulus, Paulus, erweltes fasz,
ist erst der rechte keren,
Der vns erregt den neid vnd hasz,
darnon so zornig werden
   Die welt vnd jr grosz hoffgesind,
die also toben vnd wüten:
Dann Gottes wort bleybt ewig stan,
vor den wirdt ers behüten.

O Paul, O Paul, was richstu an
mit deinem theüren schreiben?
Menschlich vernunfft hoch sichtest an,
wilt ire werck vertreiben,
   Allein den glauben richten auff,
der sols alles auszrichten,
Dann Gottes wort bleybt ewig stan,
wie wol sie es vernichten.

Petrus, Judas vnd Jacobus
folgen auch diser lere,
Das sie vns lernen rew vnd büsz
durch Christum vnsern Herren,
   Auff den sie all vns weysen thon:
on jn wirt nit geholffen!
Dann Gottes wort bleybt ewig stan
vor Löwen, Beren vnd Wolffen.

Ach mensch, ach mensch, nu schick dich drein
lasz deinen dunckel faren
Und glaub der schrifft vnd worten sein,
damit du mögst bewaren
   Dein gwissen vnd auch all dein thon
trewlich darauff verlassen:
Dann Gottes wort bleybt ewig stan,
zeygt vns den weg vnd strassen.

And Saul, God's chosen vessel he,
   His early sin repented:
He stormed and strove against the saints
   As if he were demented.
In vain the age 'gainst us shall rage,
   Our souls from Christ to sever;
In time of ill our stronghold still,
   God's word stands sure for ever.

O Paul, O Paul, what fruit of all
   Thy writings in their season!
The truth thou hast declared shall stand
   Against all human reason.
Sin is o'erthrown by faith alone,
   And, though the great and clever
Were all employed to make it void,
   God's word stands sure for ever.

And Peter, Jude, and James, all three
   Do follow in this teaching;
Repentance and confession they
   Through Christ our Lord are preaching.
In him men must put all their trust,
   Or they shall see God never;
The wolf may tear, the lion, bear,—
   God's word stands sure for ever.

Ah, man, blind man, now hear the word,
   Make sure your state and calling;
Believe the Scripture is the power
   By which we 're kept from falling.
Your valued lore at once give o'er,
   Renounce your vain endeavour;
This shows the way, no longer stray,
   God's word stands sure for ever.

O Jhesu Christ, du Gottes son,
las vns nit von dir weychen!
Das vns nit werd ein böser lon,
so menschen leer her streychen
    Mit schöner gestalt vnd wüterichs gwalt
zu tilgen deynen namen;
Dann Gottes wort bleybt ewig stan
von nun vnd ewig, Amen.

Lobt Gott, lobt Gott in eynigkeyt,
jr Christen all gemeyne!
Das er seyn wort hatt auszgepreyt,
das ist seyn werck alleyne.
    Keins menschen wan nicht helffen kan,
wie hoch er sey mit namen,
Dan Gottes wort bleybt ewig stan,
Nun singen wir fröhlich, Amen!

INDEX

A

Anabaptists, why unpopular, 1; chiliastic ideas among, 2, 161, 165 *sq.;* revolutionary views of some, 3, 162, 164; Luther's treatment of, 6; slanders against, 7, 21; Cornelius on, 7; Beck's book about, 8; Keller's researches on, 9; connection with older sects, 9–13; relation to Reformation, 13; character of, 14; their ideal of the church, 15; repudiate name "Anabaptist," 16, 204; mysticism among, 14, 17; real offence of, 19; their vindication, 20; fate of their leaders, 21; origin in Zürich, 92, 102; Hübmaier joins them, 111; charged with schism by Zwingli, 118; why deserving of punishment, 119; Denck unites with them, 142; act of baptism among, 142–145; lords of Lichtenstein join them, 151; great progress of, at Nikolsburg, 152 *sq.;* Sebastian Franck on, 159; the socialistic wing, 162; doctrine of non-resistance among, 159, 160; schism in Nikolsburg among, 167 *sq.;* charged with sedition,

171; how far socialists, 172, 176, 215, 250 *sq.;* Unitarians among, 184; ritual of 210; use of the ban, 212; singing of hymns, 214; on salvation of infants, 216; banished from Moravia, 257; their protest, 259–264; numbers in Nikolsburg, 267; their martyrs, 269; emigrate to Russia and United States, 270

Aberli, Henry, Anabaptist preacher, 124

Affusion, practised by Hübmaier, 112, 142; by Grebel, 143; by the Mennonites, 145

Albertus Magnus, 47

Albigenses, 10

Anselm, theory of satisfaction, 198

Anthropology, Hübmaier's doctrine of, 190–198

Antinomianism, 189

Apostles' Creed, Hübmaier's paraphrase of, 178

Argula von Stauff, 78, 183

Arkleb, lord of Boskowitz, 152, 275

Articles, Twelve, of the peasants, 96, 241

Atonement, Hübmaier's doctrine of, 198

Augsburg, Latin school at, 26; the Fuggerei, 39; Reichstag of 1518, 41; Hübmaier visits, 142; Ana-

323

DATE DUE